The
LAWYER'S
GUIDE
to
Writing Well

The
LAWYER'S GUIDE
to
Writing Well

TOM GOLDSTEIN
Dean, Graduate School of Journalism
University of California, Berkeley

AND

JETHRO K. LIEBERMAN
Professor and Director,
The Legal Writing Program
New York Law School

UNIVERSITY OF CALIFORNIA PRESS
Berkeley   Los Angeles

University of California Press
Berkeley and Los Angeles, California

© 1989 by Tom Goldstein and Jethro K. Lieberman

First University of California Press paperback edition published 1991.
Published by arrangement with McGraw-Hill, Inc.

Library of Congress Cataloging-in-Publication Data

Goldstein, Tom.
   The lawyer's guide to writing well / Tom Goldstein
and Jethro K. Lieberman.—1st University of
California Press pbk. ed.
      p.   cm.
   "Published by arrangement with McGraw-Hill,
Inc."—T.p. verso.
   Includes bibliographical references and index.
   ISBN 0-520-07321-5
   1. Legal composition.   I. Lieberman, Jethro
Koller.   II. Title.
KF250.G65   1991
808'.06634—dc20   90-26879
                              CIP

Printed in the United States of America

9 8 7 6 5 4 3 2

The paper used in this publication meets the minimum re-
quirements of American National Standard for Information
Sciences—Permanence of Paper for Printed Library Materials, ANSI Z39.48-1984. ∞

To Nancy and Jo

CONTENTS

PART III

Making Your Prose Serviceable
83

Authors' Note: To instruct, startle, or amuse, we have scattered throughout the text comments by judges, practitioners, professors, and others on the state of lawyers' writing. Many of the comments dated 1987 and 1988 were taken from our survey (see p. 3).

PART I

Why Lawyers Write Poorly

CHAPTER 1

Does Bad Writing Really Matter?

M OST LAWYERS write poorly.

That's not just our lament. Leading lawyers across the country agree.* They think modern legal writing is flabby, prolix, obscure, opaque, ungrammatical, dull, boring, redundant, disorganized, gray, dense, unimaginative, impersonal, foggy, infirm, indistinct, stilted, arcane, confused, heavy-handed, jargon- and cliché-ridden, ponderous, weaseling, overblown, pseudointellectual, hyperbolic, misleading, incivil, labored, bloodless, vacuous, evasive, pretentious, convoluted, rambling, incoherent, choked, archaic, orotund, and fuzzy.

Many critics amplified: Lawyers don't know basic grammar and syntax. They can't say anything simply. They have no judgment and don't know what to include or what to leave out. They do not know how to

---

*Between October, 1987, and June, 1988, we asked 650 people familiar with legal writing—practicing lawyers, judges, professors, writing instructors, and journalists who report on legal topics—what bothered them most about the way lawyers write. We do not pretend that our survey was scientific: We sent a four-page questionnaire to people listed on our Rolodexes. As journalists we have covered law and the legal profession since the early 1970s for a variety of news media, and the list included thoughtful lawyers and writers in half the states; every major city; most major law firms, scores of smaller firms, and courts; law schools; and newspapers, magazines, and broadcast stations across the country. The answers from 300 respondents form a portion of this book. People named in the text but not identified in the End Notes beginning on p. 213 were respondents and are identified in the Acknowledgments, beginning on p. 259. Likewise, unattributed statements about what lawyers, judges, professors, writing instructors, and journalists "think," "feel," or "believe" are drawn from the statements of those listed in the Acknowledgments.

3

tell a story—where to begin, when to end, or how to organize it. They get so carried away with their advocacy that they distort and even deceive.

The difficult task, after one learns how to think like a lawyer, is relearning how to write like a human being.

FLOYD ABRAMS, *1988*

So what? Does poor writing matter? It's commonplace to say that it does.

What are its consequences? That's a harder question to answer.

In the fall of 1987, Justice Alvin F. Klein of New York State Supreme Court in Manhattan embarrassed opposing lawyers in a divorce case by saying in open court that he could not understand the papers filed by either of them. He ordered the lawyers to rewrite their motions and objections.

The judge's impatience stands for more than the passing mortification of two practitioners or the wasting of several hours in drafting undecipherable papers. Judges rarely comment on the style or intelligibility of documents they read, though not for want of opportunity. Perhaps judges are reluctant to do so because they know their own prose could be ridiculed next. In admonishing the lawyers, Justice Klein rambled a bit himself: "Upon a careful reading of all the voluminous papers submitted herein, the court is frank to state that it cannot ascertain the basis for the relief sought by the plaintiff on the motion and by the defendant on the cross-motion." But Justice Klein diagnosed a soreness that afflicts the practice of law throughout the country. Perhaps it is not a fatal disease but a wasting one: a canker if not a cancer.

The consequences of poor legal writing are simple to state though difficult to prove:

- It wastes the valuable time of judges, clients, and other lawyers, who must constantly reread documents to figure out what is meant.

- It costs law firms a lot of money; they must absorb the time of senior lawyers who are forced to rewrite the work of junior ones.

- It costs society; we all pay for the lost time and the extra work.

- **It loses cases.** Briefs and memoranda and letters that do not adequately convey a writer's point give adversaries who are better writers the opportunity to portray their own positions more persuasively and sympathetically.

- **It can lead to disrespect for or indifference to law.** The public can't understand what lawyers are saying because the law itself is almost always obscure, and the lawyers' attempts to explain it are rarely clearer.

- **It erodes self-respect.** Hurried, careless writing weakens the imagination, saps intelligence, and ultimately diminishes self-esteem and professionalism.

- **It impoverishes our culture.** Writing well in a calling that prides itself on professionalism in pursuit of justice ought to be an end in itself.

Despite these consequences, many lawyers fail to connect good writing to good lawyering, probably because it is rarely possible to quantify the costs. We doubt that lawyers would offer to reveal, or that accountants would leap at the opportunity to prove, the dollar value a particular document cost the firm or the client or society because it was poorly written. And who can measure the injustice that obscurity fosters? So lawyers dismiss the consequences of their inability to express themselves well.

Writing to me is just writing—not legal or otherwise.
LOUIS A. AUCHINCLOSS, 1988

"Writing is a waste of time," said a young associate at a midsized New York firm, which had hired us to tutor incoming lawyers. "We sell time, not paper." He could not be more mistaken. Good lawyers may rightly measure the value of the paper they sell by the time it takes to put words onto it, but if the document is unreadable, clients are not impressed—or should not be—that a lawyer has spent endless hours on their behalf. Good lawyers must devote their time to producing effective prose, but that is time well spent.

> *The more important a lawyer, judge, or case, the more important clear*
> *writing becomes. One can be a good lawyer or judge and a bad writer,*
> *but not a great one without being a good writer.*
>
>   STUART BERG FLEXNER, *1987*

The good lawyer is genuinely interested in words, in their nuances, in the subtle distinctions between them, in the growth of the language. The good lawyer browses through usage books now and again, not from pedantry but from fascination with language and the power of writing. The good lawyer reveres English—and edits his work one more time to ensure that he has expressed his thought with the clarity and felicity that he owes to his client, to the public, and to himself.

Those for whom writing is unimportant are doomed to be second-rate lawyers. The connection between good writing and good professional work is not peculiar to lawyers. But because lawyers' work, more than that of other professionals, consists of writing, a lawyer's disinclination to write well is the more disheartening—and potentially the more disastrous. The bad lawyer scorns the craftsman unremunerated for his pains. This lawyer, at best, produces workmanlike prose—he knows some rules of usage—and settles for the pedestrian. The bad lawyer, neglecting his craft, risks his livelihood—or certainly his clients'.

Lawyers who ignore the art of writing, who leave their prose rough, murky, and unedited, are not simply foolish; they are guilty of malpractice. Unhappily, this form of malpractice is widespread.

George D. Gopen, a lawyer and director of the writing programs at Duke University, uses an elaborate metaphor—the "toll booth syndrome"—to describe how lawyers write. Late on an arctic night as you drive home from an exhausting day's work, you toss your last quarter at the toll basket—and miss. You can back up and pay the toll collector in another lane, or you can go through the red light just ahead of you. Your choice depends on what you think the toll is for. If it is to help finance road repairs, then you should back up and pay. But if you suppose the purpose is simply to divest drivers of loose change, you will go through the light. The money is not in the road authority's hands, but it is not in yours either.

So, says Gopen, lawyers write, without thinking about the purpose of doing so:

You cast all of your knowledge on the subject out of your mind onto the paper, not caring if the audience will actually receive your 40¢ worth of wisdom, but caring only that you unburden yourself of it. It's all out there—on the paper, in the gravel—and that is what matters.

Of course, that is *not* what matters. . . . [Lawyers] get all the relevant information down on the paper; they refer to all the possible issues and suggest a number of different approaches and counterapproaches; and all the while they have no perception of how a reader not already knee-deep in the case will be able to wade through it all.

The widespread feeling that good writing does not count is puzzling in a profession that demands its practitioners be well educated. Every state requires prospective practitioners to spend three years at law school, where students learn the substance of law. But only grudgingly are students taught the skills of practice. Enlightened schools today offer "clinical" courses, showing how to build a client's case, how to guard against an adversary's, and the like. But the schools neglect writing, the one skill that subsumes all else.

I should apologize, perhaps, for the style of this bill. I dislike the verbose and intricate style of the modern English statutes . . . You however can easily correct this bill to the taste of my brother lawyers, by making every other word a "said" or "aforesaid" and saying everything over two or three times so as that nobody but we of the craft can untwist the diction, and find out what it means.

THOMAS JEFFERSON, *1817*

When pressed, law schools offer excuses: Our professors don't want to teach writing. Teaching writing effectively is costly. Or time is limited, and students come for law, not for a refresher course in what they should have mastered years before. Teaching writing is the responsibility of colleges (or high schools or elementary schools). Students will develop their writing skills on the job.

These excuses are inadequate. The Navy scarcely tolerates a sailor's inability to swim because he should have learned it elsewhere, nor does it assume that the sailor will discover how to float when his ship is sunk.

I am not belittling my own profession when I say that lawyers and judges have a more immediate stake in what is set down on paper. I write a biography and perhaps it touches the emotion of my readers. I hope it does. But a lawyer's brief, a judge's rendered opinion leads to direct action.

CATHERINE DRINKER BOWEN, 1955

Worse, these excuses keep students from learning that most lawyers do not know how to write effectively and that good writing really does matter. The message to students is clear: Your writing is good enough for whatever tasks come your way once you leave school's sanctuary.

In practice, the problem worsens. Most firms offer only a few hours' training to their recruits, even though the best recruits are mediocre writers. Some large firms invest fair sums of money and large amounts of time on substantive training—a workshop on advocacy, a seminar in the fine points of securities trading, the art of taking depositions—a measure of what they think is valuable. Many bosses have been poorly trained themselves and cannot improve upon inept writing of their juniors, so the prose deteriorates further. The occasional partner outraged at some bit of mangled syntax might circulate a memo on "The Five Rules of Good Writing," as if these idiosyncratic rules (themselves quite likely to be wrong) solve the problem. Solo practitioners and lawyers at small firms receive little guidance; what they see is the often marginal, convoluted prose of their adversaries and judges.

The lawyer's writing problem is compounded by the different forms that poor writing can assume. When lawyers discuss bad—and good—writing, they mean diverse things. Solving minor difficulties, they may believe they have overcome all. At a prosperous West Coast law firm we visited, a fourth-year associate bragged about how well she and some of her colleagues wrote. Of her boss, she said, "He knows how to write; he knows the difference between 'that' and 'which.' "

The "that-which" distinction is an important issue in English usage, but this knowledge is scarcely the height of the writer's skill. The writer must contend with scores of other usage problems, and usage itself is only one of many elements a skilled writer must master.* Yet all too

---

*In fact, distinguishing "that" from "which" is simple. See pp. 147–148 and the Glossary.

many lawyers believe that good writing means only mastering a few simple rules.

To prove that they are good writers, or at least that they care about well-ordered sentences, many lawyers, including the West Coast associate, point to a tattered copy of Strunk and White sitting on the bookshelf. *The Elements of Style*, that venerable volume on good usage, was published in 1918 and rediscovered in 1957 when one of William Strunk's students, E. B. White, reminisced about the book in the *New Yorker*. For many lawyers, it epitomizes the craft of writing. The U.S. Court of Appeals for the Eleventh Circuit in Atlanta gives a copy to every lawyer admitted to practice. Thomas W. Evans, a senior partner in Mudge, Rose, Guthrie, Alexander & Ferdon in New York, says: "Over the years the only aid that I have found particularly useful in writing is to reread occasionally *The Elements of Style*. Immediately after these readings, my sentences seem to become shorter and clearer. In time, I drift back into bad habits until I am led to pick up that little book again."

The Elements of Style is a good "little book," as Strunk himself called it in 1919 when it was first circulated on the Cornell campus. As a brief summary of some useful rules, it does belong on a writer's shelf. We assign it to our own students. But *The Elements of Style* is also unsystematic, chaotic, limited, and sometimes unhelpful. Here, for example, is what Strunk and White say about "that-which":

> *That* is the defining, or restrictive pronoun, *which* the nondefining, or nonrestrictive.

Accurate, surely, but how does it help?

Lawyers' misplaced reliance on Strunk and White is emblematic of a limited perspective on writing. Good writing is more than adherence to elementary rules of usage. The good legal writer must consider these subjects, among others:

(1) *Vocabulary*—the choice of appropriate words

(2) *Organization*—the effective arrangement of thought

(3) *Topic flow*—the appropriate articulation of concepts

(4) *Transitions*—the connections between ideas

(5) *Structure*—the proper elements of a document

(6) *Audience*—the nature of the expected readership

(7) *Tone*—the manner or spirit of addressing readers

(8) *Style*—the types of sentences and the cadence of prose

(9) *Clarity*—the fit between idea and expression

(10) *Accuracy*—the fit between expression and reality

(11) *Timing*—when to write and when, and how often, to edit

In this book we write for lawyers who wish to improve their writing—for practitioners who seek to refine their skills and for students who hope to develop them. We look at writing from many perspectives to offer concrete solutions to difficulties of which readers may be unaware. We do not suppose that those who absorb the contents of this book will match Brandeis, Cardozo, or Holmes as stylists. But we do believe that diligent readers will become better writers and that they will be equipped with the means of improving further on their own.

Some lawyers are wonderful, some crummy; just as Lewis Thomas is a doctor who can write beautifully while other doctors' prose has all the ring of a birth-control prescription.

MICHAEL G. GARTNER, *1988*

Three more observations about the book's aims:

(1) Because writing is an art and a skill, a process and a business, an end in itself and a means to other ends, we do not confine our discussion to rules of usage. We propose that readers consider context and process as well as rules. In Chapter 2, we discuss the causes of poor writing and the historical critique of legal writing; in Chapters 3 to 7, the way writers write—individually and in the office; in Chapters 8 to 11, the rules and techniques for polishing prose; and in Chapter 12, how to make your writing memorable.

(2) Because every lawyer composes for many purposes and different audiences, our advice should not be taken to apply equally to every kind of document and under every set of circumstances. We know that lawyers are busy and that they do not have the novelist's luxury of time. The lawyer who must prepare overnight a response to a motion for a preliminary injunction obviously cannot put the draft aside for days before returning to reconsider it. Rules of grammar and usage apply to every brief, memorandum, and pleading, but the process by which those papers are composed will depend on the time and resources available.

(3) With minor exceptions, we do not consider the art of drafting legislation, contracts, or other legal instruments in "plain English," understandable to the lay public. Our premise is that lawyers' thoughts and manner of expression are so disordered that even *other lawyers* cannot understand them. This inability of so many lawyers to communicate among themselves is the focus of the pages that follow. As lawyers learn to write well, inevitably the public will learn to understand them also. But that is not the starting point. Lawyers must first learn to talk to each other.

Mindful that we have chided scores of lawyers by using their writing to illustrate problems and solutions, we have sought assiduously to eliminate our own mistakes. But writing about writing errors is always dangerous because critics invariably commit their own. Sally Powell, the book review editor of *Business Week* for many years, would never let her writers attack typographical errors in the books they were reviewing, because as soon as they did, she said, similar mistakes would creep into the magazine.

If most lawyers wrote well, I'd have to get a real job.
MILT POLICZER, LEGAL COLUMNIST, 1988

On occasion, we confess, we have led with our chins. In our survey, for example, we asked the question: "Do you have other thoughts on legal writing that you would like to share with us?" David L. Shapiro, a professor at Harvard Law School, chided: "Only that the 'sharing of thoughts' should be left to the headmasters of progressive secondary schools."

We hasten to acknowledge that mistakes are sometimes just mistakes and that not every wooden phrase or fuzzy thought means that the writer is stupid or foolish. We recognize that mistakes inevitably remain in this book too. We hope that by adhering to the principles we propound, we and you can learn to keep them to a minimum.

CHAPTER 2

Don't Make It Like It Was

AROUND THE COUNTRY, a select group of court watchers indulges an arcane hobby: collecting lawyers' dreck. Milt Policzer, a west coast columnist, sent us his nominee for the worst sentence of the year:

That on November 10, 1981, at 1:00 p.m. while plaintiff was a business invitee and customer, present at that certain real property, a Ralph's Market, located at 1725 Sunset Blvd., Los Angeles, California, and that at said time and place, the defendants, and each of them, carelessly and negligently owned and operated and maintained and controlled the said real property and particularly a shopping cart thereof, and the said cart was at said time and place in a dangerous condition, because there was no "seat flap" in the "upper" basket and a can fell through, breaking plaintiff's foot and it was unsafe for use by persons, including plaintiff, and directly because of such condition, and the negligently and carelessly maintained condition thereof the plaintiff was caused to and did sustain injuries and was proximately injured thereby as hereinafter set forth.

Fred Graham, a former Supreme Court reporter for the *New York Times* and CBS-TV, collected examples of particularly ghastly "questions presented," the required statement of the issues in each petition for certiorari, "until," he says, "I got discouraged." Here are two of his favorites:

Whether, consistently with the due process clause and the equal protection clause of the fourteenth amendment, a state court may deprive a party, without compensation of his or its constitutional

13

rights to property by validation of an invalid court determination through the aegis of res judicata, wherein such principle of res judicata was actually a premise for invalidation and nullity rather than the aforementioned validation.

Does it violate the fourteenth amendment of the United States Constitution for the highest court of the state, here the supreme court of Pennsylvania, when a petition for leave to appeal to it from a decision of an intermediate appellate court, here the superior court of Pennsylvania, to refuse allocatur even though the petition for such sets out clearly and unambiguously a claim of denial of due process of law guaranteed by the fourteenth amendment, and a claim that such refusal violated the Pennsylvania constitutional prohibition against impairment of contract, and a claim that a refusal of such a review is a violation of the corporation's right to a jury trial guaranteed at some stage of an arbitration proceeding by local case law where the jurisdiction of an arbitrator has been challenged?

Teachers, too, have their collections. On a recent constitutional law examination, one hopeful student referred to a "probable certainty." Another cleared his throat: "First of all, the first problem to address is . . ." A classmate opined that "the right to publish and distribute political ideas is a tenant of the Constitution." Another declared: "Treating AIDS sufferers and carriers as a suspect class would most likely not fly." Still another informed her bewildered professor that "the state has a valid and compelling interest in keeping its locals clean and thus affixing stickers to telephone poles and lampposts may be valid." The professor's eyes widened upon reading: "Concededly, the AIDS epidemic is a compelling governmental objective." Other students noted that the statute could not "past muster" and that an assumption may help "to access the situation." One advocated "repealment."

I want every law student to be able to read and write. Half my first year
students, more than a third of my second year students, can do neither.
                                                    KARL LLEWELLYN, *1935*

Much of the current dismay over lawyers' writing reflects a belief that their writing went to hell only recently, that lawyers were once known by their elegant style. This view misses a good deal of history. It reminds us of the story Edward I. Koch, the former New York City mayor, has often told about the elderly woman who stopped him on the boardwalk at Coney Island. She poignantly related how life had deteriorated. Crime was up, the air was dirty, the water befouled. "Make it like it was," she implored. "I'll try," Koch responded. "But it never was the way you think it was."

A Short Retelling of the Attack on Legal Prose

Historically, lawyers' prose has never been free of attack. In fifteenth-century England, Chief Justice John Fortescue declared that the judges were giving effect to forms written in unintelligible language even though none could remember the reason for the language. In the sixteenth century, the Lord Chancellor stuffed a plaintiff's head through a hole cut in a stack of pleadings and marched him around Westminister Hall with the pages drooping over his shoulders. This public humiliation was a double insult: The pleadings were drawn by the plaintiff's lawyer, who had padded them with an extra 100 pages and then had the effrontery to charge his client more. A century later the practice continued: Chief Justice Hale denounced padding as serving "no other use but to swell the attorney's bill," and Sir Francis Bacon urged editing of cases—"prolixity, tautologies and impertinences to be cut off."

In the eighteenth century, Jonathan Swift in *Gulliver's Travels* denounced lawyers for their odd speech: "a peculiar Cant and Jargon of their own, that no other Mortal can understand." Jeremy Bentham was blunter, characterizing lawyers' language as "excrementitious matter" and "literary garbage," even though his insistence on nouns in place of verbs contributed to the opaque quality of modern legal prose. Henry Fielding put in the mouth of one of his characters that "nothing is more hurtful to a perfect knowledge of the law than reading it."

In America, the critique of legal style is older than the Republic. Thomas Jefferson, a pellucid writer of legal as well as ordinary English, mocked as "lawyerish" the orotund style of the day. Late in his career,

long since retired as President, Jefferson wrote to a friend about a bill
he had drafted in simple language:

> You, however, can easily correct this bill to the taste of my brother
> lawyers, by making every other word a "said" or "aforesaid,"
> and saying everything over two or three times, so that nobody
> but we of the craft can untwist the diction, and find out what it
> means; and that, too, not so plainly but that we may conscien-
> tiously divide one half on each side.

Similar criticisms echoed through the nineteenth century, an age when
reformers began to purge from the common-law system the worst of the
archaic forms of pleading. The rules of pleading, as stylized as movement
in a Kabuki play, had contributed to the prolixity and pedantry of legal
writing. But centuries of bad habits had dulled lawyers' ears and addled
their brains. Simpler procedures would not yield simplified writing.

In this century, criticism of law language has intensified. In the early
1920s, for example, Urban A. Lavery, chief legislative draftsman for the
Illinois Constitutional Convention, scolded his fellow practitioners:

> How many lawyers ever consult once a book on grammar or on
> good use of English, where they consult a lawbook a hundred
> times? . . . The lawyer too often is a careless writer; and he,
> before all men, might write well if he but strove to do it. But he
> does not strive; he "dangles" his participles, he "splits" his
> infinitives, he scatters his auxiliary verbs, he leaves his relative
> pronouns and adjectives to die of starvation far removed from
> their antecedents; his various parts of speech are often not on
> speaking terms with their best friends.

In the 1930s, three prominent law professors deplored the general
illiteracy of the bar. In 1935, Karl N. Llewellyn, a professor at Columbia
Law School, said: "I want every law student to be able to read and write.
Half of my first-year students, more than a third of my second-year
students, can do neither." In 1936, in "Goodbye to Law Reviews," a
famous article in the *Virginia Law Review*, Professor Fred Rodell of Yale
Law School wrote: "There are two things wrong with almost all legal
writing. One is its style. The other is its content. That, I think, about

covers the ground." In 1939, William L. Prosser, then teaching at the University of Minnesota Law School, said of his students: "Very, very many of them are hopelessly, deplorably unskilled and inept in the use of words to say what they mean, or, indeed, to say anything at all." This was not an abstract generalization; Prosser proved it by reprinting this passage, among others, from a final examination:

> The buyer has an action for breech of warenty if he has gave notice to the seller in a reasonable time Uniform Sales Act sec. 48 after he knows of the defect there is a trade name here but here he does not give such he has an action no action for breech of warenty also after he reasonably ought to of known the warenty would be implied warenty of merchentable quality here thirty days is too long. You could not bring fittness for the purpose here because there is a trade name Holden's Beer is a trade name buyer took initiative in asking for it so reliance on seller's skill and judgement not here but merchentable not excluded according to Cardozo if this is sale and not service I think it is sale and merchentable quality in spite of trade name but no notice and so no action for breach of implied warenty of merchanteble quality in spite of trade name.

In 1950, Arthur T. Vanderbilt, then Chief Justice of the New Jersey Supreme Court and formerly dean of New York University Law School, acknowledged "the well-nigh universal criticism respecting the inability of law students to think straight and to write and speak in clear, forceful, attractive English."

Nine years later, another frequent critic of legal writing, Dean William Warren of Columbia Law School, said at a symposium of the American Association of Law Libraries:

> I know that some of my colleagues in other institutions have taken the position that their students are able to write. However, I can only tell you what the Bar thinks about this since I have talked rather extensively with many practitioners. Most members of law firms tell me that the young men who are coming to them today cannot write well. I think the situation has reached almost epidemic proportions.

Carl McGowan, a Chicago practitioner later to become a distinguished federal appeals judge, complained in 1961 of the inability of lawyers to express themselves in English: "Most of the time our lights are hidden under literally bushels of words, inexpertly put together."

In the last ten years, as academic and professional law journals have continued to denounce the "epidemic" of bad writing, the academy and the bar have responded by shelling out cash. Remedial writing entrepreneurs have launched businesses to tutor practicing lawyers. Law schools have added writing courses to their required curricula. A new professional discipline, the teaching of legal writing, has evolved, accompanied by its own newsletter and often unfathomable jargon. One researcher, for instance, speaks of "reader-protocols" and "revision feedback." Language columns have proliferated in bar journals, and books for students and practitioners have flooded the market.

We know that students can't read and write when they enter law school, and they can't read and write when they leave law school.

ALBERT BLAUSTEIN, *1959*

Even the government has found it politic to act. In 1978, President Carter signed an executive order that federal regulations be written in "plain English and understandable to those who must comply with them." Many states followed. During the 1970s, some large corporations began to rewrite consumer documents in plain English, both as a reaction to legislative pressures and as a public relations gimmick.

Fourteen Causes of Bad Legal Writing

Recent critics of legal writing discern not one but many causes of the "epidemic" of bad writing. To bring some order into an often confused discussion, we have distilled from the literature fourteen explanations of why lawyers write badly:

- *Sociological.* Every profession needs its own symbols and codes to set it apart from the rest of the world.

- *Professional.* Lawyers are trained to be exhaustive researchers.

- *Materialistic.* A competitive society demands prolixity.

- *Legal.* The law requires "legalese."

- *Economic.* Lawyers make more money by writing poorly.

- *Historical.* Creatures of precedent, lawyers do what was done before, solely because it was done before.

- *Ritualistic.* People must believe in the majesty of the law, embodied in its ritualistic language.

- *Technological.* Modern machines such as the typewriter are responsible.

- *Institutional.* The pressure of business is responsible.

- *Deterministic.* The way lawyers write is the best way to accomplish the law's goals.

- *Pedagogical.* Lawyers never learned to write well.

- *Cultural.* Lawyers don't read enough or know enough of their heritage to write better.

- *Psychological.* Lawyers are afraid to reveal themselves.

- *Intellectual.* Lawyers don't think clearly enough.

Sociological. To function as a profession, every group of practitioners needs its own symbols, rituals, and practices to set it apart from the rest of the world. Stuart Auerbach, who covered legal affairs at the *Washington Post* in the late 1970s, speculates that lawyers' language serves "as a secret handshake in a fraternity, letting others know you are one of the tribe." Or as Professor Lawrence M. Friedman of Stanford Law School said in 1964, a "specialized vocabulary reinforces the group feelings of members. . . . Legal style and the vocabulary of lawyers . . . are indispensable for the cohesiveness and the prestige of the profession."

They are verbose and redundant. They engage in polysyllabic obfuscation in order to convince their clients that lawyers know things that laymen don't.

JAMES SIMON KUNEN, 1987

This cultish quality of the language takes possession of all lawyers early in their training. What lawyer was not struck to learn in the first year of law school that "an action sounds in tort"? We were stepping away from our friends and college classmates, leaving them behind. They were becoming—"nonlawyers." Since they were not lawyers, they were something much less: They were laymen. Alone among professionals, lawyers exclude the rest of the world in their very name for others. Who has ever heard of a "nonteacher," a "nonjournalist," or a "nondoctor?"

"Strange style," as Professor Robert W. Benson calls it, binds lawyers, in their own eyes, into a fraternity. In short, lawyers conform to a way of writing so that colleagues will not think the worse of them.

The sociological explanation suggests that lawyers will never rid themselves entirely of their technical language. That lawyers, like all professionals, desire fraternity does not, however, explain writing that is incomprehensible even to lawyers themselves.

Almost everyone who discusses law school students—or even, it may be added, young law school graduates—has an unkind word to say about their lack of adequate powers of oral and written expression in their native tongue.

ARTHUR VANDERBILT, *1950*

It would be desirable that each student who graduates from this school know how to read and write. I do not consider this objective to be a modest one; on the contrary, it is extravagantly ambitious.

GRANT GILMORE, *1959*

Professional. The professional explanation purports to justify verbosity, obscurity, and vagueness. Lawyers are trained, as the cliché goes, to leave no stone unturned: The diligent lawyer will search through every case that even remotely bears on the problem and will digest them all in a brief or memorandum. These days it is considered less than professional—it might even be malpractice—to omit any possible strand of argument, or any case that strengthens that strand, no matter how tangential. Hence verbosity.

Likewise, lawyers allege professionalism to justify much of the cryptic quality of their prose. Knowing they have a losing case or a difficult message, they express it opaquely to keep the courts or others from acting contrary to their clients' interests. The difficulty with this explanation is that it presumes much that is cryptic has been made so deliberately. There is little evidence for this proposition. Nor is there evidence that intentional obfuscation is a sound strategy. Furthermore, purposeful obscurity is difficult to accomplish; it takes a writer who knows how to write clearly to achieve a convincingly murky style and still stay out of trouble.

Moreover, this explanation fails to distinguish between a style that is unnecessarily opaque and the expression of critically important concepts that are by their nature vague. Consider these two examples:

(1) The legal requirement that a person act "reasonably." The word expresses a legal standard impossible to define precisely. That is not a fault of the writer but a virtue of the law. Norbert Wiener, the eminent mathematician, argued that the law should always say exactly what it means; it should never use ambiguous concepts. But some legal concepts—due process, equal protection of the laws, executive power —are inherently vague; to fix their boundaries for all time would rob us of the flexibility necessary to a free society.

(2) The Supreme Court's 1955 ukase in *Brown v. Board of Education* that school desegregation proceed "with all deliberate speed." Legitimately or not, the Court chose that vague phrase to avoid the serious dangers it foresaw had its language been more concrete.

Compare these examples with this recall notice to automobile owners, a favorite example of Joseph Williams, author of *Style*, one of the best books on clear writing: "Sudden hood fly-up beyond the secondary catch while driving . . . could result in vehicle crash." The drafter masked the danger with cloudy language. Even if the client demanded this obscurity to inhibit purchasers from demanding free repairs, the notice is irresponsible and nothing in the law itself requires that kind of dismal prose.

> *As writing in general has become cheapened by television, by trendy journalism, by the desire to spout without thought, so too lawyers have become infected by the shoddy. Some, obviously not all.*
>
> HERBERT MITGANG, *1987*

Similarly, defenders of the verbose style of statutory language—those overblown sentences dozens of lines long, with series of subjects ("person, organization, company, association, group, or other entity")—insist that verbosity closes loopholes. Without this verbosity, they argue, courts would exploit the loopholes they are so adept at discerning. Sometimes that argument is true, and sometimes lengthy statutes are necessary. But this sense of professionalism does not justify the *style* in which the statutes are written or the style of documents that are not specific legal instruments.

Materialistic. In our competitive, materialistic society, the client wants every edge; no argument, no matter how trivial, should be overlooked or underdone. If contracts are to be airtight, their clauses tend to be prolix, multiple, and often redundant. Language in an adversary culture evolves into a precision tool for accomplishing a range of ends. But the symptoms are broader than the cause. A litigious society will depend on lawyers who follow every byway of a case, but it does not dictate the writing of every point at maddening length or in obscure style.

Legal. Sometimes lawyers justify legalese by pointing to the law itself. Many words have settled meanings; substituting plain language— that is, words other than those to which the courts are accustomed—can lead to litigation. For some terms, the argument has merit. The common example is the medieval requirement that a fee simple could not be transferred unless the land was sold "to X and his heirs." A sale "to X and his children" would not be effective. But the courts are less formalistic today and fewer words have rigid meanings. Moreover, few words, even the most arguably precise terms of art, have escaped being broken on the interpreter's rack: the meaning of "herein" and "whereas," for example, have stirred up plenty of lawsuits. In any event, the legal explanation is a policy at cross purposes with itself. If legalese is so refined that it prevents litigation, that means it probably will be unintelligible to the clients who sign the instruments. Because it is unintelligible, the clients may then go to court claiming that they did not understand what they were signing. At best, the term of art may win the case; but it will not prevent a case from being filed. A clearly worded contract, on the other hand, may keep the parties out of court altogether.

Economic. The economic explanation is double-sided. First, lawyers use language as a tool to maintain their economic perquisites, and second, legalese is a tool to save time and money. Steven Stark, a lecturer in writing at Harvard Law School, argues that "lawyers write badly because doing so promotes their economic interest. . . . If lawyers stopped writing like lawyers, they might have trouble charging as much for their work." Half a century ago, Fred Rodell insisted that the legal trade "is nothing but a high-class racket" because the public is "scared, befuddled, impressed, and ignorant." That is why lawyers write in legalese and produce mounds of paper—at least when paid by the hour. If clients knew what the Latin phrase meant, they would never pay for the lawyer's services.

Far too many [students] have to have blasted out of them the idea that good legal writing involves complex, polysyllabic legalese.

THOMAS D. ROWE, *1987*

These arguments amount to sheer speculation. Whatever may once have been the truth about Latin incantations, law today is so complex that clients who receive advice in the form of memoranda or letters, or who buy legal instruments such as wills, are more likely to be grateful if they can understand what they have paid for. Although lawyers were once paid by the word, in America this practice died out long before this century. Our current system is based on time, not length. It usually takes longer to produce shorter, more readable documents, so the economic incentive should lead to clearer, not more obscure, documents.

A second economic point is made by Lawrence Friedman, who suggests that legal terms of art were invented as shortcuts to save time. Legalese is thus an efficient way to write, saving the lawyer, and hence the client, money. The validity of the argument depends on how much legalese is used and if the audience for whom it is intended can understand

it. Using technical terms in front of the court surely does save time—
lawyers would appear foolish, and feel foolish, to replace such terms as
"stare decisis" or "collateral estoppel" with something else. But an
opinion letter filled with such terms is not necessarily efficient. "Why
force your reader to parse and chart your prose?" asks Mark Matthewson,
an Illinois practitioner. "The writer should be doing that work, not the
reader. Think of it in economic terms—there will almost always be fewer
writers of a document than readers, and the interests of efficiency will
surely dictate that the writers, not the readers, translate the prose into
simple form."

Historical. Lawyers are conservative, innately cautious, and often
do what was done before solely because it was done before. As Jacques
Barzun suggested to us, lawyers use strings of synonyms out of habit.
We all know that the hold of habit is strong, but it rarely justifies what
we are doing. Justice Holmes once wrote in a different context, "It is
revolting to have no better reason for a rule of law than that so it was
laid down in the time of Henry IV. It is still more revolting if the grounds
upon which it was laid down have vanished long since, and the rule
simply persists from blind imitation of the past."

Ritualistic. Because law is a system of social control, it depends in
a democracy on faith—not guns—to achieve its purposes. People must
believe in the *majesty of the law*. The language of the law is, according
to this argument, a form of magic, a ritual incantation. (Centuries ago,
the ritual function was all there was. The litigant or lawyer would recite
a formulaic defense, and if he stumbled or misspoke, his misstatement
was taken as a sign from God that his cause was wrong.) In some contexts
even today, such as the taking of an oath ("the truth, the whole truth,
and nothing but the truth"), ritual phraseology "is designed to convey,
not information, but emotion—fear, awe and respect," says Lawrence
Friedman. But in a secular age, such talismanic purposes of language
will necessarily be few.

Some defenders of legalese argue, however, that customers may draw
comfort from the archaic. Linda Ishkanian, who works at Siegal & Gale,
a New York firm that specializes in simplifying the language of legal
instruments, has suggested that some clients will not be satisfied with a

> *What is disturbing is that law schools . . . find themselves in the situation that even the good writers do not know the difference between "its" and "it's."*
>
> DAVID G. TRAGER, 1987

document unless it contains the traditional "whereases" and "heretofores." And Peter Lubin, a Cambridge writer and lawyer defending archaisms, wrote in the *New Republic* that once as a defendant in a small claims action he was quite impressed when his own lawyer produced the following lines in answer to an unfair suit filed against him: "Now comes the Defendant and for his answer denies, Each and every allegation of the Plaintiff's complaint. And further answering says, that if he ever owed the Plaintiff anything, he owes the Plaintiff nothing." Lubin extolled this language as "beauty on the level of the Bible and Shakespeare, . . . part of what creates the mystery and majesty of the law."

This is more whimsy than sense. There are few such phrases and, we suspect, even fewer admirers of them. Again, magic explains only phrases, not the panoply of writing faults in which lawyers regularly engage.

Technological. The typewriter has led directly to verbosity, suggests David Mellinkoff, professor emeritus at the University of California at Los Angeles Law School. With the hand no longer so liable to cramping, the fingers could waltz along a keyboard turning out far more copy in a shorter time than they ever could with the pen and inkstand. Other modern machines—the copier, the word processor, the optical scanner, the facsimile machine—have also contributed to sprawl. As long ago as the early 1960s, Mellinkoff noted that electronic data retrieval, like its predecessors "in the arts of availability," is "ruled by a corollary of Parkinson's Law: the data to retrieve increases as it becomes more retrievable." Because they can get words down on paper so easily and without scanning every line, lawyers may be less likely to take the time to consider what is being imprinted.

Institutional. Modern law practice is a business, with institutional imperatives of its own. Few law firms working at a leisurely pace survive. From the most senior partner to the most junior associate, private law firms (and most public law offices too) are pressured to crank out paper. The pressure of business means that human energies are focused more on technical matters—meeting deadlines, checking footnotes, getting documents printed—than on thinking. Fewer and fewer hours are available for thinking through a problem, writing it down, and editing the results. It is thus far easier, and seemingly safer, to borrow from previous documents than to rethink and rewrite. Add the lawyer's fear of originality, and the consequence is that lawyers reproduce not just words from a document but its tone and style as well. To be sure, boilerplate may be appropriate, but it does not belong everywhere.

Students seem more than ever to think that some kind of human right is violated when we hold them to high writing standards.
                                        RICHARD K. NEUMANN JR., *1987*

The institutional pressure can be even more unremitting on the small-firm and solo practitioners. Always pressed for time, often competing with large firms that can drown them in paper, the small-firm practitioners understandably, if unfortunately, are inclined to regurgitate old copy.

Other institutional habits also diminish the quality of writing. One is the tendency, observable at nearly every level of every institution (it is by no means confined to law firms), to ask someone lower on the organization chart to write for someone higher. Outside the legal profession, this practice often goes by the name ghostwriting. A generation ago, Carl McGowan commented on "the extraordinary degree to which the successful lawyer may get out of the habit of writing anything himself. . . . Some of our best men at the bar may be doing very little initial composition; and we all know how the first draft tends to set the style and tone of any piece of writing."

Still another development that multiplies words is the expansion of staff. Many of our respondents pointed to the baneful effect of more law clerks on the length and quantity of judicial opinions. Justice Richard Neely of the West Virginia Supreme Court said that hiring more clerks increases the level of "pseudo-scholarship": "While judges used to be good old boys who penciled out their opinions in long hand, now they simply figure out the bottom line and tell some magna cum loudmouth smartass clerk to cobble up the reasons in an opinion. The clerk has little idea how everything comes together. But he knows how to use a library. Thus, the ever rising level of crap in reported cases.'' Similarly, Patricia M. Wald, Chief Judge of the U.S. Court of Appeals for the District of Columbia Circuit, told us that judges are understandably reluctant to disappoint the clerk who has researched and written a lengthy memorandum about a pending case. So they incorporate the pages in the opinion.

Deterministic. Some critics say that lawyers talk and write abstractly because that is the way they think about the world. Condemning their abstract approach, Steven Stark argues that ''poor writing is as much a consequence of the way lawyers look at the world as is their ability to read a contract and find consideration.'' Because lawyers view the world abstractly, Stark theorizes, they cannot not tell stories that would make their writing concrete.

In the heels of the higgling lawyers, Bob,
Too many slippery ifs and buts and howevers
Too much hereinbefore provided whereas,
Too many doors to go in and out of . . .
CARL SANDBURG, *1920*

Stark's theory is disputed by Richard Hyland, a practitioner in Washington, D.C., who in 1986 offered a lengthy defense of legal writing. Instead of blaming lawyers for writing what the public cannot understand, Hyland suggests that the public is at fault for not understanding the conceptual complexity of what lawyers write. Storytelling is only one of many levels of discourse, he says, and it is not the level on which lawyers should be spending their time; they must aim for the higher, conceptual level, a place where, almost by definition, the uninitiated will feel uncomfortable or lost.

But even at this level, lawyers fail. Lawrence Grauman Jr., a San Francisco–area writer and editor with a special interest in law, expressed it best: ''Most lawyers appear to regard language and prose as merely an inconvenient vehicle (what they would term 'style') for the accommodation of ideas or argument (what they think of as 'content'), rather than as the very fiber of, and inseparable from, thought (or at least distinctive perception) itself. Few lawyers would wear a second-hand suit, but most are comfortable wearing well-worn or mass-produced language. And frequently the same lawyers who select their clothes to make a visual impression use language merely to make a verbal impression or to inflate their self-importance.''

Every time a lawyer writes something, he is not writing for posterity, he is writing so that endless others of his craft can make a living out of trying to figure out what he said.

WILL ROGERS, 1935

Whether or not the public should be expected to understand is not the critical point. Obviously much of the complexity of law will try the public's patience, even if the law is expressed plainly. The real problem is that even *other lawyers* cannot fathom what their colleagues are writing.

Pedagogical. The simplest explanation of why lawyers write badly is that they were never taught how to write well. Participants in a symposium in the *Yale Alumni Magazine* in 1976 expressed a familiar complaint of the 1970s and 1980s: ''Anyone who reads student writing today knows that students can't write.'' The students of 1976 who could not write are today's junior partners who, in turn, are responsible for supervising the writing of new associates. At that symposium, A. Bartlett Giamatti, then professor of English and comparative literature, explained how cultural longings denied students their ability to express themselves:

Today's college students—the former grammar and high school students of the late 1960's and early '70's—have lost touch with the language. . . .
. . . They have come out of the sentimental '60's . . . out of a primary and secondary world where ''personal development'' was said to be worth more than achievement, where ''creativity'' was the highest goal and was often completely divorced from one of its essential components: discipline. . . .
What has happened? I believe that of all the institutions at-

tacked in the past dozen years—governmental, legal and educational—the one that suffered most was the institution of language itself. . . . This institution—language—was perceived as being repressive. It was thought to be the agent of all other repressive codes—legal, political, and cultural. Language was the barrier that blocked—blocked access to pure feeling, blocked true communal experience of the kind that flowered at Woodstock, blocked the restoration of Eden.

Though the student rebellion has subsided, some of its legacy lingers. Many schools are now focusing on language skills courses, but their rigor is open to question.

Still, too much can be made of what happened in the late 1960s. Even a nodding acquaintance with the complaints of educators over the years shows that the quality of too much student writing, in general, and law student writing, in particular, has always been problematical. In 1953, speaking of past generations, Jacques Barzun asked how "people write who are not professionals or accomplished amateurs?" His answer: "Badly, at all times."

The time traveler can easily confirm Barzun's observation. In the seventeenth century, leading British intellectuals clamored for admission to the new Royal Society, dedicated to scientific discovery and invention. In their history of the period, Jacob Bronowski and Bruce Mazlish have said: "More important than any formal symbolism, however, scientific work, to be understood, needs a clear expression in words. This the Royal Society stressed from the outset. . . . The Fellows of the Royal Society were exhorted to report their findings 'without amplification, digressions, and swellings of style.' " When the poet John Dryden was admitted to the Royal Society, he was promptly put to work simplifying the scientists' prose.

Each generation of critics has despaired anew over the ostensible decline of English and has blamed the deterioration on the failures of an earlier generation to teach it well. Writing in 1985, two law librarians, Kathleen M. Carrick and Donald J. Dunn, observed that the study of English was downgraded in secondary and high schools and colleges during the 1930s, posing writing problems for a generation of law students in the 1940s. "Law faculties," Carrick and Dunn assert, "resented being English grammar and composition teachers at the expense of substantive and adjective courses," and so separate law school writing courses, with all their problems, were created, first at the University of Chicago Law School in the late 1930s and at many more law schools in the late 1940s.

In legal education, even in most legal writing courses, little attention is given to reading good works and criticizing bad writing. During three years of law school, the basic reading materials of the student—judicial opinions—are selected for their substantive meaning, not for their quality of expression, and most judicial opinions are dreadful. They are poorly written in no small part because the profession contains no mechanism for criticizing the prose style of opinions.

Professor Robert Leflar of the University of Arkansas Law School has observed that the opaqueness of judicial writing is rarely challenged or criticized. The judge "may receive no real criticism of his writing for months or years," Leflar, a former justice of the Arkansas Supreme Court, wrote in 1961. "Unlike ordinary editors or publishers, the state reporters and the West Publishing Company never refuse to print his opinions, nor do they even edit them. His writing is published whether good or not. Almost no one except law review editors and losing litigants criticize his work, and even these critics usually dwell only on the correctness of his legal analyses rather than on the quality of his presentation."

Lucidity does not come naturally to most law students, perhaps because they have been forced in their legal studies to read so much bad writing that they mistake what they've read for the true and proper model.
                                              PAMELA SAMUELSON, *1984*

One style is held out as a model—the law review essay. It should not be. In his characteristically blunt fashion, Fred Rodell blamed legal style on what lawyers learn as law review editors, when they are "brainwashed" into thinking they must write in a "straitjacket" style, the lawyers' "brand of professional pig Latin."

Like judicial opinions, law review articles are seldom criticized for their density and opaqueness. As law reviews proliferate—more than 250 are now being published—the law review style spreads. Journal editors move on to clerkships, and in those jobs they re-create what they have learned: unending essays, numerous footnotes, suffocating prose—all taught by people who are themselves far from being students of good writing. Many of our respondents said they learned how to write and edit on a law review. But the question is *what* they learned. If you are being taught by people who prefer long-windedness, you will likely adopt that long-windedness. In criticizing law review writing, we do not mean to be anti-intellectual, but we do mean to observe that good writing is rarely taught, bad writing usually absorbed. Although many of these same people (and plenty of others) privately deplore the style of law reviews, few suggest how to change it or declare that they will refrain from writing for them.

Cultural. Two centuries ago, the tiny social elite that could write also tended to read. The intellectuals of the day, including the learned professionals—lawyers, clergy, and doctors—read the classics and the leading contemporary works. Today a common culture has nearly vanished; few professionals (who are drowning in technical literature) read works outside the law. As a consequence, they have little or no breadth. This is a complaint we hear frequently from senior partners about their younger associates, but it is not new. In 1950, Arthur Vanderbilt asserted that "no instructor in any class in any law school can make a reference to Plato or Aristotle, to the Bible or Shakespeare, to the *Federalist* or even the Constitution itself with any real assurance that he will be understood."

Without a reading habit, lawyers fail to develop the nimbleness of mind that distinguishes good from bad writers. Carl McGowan recalled the comments of a Supreme Court justice (whom he did not name) who had said that the quality of briefs and oral arguments before his court "is, on the whole, distressingly low. The justice in question has speculated that this is due to the narrowing cultural range of the profession, which in turn is a result of the restricted reading habits of lawyers, both in terms of the small amount of time devoted to general reading and the ephemeral character of what is read."

They have no lawyers among them, for they consider them as a sort of people whose profession it is to disguise matters.

SIR THOMAS MORE, *Utopia, 1516*

In answering our survey, many respondents referred to George Orwell's 1946 essay "Politics and the English Language." Orwell pointed
out that modern public discourse has been caught in a vicious circle that
continually corrupts the language: "It becomes ugly and inaccurate because our thoughts are foolish, but the slovenliness of our language makes
it easier for us to have foolish thoughts." Orwell blistered British bu-
reaucrats in particular. Anyone who reads newspapers knows that his
condemnation of Newspeak is as pertinent now as when he wrote it, forty
years ago. McGowan noted that lawyers are particularly exposed to the
double-talk of the bureaucracy; he offered the Pentagon's description of
appropriations not already spent as "unprogrammed in no-year ac-
counts." Since then we have had the euphemistic "terminations with
extreme prejudice" of Vietnam, the "inoperative statements" of Watergate, and the obfuscation of "revenue enhancements."

Psychological. As representatives, lawyers hesitate to intrude their
personalities into the affairs of their clients. Trained to identify more
with process than value or outcome, exhorted to refrain from vouching
personally for their clients' bona fides, lawyers are distanced from the
merits of their causes. But writing is a personal act, which reveals the
writer in the act of writing. To avoid or minimize the revelation, lawyers
transport the masks that they wear in public to the prose that they put on
the page. The passive voice, the fuzzy phrases, and the circumlocutions
that permit the lawyer to sidestep the simple "I" may all be understood
as lawyers' attempts to keep themselves from being on display. Stretch-
ing this point a bit further, we can hypothesize that lawyers, resistant
to changing themselves, exhibit that hesitancy in their general disdain
for editing. To edit is to probe; the insecure feel safer with surface
appearance.

Intellectual. The final explanation is the most devastating: Lawyers
lack the aptitude, or at least the training in logic, to think clearly. Richard
Hyland grounded his critique in the equation of thought and expression:
Lawyers, he said, cannot possibly hope to write clearly unless they can
think clearly. The real problems of legal writing, Hyland concluded, are
far more serious than technical problems of prose style: "They are the
irrelevancies that reveal the absence of disciplined thought." Stated that

baldly, it is hard to disagree with Hyland's proposition. Muddled thought can never be papered over—in law or any other discipline. Many lawyers toss out any and every argument, hoping one will capture the justices' fancy. Lawyers who grasp their arguments do not make such mistakes.

I know you Lawyers can, with Ease,
Twist Words and Meanings as you please;
That Language, by your Skill made pliant,
Will bend to favour ev'ry Client;
BENJAMIN FRANKLIN, EIGHTEENTH
CENTURY

Hyland pessimistically concludes that most lawyers are incapable of thinking clearly on the astonishing ground that they have not been trained in Latin, Greek, or comparative law. Though it is true that the more difficult a legal problem, the more likely a lawyer will flounder, Hyland's conclusion is flawed. Many legal problems are simple enough for any practicing lawyer to grasp. Failure to organize a document logically cannot be attributed solely to an empty head. Poorly organized thought and cloudy concepts are also products of laziness and inadequate grounding in what constitutes clear expression.

The most sophisticated commentators have recognized a deep duality that runs through the argument about legal writing. Thus Professor Ray J. Aiken of Marquette Law School, after defending the legalese that drafters use, concedes what "I, too, regard as a rampant and progressing decline of legal literacy, characterized by redundancy, obscurity of meaning, poor grammar and practical abandonment of every classical virtue of the compositional art." Professor Lawrence Friedman, after noting the purposes that legal language rightly fulfills, goes on to say that "law books are full of incredible quantities of plain bad style—clumsy, pompous legalese and tedious, obscure prose—which is neither good law, good magic, nor good history."

That it is imperative for lawyers to learn how to express themselves more clearly—against all the social and personal forces we have just explored—is, we think, almost a tautology. In his law review article defending the status quo of legal writing, Richard Hyland glibly concludes that good writing makes little difference because ''prose itself seems to be losing its hold as the prime medium for the communication of thought.'' We reject this 1980s' ''McLuhanacy'' out of hand. The lawyer's job is, as it always has been, to communicate legal thought in understandable prose.

PART II

The Process of Writing

CHAPTER 3

Ten Steps to Writing

"W HAT IS writing for?" we ask a roomful of lawyers.

"Communication," someone pipes up.

"Anything else?" we continue.

Blank stares. Determined to get an answer, we change our question.

"Quick now, how much is two plus two?"

Singled out by name, the lawyer hesitates, weighing the simplicity of the question against the odious possibility of a complex trick. Finally, the answer: "Four."

"Good."

Singling out another lawyer, we ask: "How much is ten times five?"

"Fifty," hurled back in the next breath.

"Very well, then," pointing this time to a lawyer who has sat silent all afternoon, "how much is 1324 times 967?"

The wiseguy, overcome with his brilliance, announces that the product is 57,246,589. Polite laughter, from us too.

We point again to the perplexed lawyer, who stares ahead gloomily, not understanding what has turned a writing tutorial at a law firm into a mathematics exercise from which he had fled years before.

"I cannot do that math in my head," the wriggling lawyer grunts. "I'm no idiot savant."

"What, then, should you do? We want an answer."

"Multiply," he replies, still resisting the obvious.

"Multiply where?"

In the hardcover edition, we called this chapter "The Ten Steps of the Writing Process." Jacques Barzun wrote us to complain of the unnecessary use of "process."

37

"Here," he says, stabbing at a notebook.

"Oh," we say, "you mean on paper!"

We've engaged in this colloquy dozens of times to show that before communication is possible, the writer must know what he wants to say. Just as most of us cannot solve a complicated math problem in our heads, so most of us need paper to solve the problems that are put to us as lawyers. Before communication, in other words, comes *problem solving*.

Every writer from the beginning of time . . . has learned the art of writing by ceaseless toil and practice. The lawyer alone thinks himself immune.
                                                              URBAN A. LAVERY, *1921*

How much anguish we would all have been spared had we known when we were young what we do when we write. Told to compose an essay on Shakespeare, Charlemagne, or the Declaration of Independence, we gnawed at our pencils, wondering how to get words to resemble the essay example in our textbooks. The methodical writer constructed an outline, dutifully scribbling after Roman numeral I, "Shakespeare, the Man." The impatient jotted down thoughts in spurts and whooped when the last ruled line was filled in. The furtive pulled down the encyclopedia, copying the most relevant article, aware on occasion of the need to paraphrase, though unclear why. Wasn't the object of the exercise to make sure we stayed in at night? Any words on the page would prove the next morning that we had.

When the papers came back to us, the teacher annotated in bold marginal red about the need to avoid so many irrelevancies, or to organize our thoughts better, or to refrain from copying quite so liberally, but few teachers could explain what we were supposed to do and why we couldn't seem to do it. Even fewer acknowledged the pain of writing and showed us how to deal with it.

Lawyers need to know what writing is about and how to vanquish the pain, without aspirin. You need to know that you are not the only one who suffers from chaos, uncertainty, and false starts. All writers do, and there is a sound reason for your difficulties in writing clearly and smoothly and logically on demand. That reason lies in the very nature of writing.

Writing is a twofold process: First, in the composing stage, you think through a problem and get your thoughts on paper. Second, in the editing stage, you shape what you have written to communicate it to an audience. When you sit down to compose, you have nothing to communicate, nothing, at least, about a subject of even moderate complexity, for you have not yet figured out what to say or even what you know. Just because you stare blankly at a piece of paper does not mean that your mind is defective; it is not a warning to take up another line of work. It means that your work *as a lawyer* is about to begin. Writing is thinking on paper.

Though problem solving is the essence of a lawyer's job, that skill is barely taught in law school. Classroom discussions focus on small points. Indeed, you cannot expect more from classroom time: To take on a larger problem, you would have to write it down, and no time in the classroom is set aside for that. Only on final exams do law schools call on students to solve problems, and by then class has been adjourned for the semester. Students thus learn little writing from exams. The schools teach doctrine, not skills.

Different skills are required at the two stages of writing. The goal of the first stage, *composing*, is to solve problems; the goal of the second stage, *editing*, is to express the solution clearly, to communicate. Most instruction in writing emphasizes the second stage—communication— by teaching rudimentary tools of editing. Writing instruction, at least in law schools, rarely emphasizes the first stage—problem solving or composing.

Skill in composing is proficiency in thinking: First, you must have the talent to put concepts in words—to wield logic, use analogy, and employ metaphor. Second, you must exercise judgment—to evaluate, select, and weigh.

There is an accuracy that defeats itself by the overemphasis of details . . .
The sentence may be so overloaded with all its possible qualifications
that it will tumble down of its own weight.

JUSTICE BENJAMIN CARDOZO, *1925*

In solving math problems, you needed plenty of scrap paper because you quickly learned, at least beyond simple arithmetic, that the solution was uncertain and mistakes were unavoidable. So, too, in solving complex verbal problems, you will rarely get it right the first time. You stumble, you back up, you weave this way and that because you are hunting for the solution as you go. That is why the most successful writers are those with well-stocked minds open to experimentation.

Few people solve problems the same way. Carl Stern, the law reporter for NBC-TV, compared how two Supreme Court justices with different approaches arrived at the same conclusion. They were dissenting from the Court's ruling that the Sierra Club had no standing to challenge the Forest Service, which had approved a plan to build a vacation complex in California. "When I think how different styles of writing can be, and ways of thought, I always recall the dissents of William Douglas and Harry Blackmun in the 1972 Sierra Club case," Stern wrote us.

"Douglas wrote passionately of 'these priceless bits of Americana' which might be forever lost. He eulogized the 'valleys, alpine meadows, ridges, groves of trees, rivers, lakes, estuaries, beaches, swampland or even air that feels the destructive pressures of modern technology and modern life,' of water ouzels, otter, deer, elk and bear, and of the Tuolumne Meadows and the John Muir Trail. He wondered who would speak for 'the core of America's beauty' before it is destroyed?

"Justice Blackmun, on the other hand, a one-time Harvard math major, computed the number of cars that were likely to pass a given point in the road each hour (300). 'This amounts to five vehicles per minute,' he said, 'or an average of one every twelve seconds.' Really, one every six seconds, he noted, because cars must return to leave the park. And that does not include service vehicles and employees' cars, he added, in his concern about preserving the beauty, solitude and quiet of the wilderness.

"Two judges with one point of view, but vastly different writing styles."

Diversionary tactics on the part of lawyers come from their fear that their expertise won't seem very special if they write it down in plain English.

ANDY ROONEY, *1987*

The ability to write is neither an innate talent nor a learned skill, concludes Susan R. Horton, an English professor at the University of Massachusetts and a perceptive student of the subject. "It is," she writes, "more a matter of attitude than of skill, and the attitude most essential is that of welcoming the mess and the mystery" that make up the writing process:

> If you are uncomfortable getting your hands dirty and your desk messy, you will cheat yourself out of the chance to discover something new and wonderful to say. Mess is material: material for thinking; for shaping into essays. . . .
>
> We know that "writing" does not begin when we first put pen to paper. Instead, writing is actually only the final stage of a long process. Ideas are born . . . partly in the act of writing— writing itself generates them—but they are also born out of that rich, primordial slime where we alternatively go after them with our big guns (like definition, compare/contrast, distinction-making) and lie in wait for them to raise their heads out of the smoky swamp like some Nessy. The truth is that all of the lists of procedures in the world will not help you write better if you do not acknowledge that the idea, the hypothesis, the new synthesis, the organization for an essay is likely to appear not so much as a result of applying a rigorous set of procedures, but just when you were not looking for it at all; as you stumbled half asleep to the front door at 4 a.m., to let the dog in, or out.

Once you understand that composing is a messy hunt for a solution to a problem, you should feel less frustrated over the stubborn refusal of the first draft to write itself. If you find it slow going, it is because you are wrestling with unyielding concepts, not because you are foundering on the words. That is why you cannot sensibly begin with a formal outline, as some teacher somewhere along the way insisted you must (even though an informal outline is usually helpful). An outline represents an ordered and logical structure, an organization that will not have come before the solution.

Since composing is thinking on paper, a first draft can never be your final product. At best it is the scrap-paper solution to your problem, showing the signs of trial and error. You can never count on a first draft's successfully communicating a solution to your intended audience.

From these considerations emerge two key principles to mastering writing:

- Compose early.

- Edit late.

These two simple principles, strictly adhered to, will promptly produce results. There is no trick here, but rather a recognition of the twofold purpose of writing. Solve your problem as early as possible; then delay rewriting as long as you can so that you will best communicate that solution to your audience.

The writing process consists of ten steps:

1. Develop a theory.

2. Research.

3. Jot down a rough outline.

4. Reassess your theory.

5. Set down a more formal outline.

6. Compose.

7. Reorganize.

8. Rewrite.

9. Edit.

10. Edit again.

Because we are discussing these steps in linear fashion, they sound more coherent and discrete than they will be in practice. For the most complex assignments you will necessarily proceed step by step as we have outlined. For less complex assignments, the steps may be all jumbled up, undertaken continuously, and repeated many times.

Step 1: Develop a theory. You must begin with some idea of direction, purpose, or goal, though you need not know exactly how you're going to get there. When Jessica was in the eighth grade, her history assignment was to write a thousand-word essay on "the impact of European colonialism on African economic development." She didn't know quite what that meant, and she didn't ask. Consequently, her research amounted to no more than a random collection of quotations that she jerry-built into an answer. She gave the draft to her father, the writing teacher. He didn't take kindly to it. She didn't take kindly to him. Moral: Know where you're going.

Too many young lawyers today are afraid to show strong feelings of any kind; the jargon in which they write illustrates all too graphically their insecurity about stating what they believe in. They rarely use a straight declarative sentence or the pronoun I. The passive tense sanitizes and institutionalizes their writing, and often anesthetizes the reader: all views are attributable to an unknowable "it." "It is said, it is reported, it is argued," etc.

JUDGE PATRICIA M. WALD, 1988

Ordinarily, Step 1 in legal writing is the easiest step because the nature of the case or your discussions with the client or a supervising attorney determine the objective: "We want summary judgment"; "he breached the contract"; "let's see if we can get specific performance"; "do we have a good case of copyright infringement?" You will surely fail if you do not know at the outset what your aim is. If unsure, ask. Lawyers who fail to ask questions, fearing to look stupid, are doomed to prove that they are stupid when the draft is turned in. Of course, you want to be intelligent about the questions you ask. The young lawyer who wonders "what exactly is summary judgment?" will raise a supervisor's eyebrow. But to wonder "why exactly do you think we should seek summary judgment in this case?" will force the supervisor to articulate a theory, a starting point for the work to come.

Step 2: Research. With a goal in mind, you can begin to research. You are not looking just for quotations to adorn your brief. Writers absorbed in hunting for quotations sacrifice time for thought; the more sparingly you quote, the better your writing. The library should stimulate thought; you read cases not to write a history of the law but to force your mind to react to something relevant, to begin thinking about the problem at hand, to let ideas flow.

As you research, keep your mind open to all possibilities. In a letter to a friend who had complained of an inability to write, the German poet and dramatist Johann Christoph Friedrich von Schiller acutely diagnosed the problem and offered advice that remains sound two centuries later:

> The ground for your complaint seems to me to lie in the constraint imposed by your reason upon your imagination. . . . Looked at in isolation, a thought may seem very trivial or very fantastic; but it may be made important by another thought that comes after it, and, in conjunction with other thoughts that may seem equally absurd, it may turn out to form a most effective link. . . . Where there is a creative mind, Reason . . . relaxes its watch upon the gates, and the ideas rush in pell-mell, and only then does it look them through and examine them in a mass. . . . You critics . . . are ashamed or frightened of the momentary and transient extravagances which are to be found in all truly creative minds and whose longer or shorter duration distinguishes the thinking artist from the dreamer. You complain of your unfruitfulness because you reject too soon and discriminate too severely.

How the mind solves a problem remains mysterious, so no one can give you a formula for telling how many pieces of the puzzle you need and how to lay them out. But we do know that it is crucial to begin the writing process early. You need not actually sit down to compose, but you must put the project in mind. The sooner you think about the assignment, the sooner you start reflecting on the variables and the sooner your subconscious mind can begin to focus on the problem. That is why a paper due on Monday morning should never be first undertaken on Sunday night; you have left no time for reflection, for mental processing, for second thoughts, or for intermediate solutions that lead to still better solutions. Even if you do not have the time to start *composing* until Sunday night, you should at least have read over the assignment and begun thinking about it the instant you received it.

Step 3: Jot down a rough outline. Before you progress too far in your research, you should begin to jot down notes for a rough outline. It's

> *Some lawyers use language to keep civilians at bay. Other lawyers are just not smart enough to overcome the technical gunk in the profession sufficiently to use language to communicate clearly.*
>
> ROGER WILKINS, 1987

still too early to have the complete structure of your solution, so you cannot compose a complete formal outline. But you can begin to assemble the topics you will be discussing, so that later, when you are sure what your topics are, you can rearrange them into a proper sequence. Even a rough outline helps direct and organize further research.

Step 4: Reassess your theory. Your initial theory of the case suggested certain avenues of research. Your research may have suggested new avenues. You should constantly be asking whether your initial assumptions were correct and looking consciously to see whether what you have so far uncovered requires that you change them.

Step 5: Set down a more formal outline. When you are satisfied that your research has shown the main direction—and that no unexpected byways are in store—you should write a formal outline. By now you will know, for instance, that there are two elements to proving copyright infringement, that courts have accepted six circumstances in your case as proof of those elements, that there are several procedural hurdles, that you have ways to surmount each, and that none of the available defenses is well-founded. You may have solved your problem already; you may solve it as you think through the outline of the discussion you will shortly write out. But even here, you should never suppose that this outline is the final one.

Step 6: Compose. You are halfway through the ten steps of the writing process, and only now should you begin to compose. Only now will you see whether the solution you have found actually works. Or if you are not conscious of possessing a solution, only now will you begin to work toward it.

The time it takes to reach this step depends on the complexity of the assignment and the amount of research you must undertake. But it is essential to leave plenty of time for steps 6 through 10, regardless. By composing, you will learn what you know and, even more important, what you have yet to discover. The sooner you start writing, the sooner you can see the holes in your argument. You can read forever, but you can never really test whether your reading is sufficient or germane until you try to make sense of it by assembling it in your writing.

What we were going through seemed like a kind of Berlitz assault in "Legal," a language I didn't speak and in which I was being forced to read and think 16 hours a day. Of course Legal bore some relation to English—it was more a dialect than a second tongue—but it was very peculiar.

SCOTT TUROW, 1978

When you now sit down to compose—or stand up, if you are like Justice Holmes, who said "nothing conduces to brevity like a caving in of the knees"—you may experience a "block." "Mental block" is a term that writers glibly mouth, as if it explained an extrinsic difficulty. But a block is not a single mental event, nor is it merely a nuisance unconnected to the composition. A mental block is a vital clue to the state of preparedness.

We distinguish two kinds of mental blocks. The first is the psychological difficulty many people have in *beginning* any difficult mental effort. The second kind of block is not psychological but conceptual. You stop because you are missing information about the law or circumstances of the case, because you do not know how to make logical connections between the material you have gathered, or because you have not sufficiently weighed the ingredients you do have. If the gap is big enough, you may be unable to continue writing until you have done further research. Or it may be signaling you where to direct your thought: How does *this* fact connect to *that* rule? Again, the earlier you start to compose, the earlier you will encounter these blocks, and the more time you will have to research more law, interview more witnesses, re-question the client, or rethink some aspect of the problem. If you have waited until Sunday night, you will be denied these options, and your document will be empty—or late.

You can learn to write around minor blocks. If you are missing a minor fact, one whose presence will not affect the concepts you are developing or their consequences, you can skip over it as you compose for the first time. Once you begin to compose, you should not interrupt a train of thought to locate a date, a name, a middle initial, a line of cases, or the "right" word. Give yourself as much uninterrupted time to compose as possible.

A simple trick, used routinely by journalists, should help. When journalists come to a place where they are momentarily stumped, they fill it in with a marker—the idiosyncratic "TK," meaning "to come." So a sentence in your first draft might read like this: "On May tk, 19tk, a witness, tk Jones, saw the defendant step out of the drug store wearing, in Jones's words 'tk.' " These missing points will not affect your argument, nor will their absence disable you from proving your point. The important thing is to write. Don't hold back the big ideas; don't bog down in minutiae. Shut your door, turn off your phone, keep the radio low, tell your kids to play in the street, don't get up to sharpen a pencil or look up a word in the dictionary—just write.

If you can avoid it, don't even look at your notes. You have spent time in the library reading through cases, previous memos, and the record of the case. You have a general impression of the facts and the law. Let that impression suffice as you strive to make sense of the whole. Usually the important points will rise to the surface, and you'll be less bogged down in details. You can always go back later and add what's missing.

Too many lawyers have lost the capacity or interest in exercising independent legal judgment. Rather than conceiving of themselves as teachers of the law to their clients as well as their adversaries, they believe their clients' position defines entirely the relevant legal terrain. Unable to fairly evaluate the contrary views, their writing is shallow and their advocacy ineffective.

JUDGE WILLIAM G. YOUNG, 1987

Step 7: Reorganize. Let's assume you have solved your problem. You know just why summary judgment should be granted, why your client's copyright has been infringed and how to prove it, why your client was not an inside trader after all. You may have reached the solution in a single burst, or you may have repaired to the library for more research. Your draft means that you have completed the first stage of the writing process. Now it remains to communicate that solution to your readers.

The first step in communicating is to ensure that you have organized your thoughts in a logical way. When you did your algebra homework, you scribbled the steps of your solutions all over the scrap paper. To demonstrate your solution formally, you rewrote the answer, putting each step in a logical sequence. You do the same with your draft. Read through the whole draft, and ask whether its major parts are properly related, whether the presentation within the major parts are tied together or should be repositioned in tighter order somewhere else. One simple trick: Jot down in the margin of each paragraph its main points and compare these marginal headings throughout the document. You should quickly see what belongs together and what is out of order (see Chapter 9).

Don't fret if much of your draft is jumbled. In fact, be suspicious if everything seems well ordered. Problem solving is messy, as Susan Horton suggested, and as you compose you will rarely think of every issue and every fact in time to place them just where they belong in the polished document.

Move your sentences and paragraphs around. Draw arrows; use scissors and tape or the handy "move" program on your word processor.

Confusion of expression usually results from confusion of conception. The act of writing can help clarify one's thoughts. However, one should spare the reader having to repeat one's own extrication from confusion. The object is to be clear, not to show how hard it was to be so.

GEOFFREY C. HAZARD JR., *1987*

Step 8: Rewrite. Read through the document again. This time you should look at the major segments: lead or introduction, conclusion, topic sentences, transitions. Have you given your readers a sufficient road map to your entire document (see Chapter 8)? Is your conclusion obvious and inescapable? Does each paragraph contain only one major point, does the topic sentence state that point, and do the sentences that follow make the point? Are your paragraphs tied together in a sensible way? Do you understand why paragraph 24 follows paragraph 23? Can the reader? Although *you* now know what the question is and how to answer it, remember that the reader remains to be convinced. You have satisfied yourself; now satisfy the reader.

Step 9: Edit. The first draft is *your* solution to the problem; the final draft must be the *reader's*. A gulf now stands between you and the reader, and you have much to do to bridge it. The gulf arises from the looseness of English, which contains more synonyms and opportunities for nuance than any other language. When you compose, you are not merely putting words down on a page. You are also investing those words and phrases with a meaning that is personal to you. What may be clear to you may appear ambiguous to a reader who does not know how you think, why you wrote it, and what you intended. Your readers' only window into your thinking is the words themselves, the writing without the meaning you invest in it when *you* read it.

Your business as thinkers is to make plainer the way from some things to the whole of things.

OLIVER WENDELL HOLMES, JR., *1886*

That is why you must *edit late*, why you must allow as many hours or days as possible to elapse after you have reorganized your document so that you still have time to prepare a final product on deadline. For as time passes, as your words grow colder, your memory of what you intended will dim. The halo of meaning will dissipate. After enough time has passed, you will read the document more as an outsider would, seeing the ambiguities and having to guess at the meaning. Edit a paper five minutes after you have drafted it, and you will not see how it flunks its ultimate mission, to communicate your solution to its readers. Edit five days (or even five hours) later, and you will begin to see where it is murky and how to clarify your thought.

John Kenneth Galbraith tells that he was about to send the manuscript of *The New Industrial State* to his publisher when President Kennedy called, asking him to serve as ambassador to India. Galbraith put the manuscript in a drawer and returned to it two years later, appalled to discover deficiencies he had never imagined. He rewrote it. He therefore recommends that the best thing for a writer is to accept appointment as an ambassador for a couple of years.

Failing that, allow as much time as possible for the document to sit in a drawer, out of sight and out of mind. That is another reason that you should begin your writing early. The earlier you write, the more time you will have to delay your editing so that you can clear your mental registers of unwanted meaning.

Step 10: Reedit. Editing is not simple work, nor is it a one-step task. As we discuss in Chapter 11, editing is best accomplished by doing it several times, checking over your copy for a single set of errors or difficulties in any one pass. You should edit until satisfied, or until you run out of time. You should press on friends and colleagues as many of your documents as their time and patience will permit. No matter how long you let your own writing lie inert, you will still retain some faint wisp of meaning that your audience can never have. An outsider who tells you that something is unclear is therefore a valuable ally. There's little point in arguing with someone who says, "I don't understand this." *You* may fully understand it, but *your* understanding is not the goal. If one person misunderstands, others may as well. Rewrite some more.

The hardest lesson of all remains: You must reallocate the time you spend at each stage of the writing process. Lawyers widely misconceive the relative importance of the different phases of writing. We have talked to enough lawyers to conclude that most lawyers, when presented with novel issues, spend between half and three-quarters of their time on research. That is a mistake. Research in a vacuum, without the hard thought that comes from composing, is often a wasted effort. Information is useless if it remains in your head, if it is not effectively communicated to judges, adversaries' lawyers, or clients. If you are responsible for producing a first draft from scratch, you should devote no more than 30 percent of your time to research and up to 40 percent to composing. During part of your composing time, you may be forced to return to the library. That's not only permissible, it's imperative, as long as you are continuing to compose while researching. The remaining 30 percent should be spent editing. Editing is that important, and it's likely that you will fail in your most important task of effectively representing your client if you do not reserve the time to polish your prose.

Writing is hard work. But that's what you do. It's why you're paid.

CHAPTER 4

Of Dawdlers and Doodlers, Scrawlers and Brooders, Pacers, Strollers, and Joggers —Getting Started and Overcoming Blocks

J AY TOPKIS, who has represented Spiro Agnew, large corporations, and death row inmates, is a tenacious courtroom advocate and an elegant craftsman admired for his spare prose, apt analogies, and colorful images. This is how Topkis, who has practiced in New York at Paul, Weiss, Rifkind, Wharton & Garrison since 1950, starts writing: "I wait, or, as Red Smith once said, I sit down and think until beads of blood form on my forehead. Mostly I procrastinate."

Writing is not easy. Getting started can be especially wrenching. But procrastination rarely is the wisest course. It only makes writing harder.

"Plunge in," advises Evan A. Davis, a one-time partner in Cleary, Gottlieb, Steen & Hamilton, and now counsel to Governor Mario Cuomo. That sounds right.

On the other hand, maybe it depends. As William J. Jones, general solicitor of American Telephone and Telegraph, warns, "A long walk is a good idea, but that *should* vary with individuals. Beethoven and Dickens did extensive rewriting and editing; Mozart and Shakespeare rarely rewrote a line, but you can't tell from the final product. That's what 'counts.' I personally get in mind what I want to say and rarely rewrite. It is a great mistake to force one person's method on another.''

We asked lawyers, judges, and professors how they start writing, and they described dozens of different approaches. Their methods can be grouped into categories:

(a) The dawdlers and their opposites, the plungers

(b) Those who scrawl or spew out words as fast as they can

(c) Those with only a hazy sense of organization and those who outline meticulously before they start

(d) The perfectionists who think long and hard before they begin and the stream-of-consciousness writers who think only as they compose

(e) Those who begin at the beginning of a document and those who start at the end

(f) Those who start by editing other people's words

(g) Those who adopt different strategies according to the complexity of the project

(h) The doodlers, brooders, pacers, strollers, and joggers

Some of these approaches are idiosyncratic, some overlap, several conflict, and many may not be worth emulating. But we set them forth because (1) misery loves company and (2) you may be able to adapt one of these strategies to your own habits and needs.

When [lawyers] face a typewriter and blank sheet of paper, a strange metamorphosis occurs. The language that has served them well as ordinary men and women, husbands and wives, lovers, sisters, brothers, aunts, uncles, dinner companions and neighbors, suddenly abandons them.

JAMES RAYMOND, *1978*

The Dawdlers

Thomas D. Rowe, Jr., a professor at Duke Law School, reads, thinks, and then organizes. "I dither a lot to force myself to do it, and I sit down at my word processor and type, taking lots of breaks." R. Edward Townsend, Jr., a litigator in Manhattan, does everything he can "to keep from starting," and then he dictates "a stream-of-unconsciousness first draft, from which I create the final product." Jerry W. Ryan of Washington says: "First I procrastinate. Then I worry, during which exercise the structure of the writing really forms at a less than conscious level." Zick Rubin, a recent graduate of Harvard Law School, says: "I delay a lot and then force myself to plunge in." Rubin, a professor of social psychology at Brandeis University before he entered law school in 1985, adds: "Having more than one project helps—you start writing one thing in order to avoid writing another." William Hughes Mulligan, a former professor, law school dean, and federal appeals judge in Manhattan and now a partner at Skadden, Arps, Slate, Meagher & Flom, offers a similar approach: "I wait for a deadline I can't escape."

Early Risers

Federal District Judge Avern Cohn of the Eastern District of Michigan says he frequently finds inspiration at 4 a.m. For Weyman I. Lundquist, who practices in San Francisco and is also an author, "usually the thought process occurs between 4 and 5 a.m." Not a single lawyer preferred writing late at night, even though many said they were forced to work late because of deadlines.

Scrawlers

David G. Trager, the dean of Brooklyn Law School, tries to get as many ideas as he can on paper "without regard to order or logic." Eric D. Green, professor at Boston University Law School, "lets it percolate. Then I blast it out and revise it later as many times as I can." Justice Richard Neely of the West Virginia Supreme Court, who has written several books, says: "I usually vomit a first draft onto the page to see where I am going, and then rewrite and rewrite."

Outliners and Nonoutliners

Those who plunge in usually skip the outline stage. "I envy those who use outlines and think through what they want to write," says Gerald Stern, administrator of the New York State Commission on Judicial Conduct and, for a public official, an unusually gifted writer. "I think while I write. I write quickly and in volume, and then make many changes in drafts 2, 3, 4, 5, 6, and 7." Marvin E. Frankel, a former professor and federal district judge in Manhattan, author of many books, and now in private practice, simply starts "writing by starting to write. I don't normally make outlines." Albert Beswick, senior counsel of International Telephone and Telegraph, said: "I write via stream of consciousness, with an apparent outline of sorts in my head. I revise and do a reorganization of ideas once I have them on paper." John H. Stassen, a Chicago lawyer, never writes an outline, but he does prepare "a points list." He uses that list as a springboard, starting "with the easiest point first," to ease into "the always painful process of putting words on paper. That starts the creative/analytic juices flowing."

But there are plenty of outliners, and they usually spend plenty of time redrafting. James H. Carter, a Wall Street lawyer, outlines "for anything complicated" and then tries "to get something on paper as a first draft as quickly as possible, no matter how rough. I then edit extensively. I often have a 'moaning and groaning' period at the outline/first-draft stage of two to three days of avoiding putting much on paper, building up guilt to get going." Pete Putzel of New York said: "I think hard about the outline of the argument. Then I draft on a yellow pad, taking frequent long walks. I then revise drafts on the word processor."

Among the most meticulous outliners is Randal R. Craft Jr., a New York City litigator. His strategy is to "outline, outline, outline. For documents whose organization is relatively simple, I outline them by making a list of the topics to be covered, and then I go back and put in the margin each topic's appropriate numerical sequence. For more complex documents, I usually use index cards for the various topics, subtopics, etc., and then, on a conference room table, I put them in various arrangements, in order to determine which arrangement appears to be the most effective. The authorities and sources to be cited or quoted are listed on the cards. After the outline of cards is completed, I usually dictate my first draft directly from the outline, having my authorities and sources at hand for ready reference. While I dictate, I frequently pace around the room."

Shuffling index cards is a crude form of moving blocks of text on a word processor, and some lawyers have adopted sophisticated software programs specifically designed for outliners. Jay F. Lapin of Washington, for example, usually outlines "using a personal computer outline program. . . . I also take walks, think about my approach in the shower and while falling asleep."

Perfectionists and Thinkers

A few lawyers said they aim for a polished first draft. "Generally speaking, I have written a lot of it in my head before I actually sit down and start writing," said Daniel H. Lowenstein, a professor at the University of California at Los Angeles Law School. "I tend to start at the beginning and work my way through. I am pretty compulsive about being fairly polished at the outset. For example, I almost always write my footnotes as I go along. I even write my introduction at the beginning. . . . I do not recommend this method to others. It is simply how I work."

Some lawyers emphasize thinking long and hard before writing. "A long period of thought preceding the writing is important," says Justin A. Stanley of Chicago. "Sometimes I just start writing and rewriting and rewriting. Ultimately, thought and writing must come together."

Leads and Conclusions

Some lawyers work on leads first, others start with conclusions, and some work on both. "Work a first paragraph to death and take it from there," says James J. Leff, an experienced trial judge in Manhattan and well-known gadfly of the court system, who is famous for his acerbic and literate letters to the state's administrative judges. J. Anthony Kline, a California appeals judge, states "the threshold question as succinctly as I can and then proceed to answer it."

Still others begin by focusing on both last and first paragraphs. Herald Price Fahringer, a flamboyant trial lawyer who has represented Larry Flynt and Claus von Bülow, says he tries "to write the opening and the closing first because I believe they are the most important parts of a brief or legal presentation of any substance." Similarly, Martin Garbus, who represents publishers and authors and is the author of two books himself, drafts the first and last paragraphs and then outlines.

Eugene R. Fidell, a Washington lawyer, writes his conclusion first, then his introduction, "then [I] settle down on the questions presented, then work up argument heading and subheadings, then write the textual parts of the argument, then go back and tinker with introduction, questions, conclusions, etc. so it all fits together." Before he begins, he often makes notes, though not a strict outline. "I will jot down the ideas that I think are interesting or likely to catch the reader's attention. Inspiration comes in bits and pieces for me, and I commonly have a lot of scraps of paper floating around—some of them written in the darkness when the idea comes to me in a wakeful moment at night."

Rewriters

A few lawyers prefer to act like newspaper rewriters, taking the copy of others and massaging it. David A. Barrett, a professor who recently started his own Wall Street firm, finds "the blank page terrifying." He prefers "having a draft from someone else to work from, even if I completely rewrite it."

I doubt that there are so many as a dozen professors of law in this whole country who could write an article about law, much less about anything else, and sell it, substantially as written, to a magazine of general circulation.

                                            FRED RODELL, *1962*

Strategists

George Gopen's strategy differs according to the document he is drafting. For a letter, Gopen, of Duke University, merely turns on his word processor and sits down. "For an article or a book chapter," says Gopen, who also runs writing seminars for practicing lawyers, "I do a great deal of putting the rest of my life in order (make the phone calls, prepare the diet Coke, put on the music, etc.), do a great deal of pacing about, get intensely tense, and hope to sit down.''

Doodlers, Pacers, and Brooders

As an aid to getting started, Donald G. Leka, general counsel at Teradyne in Boston, uses ''walks to the water cooler.'' James M. Klebba, dean of Loyola University Law School in New Orleans, does a ''lot of floor pacing.'' Beryl A. Abrams, associate general counsel at Columbia University, says that at her office she starts to write immediately, but at home, ''I make many trips to the refrigerator.'' When he works on a problem out of the office, Howard Burnett, a practitioner in Pocatello, Idaho, says he ''broods.'' Then, he adds, ''I think about key concepts and phrases, and then I rough out an outline.'' To get his thoughts in order, Michael Meltsner, of Northeastern Law School and author of novels and books, says: ''I do anything I like to do—run, walk, read.''

Many lawyers connect perambulation to the writing process. To start his thoughts flowing, Simon H. Rifkind, now in his sixth decade of practice, says he doodles, outlines, and takes long walks. Eric A. Seiff of Manhattan may ''spend minutes or even hours contemplating the phrases, sentences, tone, and substance of my statement during my daily jogs in the park.''

Lawrence F. Henneberger, a Washington lawyer, says: ''A long (10 to 15 miles) run usually gets me in shape for a difficult writing assignment—then an outline to put together my thoughts.'' Paul Bateman, codirector of the Legal Communications Skills program at Southwestern University Law School in Los Angeles, takes his long run after he has done much spadework. ''I write what might look like a 'final' draft,'' he says. ''Then I do one of three things with this draft. 1. Throw it away. 2. Revise it (usually the case for letters). 3. Begin outlining— but I use very *large blocks* for outlining—it doesn't get detailed. Finally I take a long run—it really works for me.''

In their sometimes zany approach to getting words on paper, lawyers join a distinguished group of writers. Samuel Johnson needed a ''purring cat, orange peel and plenty of tea.'' Ernest Hemingway stood while writing, typewriter and reading board chest high opposite him. For years, Raymond Carver worked at his kitchen table, a library carrel, or in his car. In *Thinking through Writing*, Susan R. Horton compiled a splendid list of idiosyncracies employed by major authors. Balzac wrote only at night, while Emile Zola worked only in the daytime, but he drew the blinds because he could not write without artificial light. Carlyle craved an atmosphere without sound. For inspiration, Schiller needed to catch whiffs from a drawerful of rotting apples. Stephen Spender needed tea, while W. H. Auden relied on coffee and tobacco. Only black ink would do for Kipling. Malcolm Lowry could only write standing up, dictating to his wife, and leaning with his knuckles against a lectern.

The point of these stories—and of the admissions by lawyers of how they start composing—is that no one has a single correct way to begin. The most dangerous approach is not to begin at all. Procrastination may be the surest sign that you have not worked through what you wish to say. It is better just to plunge in. Yield to your quirks.

Overcoming Writer's Block

Writer's block, the occupational hazard of those who earn their living by the word, can strike at any moment—at the start of a project, in the middle, or even near the end when you are trying to fashion a stirring conclusion. It can happen when you have not fully researched your topic or when you have had a lot of time to think before writing or when no deadline exists. You may be suffering from too much choice. Or you may just be too much of a perfectionist.

In *Thinking on Paper*, two educational researchers at Harvard, V. A. Howard and J. H. Barton, call the single greatest block to getting started "the self-defeating quest to get it right the first time." Establishing an unrealistic goal can do you in. Lower your standards—temporarily. Arrange your writing schedule so that you are not pressured into equating your first draft with the finished product.

You can conquer writing blocks in many ways. If you ordinarily write at midday, write in the morning. Change your tools. If you dictate or write longhand, try typing. Keep scraps of paper wherever you go, and jot down thoughts or fragments of sentences. Change your location. Try writing at the public library. Set intermediate deadlines. Do not get bogged down in your lead paragraphs, which need not be written first. Indeed, they often should be written last and then be rewritten and rewritten.

In *Writing for Your Readers*, Donald H. Murray, a professor of English at the University of New Hampshire and a former writing coach at the *Boston Globe*, offers other tricks to overcome writer's block:

- Write a letter. "Many writers, including Tom Wolfe," Murray says, "have fooled themselves into writing by starting the first draft "Dear . . .""

- Write the end first. "This is a technique used by John McPhee and other writers," according to Murray. "Once you know where you are going, you may see how to get there."

- Read. "One writer friend reads the King James Version of the Bible when he gets stuck," Murray recalls. "It is amazing how stimulating the flow of fine language can be to the writer."

- *Nulla dies sine linea*, meaning "never a day without writing," a saying attributed to both Horace and Pliny. This phrase "hung over Anthony Trollope's writing desk, John Updike's and mine," notes Murray, who advises that by exercising the writing muscle every day, writing becomes "a normal, not an abnormal form of behavior."

The lawyer who procrastinates at the start may be resisting for any number of psychological reasons the hard work of articulating thought. The lawyer who is blocked in the middle of writing or near the conclusion may have the will to continue but not the facts. If you find that your power to compose suddenly wanes, that you are spinning out aimless and meaningless sentences, or that you are repeating yourself, you have probably exhausted your knowledge of the subject. You might need to revisit the library or return to your notes or the case file—but not before you analyze the stopping point to see what information is missing.

Interrupting the act of composing should be your final refuge. Before you leave your desk, you should try alternative strategies to test whether the block is caused by a lack of information. Try writing yourself a memorandum that addresses the problem you are facing: "I have reached an impasse here because I can't figure out how to go from this point to that one. Perhaps if I . . ." The change of tone might rejuvenate your thinking or help you pinpoint the missing material. If a self-addressed memorandum does not work, the block might be caused by fatigue; a brief rest could very well provide the cure. Or you might be bored; a change of topic might refresh your capacity to think. Instead of finishing the subject on which you are stuck, move on. Ignore the unsolved problem and tackle the next one; solutions to mental problems often come when you are not directly focusing on them. Or copy over a passage you've already written. "Many times," says Donald Murray, "it helps, when stuck in the middle of a piece, to copy over a part of the writing that has gone well. This helps you recover the voice and flow."

If nothing works, you're through for the day. Sleep on it.

CHAPTER 5

The Mechanics of Getting It Down

AT THE END of the last century, when most secretaries were male and clerical work was still part of a legal apprenticeship, touch typing was introduced into offices around the country. The earliest typewriter manufacturers thought that authors, clergymen, and telegraph operators would be their natural market; they ignored journalists and secretaries. Businessmen were suspicious of typewriters when they came on the market in the 1870s but were soon convinced of the machines' utility when they read endorsements by luminaries such as Mark Twain, the first author to send his publisher a typewritten manuscript (*Tom Sawyer*), and Lloyd George, the future British prime minister who had learned to type as a young lawyer. But businessmen were unhappy with the slowness of typists, who hunted for and pecked at keys with two or, at the most, three or four fingers, no faster than an accomplished office stenographer could write in longhand.

But in 1888, Frank E. McGurrin, the federal court stenographer in Salt Lake City, amazed the stenographic world by demonstrating that he could use all ten fingers without ever looking at the keyboard. He had invented his system in a Grand Rapids, Michigan, law office where he worked as a clerk. In a widely publicized contest, McGurrin emerged the fastest typist in the world. "Touch typing" was born.

The tedium and expense of handwriting disappeared, and "verbosity was within the reach of everyone, especially lawyers," noted David Mellinkoff, the chronicler of the use and misuse of law language, in a decidedly curmudgeonly mood in his pioneering 1963 book, *The Language of the Law*. Producing words by machine, Mellinkoff added, is "so fast, so effortless, that one inclines to lavishness, and forgetfulness."

The writer who uses words unknown to his readers might as well bark.

CHARLES BEARDSLEY, *1941*,
QUOTING APPROVINGLY AN EDITORIAL IN THE SAN FRANCISCO CHRONICLE

A quarter of a century later, Mellinkoff, an energetic man in his seventies, has not mellowed in his views about lawyers' sloppy prose. "Exposure to three years of law school will hurt rather than help an ordinary person's writing," said Mellinkoff as he sat surrounded by oversized leather dictionaries and bulging file folders in his office at the law school at the University of California at Los Angeles. When discussing a recent book on lawyers' prose by another professor, Mellinkoff cited the precise page where his name appeared—and had been misspelled.

For the last several years, Mellinkoff has been busy writing a new book of his own—a law dictionary. He is composing on a typewriter. A spare stylist, he has avoided the pitfalls he complained about in *The Language of the Law*. "I write and rewrite and rewrite," he said. A typist since the sixth grade, he is preparing the dictionary on the Royal 440 that he keeps on a rickety table in his office. At home, he uses an Underwood. A monitor from a computer sits on a desk at his office, unused and detached from a keyboard. He once composed on a computer but abandoned it because he found the software wanting.

Gentlemen?
In re yours of the 5th inst. your to hand and in reply, I wish to state that the judiciary expenditures of this year, i.e. has not exceeded the fiscal year—brackets—this procedure is problematic and with nullification will give us a subsidiary indictment and priority. Quotes, unquotes and quotes. Hoping this finds you, I beg to remain as of June 9th, Cordially, respectfully, regards.

GROUCHO MARX, *1928*

Once the target of reproach, typewriters today rarely attract comment. Lately, it is their much fancier and sophisticated offspring, word processors and computers, that have drawn rebukes. Although no law office could operate for very long today without electronic machinery, lawyers have only hesitantly adopted word processors for themselves. Disapproval of new technology pervades the profession. In 1975, the New York Court of Appeals was distressed by a 284-page brief that had been submitted. "In recent years, we have witnessed great technological advances in the methods of reproduction of the written word," complained Judge Matthew Jasen. "Too often this progress is merely viewed as a license to substitute volume for logic in an apparent attempt to overwhelm the courts, as though quantity, and not quality, was the virtue to be extolled." In his opinion, Jasen referred to a 1902 decision of the New York court, which noted that the problem of prolixity had not arisen when "every lawyer wrote his points with a pen."

Those who distrust computers are not Luddites; they do not advocate a return to the ballpoint or quill or the hammer and chisel. Their concerns are genuine and cannot be dismissed summarily. Echoing the New York court, Mary Frances Edwards, a Washington writer, wrote in 1987 that "the ease of word processing has generated a barrage of paper. American lawyers bombard each other with lengthy memoranda, attachments and appendices. The miracle of word processing has also turned many lawyers into mere mechanics. . . . Due to word processing, some documents which were formerly individualized are recycled from case to case and client to client, like soft drink bottles." Vivian Dempsey, who has taught legal writing at law schools in the San Francisco area, also feels that computers tempt lawyers to write as if they were automatons. "Like the harried white rabbit in *Alice in Wonderland*, the attorney who borrows from existing documents may look at his watch and scurry off to more pressing matters instead of taking the time to tailor computer-made documents to a particular use."

David S. Levine, a lawyer and critic, acknowledges that "the new technology gives us opportunities for thoughtful language and style." But, he adds, "the result tends to be prose that is both over-manicured and, as always, turgid." Avern Cohn, a federal district judge, predicts: "If all papers were required to be generated on old-fashioned typewriters, and text was eliminated from footnotes, writing would improve." Another federal judge, William G. Young of Boston, raises similar objections: "Word processing available to lawyers assists them in raising a plethora of points. Judges feel they must deal with each of the points raised even if they are minor."

The same lawyers who write clear and interesting letters to a kid in camp or a mother in the hospital go through a Jekyll-and-Hyde mental transformation when they sit down to write (or dictate) a business letter, a law review article, a judicial opinion, a law, a regulation, a contract, whatever. They begin writing the way they think lawyers are supposed to write. The result is stark and ludicrous.

RICHARD HYLAND, *1986*

Word processors, like typewriters, or even ballpoint pens, can be used improperly. When misused, they contribute to sprawl. Correctly used, though, they can provide extraordinary benefits. They save time, freeing more time for redrafting. "A first draft produced on a word processor," says Fran Shellenberger, a law office management consultant from Maryland, "will have the quality of a second or third draft produced with machine dictation or longhand."

Erasing, deleting, and substituting are far easier on computers, and the writer can quickly move text where it fits best. We find this electronic pasting and cutting immensely satisfying. We think we are better writers because of computers, as do many other people who spend the few hours it takes to learn how computers work.

Word processing may not work for everyone. In a widely discussed speech delivered in 1987, Louis Simpson, the poet and teacher, doubted whether "Flaubert would have written prose more easily if he had owned a word processor—he complained that sometimes it took him a whole day to write a sentence." But critics of the new technology blind themselves to what seem to us to be the obvious advantages of word processors.

After an initial wariness that bordered on fear, William K. Zinsser, an elegant stylist, has become an enthusiastic booster of word processing. "Not since the typewriter replaced the pen has a more exciting tool come along," he wrote in the 1988 revised third edition of *Writing Well*, his best-selling guide to writing nonfiction. "The word processor can concentrate your mind on the craft of writing, revising and editing—much more powerfully than this has ever been possible, because your words are right in front of you in all their infinite possibility, waiting to be infinitely shaped. Technology, the great villain, turns out to be your friend.''

One hundred years ago, typewriters introduced the low-cost word. Chatty executives could dictate to their secretaries who had lost their right to plead writer's cramp. But if typewriters are responsible, as Mellinkoff suggests, for verbosity, word processors promise a cost-effective cure. Bruce Bliven, Jr., a magazine writer and historian of the typewriter, noted in 1954 that when the typewriter first came to the office, it relieved businessmen "from having to trace out the letters with their own fingers, and saved them from the dangers of ink blots, stains and splatters" but as a consequence they "fell into all sorts of evil practices, particularly the sin of starting a sentence without a plan for finishing it":

> We are pleased to forward to you the merchandise referred to in your valued order of the 21st except that, on account of unforeseen difficulties in the supply of materials, we have substituted light blue for navy hoping that this will not inconvenience you rather than cause further delay which, as you know, we are as anxious to avoid as you are in view of our pleasure during these past months of being of service to your esteemed organization as well as personally.

Retyping, though less costly than rewriting a letter longhand, was nevertheless an expense. Today that expense has vanished. The writer who composes on a word processor may erase, reorder, rewrite, and replace at a cost so low that even a state-of-the-art computer, together with its word processing software, will pay for itself within weeks at a moderately busy law office. The lengthy document can be mechanically shortened in seconds. And because word processing permits any writer to begin composing easily at any point in the document, the lawyer who masters it should finally lose all fear of starting, composing, and editing. A new age has dawned for the legal writer, but many lawyers still resist.

One reason that many lawyers have yet to accept word processors is that they cannot type. They may never have learned, they may feel they are too advanced to learn now, or if they do know how, they may feel

Why is it that the lawyer, who thinks and speaks the King's English better than his fellows, falls below them when he writes it: Why does the lawyer seem to lose his mastery of words when he puts his pen, instead of his tongue, to the task of expressing them in statutes, in judicial opinions or in legal documents?

URBAN A. LAVERY, 1921

it is beneath their professional dignity to touch fingers to keys. Some women lawyers we interviewed said they have hidden their typing skills because they did not wish to be mistaken for secretaries.

Our survey suggests that most lawyers still compose by dictating into a machine or to their secretaries or by writing longhand, usually on a yellow (never, never white!) pad. A few said they typed. A few more—mostly younger lawyers—reported that they are adopting the new technology of word processing, but they remain a minority—albeit a growing one.

These results were borne out by our visit to a bustling and growing West Coast law office where most of the lawyers still wrote longhand or dictated. Most of the lawyers were young. About a quarter of them owned their own computers. Many said they were bad typists, if they could type at all. The firm, which was automating writing and document production, would not provide typing tutorials (as we suspect most firms do not). That refusal is a false economy. Lessons are essential if busy novices are to feel comfortable using word processors. Many of the lawyers enthusiastically greeted the introduction of computers into the firm. All who had mastered word processing, including some who thought they never would, regretted the time they had wasted dictating and writing longhand.

Another reason law firms resist computers is that senior lawyers prefer to compose the way they always have. Arthur H. Christy, in practice in New York for forty years, lamented that lawyers are losing the facility to dictate. For him, dictating well is a badge of accomplishment. He observed about young lawyers: "Very few of them have the ability to dictate face to face, preferring to resort to the little black box with controls for starts and stops. Part of this may be that in the changing legal world there are fewer and fewer secretaries who take shorthand. It seems to me that if a young lawyer, particularly a litigator, can organize his thoughts, he should be able to dictate steadily without having to start and stop.''

What Christy sees as a virtue, others view as a vice. Writing usually gives unmistakable internal evidence of having been dictated. As William Zinsser suggests—''Don't say anything in writing that you wouldn't comfortably say in conversation''—writing should resemble the spoken idiom. But writing surely is not transcribed conversation. In 1942, Professor Edward H. (''Bull'') Warren of Harvard Law School advised lawyers never to dictate anything that ''calls for careful thinking.'' If you dictate, he said, ''you are likely to get into a habit of using words of many syllables like 'formulate' or 'constituted.' If you write in longhand you are likely to get into a habit of using words of one syllable like 'made' or 'was.' '' Sandra Gamow Goldenfarb, a Clearwater, Florida, practitioner, thinks ''dictation may well be the single most significant contribution to poor legal writing—especially when a document goes out directly after being transcribed, with no editing except perhaps proofreading (for typos only) by the secretary who typed it. Dictation of legal work results in wordiness, repetition, poor grammar, misuse of words, and sheer legal gobbledegook. Dictating machines should be abolished.''

In West Palm Beach, Florida, Anthony E. Pucillo, a lawyer in his late thirties, presides over a hectic litigation practice in an office tucked behind a small hill off the interstate highway. Pucillo does not own a dictating machine, but he has six computers—two in his office (one sitting atop a rolltop desk), two for his secretaries, and two for his use at home. In 1986, he was a computer illiterate. ''I needed to be efficient, but I thought I was too busy to learn,'' he recalled. Pucillo taught himself, without a consultant. ''I have a perverse need to understand and not to have anyone put anything over on me,'' he said. His premise was: ''If any idiot can do it, I can, too.'' The result: He thinks he has become a more efficient, less pretentious writer, and paperwork in his office moves faster. ''I am able to charge more for my time because I'm more productive,'' he said. ''And I'm able to handle more cases.''

CHAPTER 6

Writing in Law Practice I: Lessons from a Writing Audit

In early 1988, a senior partner invited us to his medium-sized law firm on the West Coast to audit its writing process. As an experiment, we were to interview a cross-section of the firm's entire work force (partners, associates, paralegals, secretaries, and support staff) and then assess how effectively the firm's written assignments were carried through.

A fast-growing group of corporate litigators, the firm annually hires a large number of associates who understand that they will be spending long hours, often under intense pressure, in the office churning out documents. Senior members of the firm say that good writing is appreciated and rewarded, and because the firm is growing so rapidly, they worry about the quality of briefs, memoranda, and other documents drafted by new associates. But the partners are too busy practicing law themselves to devote much time to training their younger lawyers. They are too busy even to review writing samples when recruiting new lawyers. Although no two firms are identical, this firm resembles many other growing firms with active business practices, and its deficiencies in writing are representative of many law offices.

We found that the firm fell short of its professed goals. It tended to have higher-priced people doing lower-priced work. For example, several associates acknowledged that they overwrite documents, expecting partners to edit and revise. Much of that editing and revising should have been completed early on, by the associates themselves. Similarly, one associate said he would prefer to proofread documents himself than to send drafts to central proofreading because it takes too long to walk the papers to the appropriate geographic spot.

Although many associates said they believed the firm held good writing as one of its highest values, others said they thought the partners were whistling in the dark. We found a discrepancy between the partners' perception and that of the younger lawyers on the importance of good writing. This discrepancy arose because the senior partners differed about what constitutes good writing. For some, it meant spelling words correctly and capitalizing properly; for others, it meant well-reasoned, tightly written documents. The differing perceptions also arose because the partners were too busy to convey explicitly to associates that they valued good writing or what they meant by it. We concluded that unless the firm demonstrates in every possible way its commitment to good writing, much of its written product, at least at the draft stage, will continue to be shoddy.

We found several ways that this firm—and other firms as well—can make explicit their commitment to good writing and substantially improve the skills of their lawyers.

1. Upgrade proofreading and establish an in-house editing office. Law firms are publishers, and they err when they neglect to assume the tasks that publishers must undertake. The most significant missing position in most law offices is that of editor. (Because the concept is so important, we examine it in detail in the next chapter.) Proofreaders are underemployed by some, employed badly by others. Lawyers are divided on the usefulness of proofreaders—those who object do so in part because they are confused about the proofreading function. Several younger lawyers suggested that their prose would not benefit from having a fresh pair of trained eyes look at it. That is a bizarre notion. Senior partners should discuss the proofreaders' function with all incoming lawyers and, to the extent possible, standardize the proofreaders' tasks.

Beyond proofreading, law firms should consider routinely sending more drafts to copy editors, who would provide a more substantive check on written work. Some lawyers already have their office proofreaders assume this extra function ad hoc. But copy editors perform a separate function: they check for a host of writing difficulties—syntax, grammar, organization, word usage, questions of fact—that proofreaders do not.

2. Write and employ a stylebook. Lawyers are stylistically ineffi-cient, their prose riddled with inconsistencies. Few firms have a stylebook or even a uniform style informally adhered to—lapses unthinkable in publishing houses, newspapers, or magazines. It is wasteful for highly paid lawyers to worry about the simplest style considerations. Should the "c" in "court" be capitalized? Should the number "10" be written out? How should various documents be formatted? Like publishing enterprises, law firms need to make style decisions and then stick to them.

These decisions can easily be embodied in a uniform stylebook, dis-tinguished from the *Blue Book*; it would include rules peculiar to the firm's practice and particularized to its sense of style. It would be much shorter than the *Blue Book*, and not only lawyers but also proofreaders, word processors, and secretaries would rely on it heavily. Because it would answer many niggling questions automatically, a stylebook would save considerable time.

I know of no field of learning so vulnerable to burlesque, satire, or occasional pokes in the ribs as the bombastic pomposity of legal dialectic.
FRED RODELL, 1936

Many lawyers to whom we have spoken think that a written stylebook is a sound idea. Others are more skeptical. They feel they might be forced to memorize a host of useless rules. This objection is groundless, since the rules would ultimately be employed by others—proofreaders and secretaries. The skeptics also feel that the firm might never agree on what the rules should be. While a potential difficulty, this objection is wholly surmountable. The partner in charge, in consultation with an editor, would set style policy, just as other policies at the firm are established.

3. Start a writing newsletter. Considering the number of memo-randa that float through even the smallest law offices, most large firms could easily produce a newsletter dedicated to writing. It would include samples of fine writing within the office and cite or reprint examples of persuasive or otherwise well-crafted briefs and documents written else-where. It would identify by name those whose writing is worthy of praise. It would also quote examples of bad writing (though names would not be attached) and explain the error and show how to avoid it. Everyone we talked to thought an in-house writing newsletter worth launching. It could be edited and produced by an in-house editor or by a partner with an interest in writing. That partner's time spent in producing the newsletter should be billed to the same extent as the managing partner's time is billed when doing administrative work for the firm.

4. Orient incoming lawyers. The firm we visited has a sink-or-swim approach to incoming lawyers, perhaps because many of the newly employed professionals are "lateral hires" from other firms, and it is assumed that a lawyer who has been practicing knows how to write. That assumption is faulty. Even a day spent discussing the importance of writing—the firm's expectations, how drafts are edited, what style to use, how to use proofreaders—will pay off later.

5. Launch a brown-bag lunch series. Law firms should consider inviting outsiders, such as writing specialists and judges, as well as partners or senior lawyers with a special interest in the written word, to talk over an informal lunch about the imperatives of writing. Topics might include what a judge looks for in a brief, how judges read briefs, how to focus on the important topic in the fact statement, or how to avoid writer's block.

6. Run regular writing workshops. Law firms should institutionalize writing workshops designed primarily for newer lawyers, though everyone could benefit. Running writing workshops would be a major task for a full-time editor, though they obviously can be undertaken without an editor on staff.

7. Create a quiet room for composing. Law firms should consider creating a quiet refuge where lawyers can work on larger writing projects without being distracted but where they are available for emergencies. The composing room would avoid the problem of working at home— inaccessibility—but offer at least some of its advantages.

8. Establish a work-product repository. Law firms should systematically collect all work products and computerize them thoroughly. Most lawyers we interviewed said that a work-product repository would save a great deal of time and energy, which could be better devoted to editing and rewriting. For example, associates are often called on to research a question similar, or identical, to one that another lawyer has already examined. "Obtaining summary judgment" was an assignment we heard associates discuss frequently. It is foolish to send yet another associate to the library to begin at square one when the fully developed argument, supported by all the cases, submitted to some other courts, sits in a manila file nearby and need merely be updated.

The job of collecting documents and overseeing the repository should not be casually undertaken by someone responsible for other tasks. In firms of more than twenty-five lawyers, tending the repository should be a full-time job. (Obviously, not every piece of paper need be collected; each office defines for itself what ought to be included. But it seems essential to us that the repository include all papers filed in court and with agencies and all substantive research memoranda.)

Even a solo practitioner can create a small but useful repository by investing in an inexpensive word processing program that will enable a secretary to retrieve an indexed file of documents quickly.

9. Reallocate the division of labor. Law firms are profitable to the extent that they can delegate work to those who cost the firm less. Our audit uncovered several instances of work moving in the opposite direction: those whose time is relatively more expensive doing work that others should do. Junior associates write long-winded documents that senior lawyers then must spend extra time editing. Some lawyers refrain from using proofreaders because the proofing offices are inconveniently located, when a simple messenger system would suffice. All associates must be shown the necessity of exercising judgment and spending their own time, rather than the more expensive time of partners, in composing and editing drafts. The original writers must learn to draft documents much closer to their final form than they do now.

10. Review writing samples from applicants. Reviewing writing samples of applicants is time well spent. If associates are to be hired on paper credentials, the screening process ought to include the paper that counts. The editor, or the recruiting partner, should routinely collect and review writing samples before inviting an applicant for an interview.

11. Give word processing courses. Many of the lawyers we talked to were enthusiastic about learning to use computers. A few were reluctant because they thought their typing skills were deficient. Law firms should enable every lawyer to take first-time or refresher courses in typing and word processing. We emphasize the plural "s" in courses. Learning word processing in many ways is like learning a new language (though much easier), and no lawyer should be expected to master it in one try. In the long run, these skills will save time that will dwarf the short-term training cost.

These recommendations obviously do not exhaust what can be learned from a writing audit. We encourage all law offices to audit their writing process by adapting our questions and adding their own. But every audit should start with a basic premise: Law offices are publishers and should therefore adopt the practices of publishers.

Questions for Law Firm Writing Audit

1. How do you write? By longhand, typewriter, word processor, dictate, other? Do you know how to type? If not, will the firm give you lessons? Would you use some other type of machine if you had it?

2. Are you encouraged to ask questions when receiving an assignment?

3. Are page lengths assigned? If not, how do you decide how long to make a document?

4. Are you given a deadline? Do you set your own deadlines? Do you have enough time to write? Edit? If not, are the assigned deadlines too short or do you tend to wait until deadline to write?

5. How many times do you edit your drafts? How many times is your work edited or rewritten by others? By whom?

6. Have you ever curbed the time spent on composing or editing because you felt you could not justify billing your client for more time?

7. Do you see the document again after you turn it in? Does the person who assigns it or anyone else discuss the edited work with you in detail?

8. Who reviews a document once it leaves your hands? For example, who does the heavy editing, the retyping, the proofreading, and the formatting?

9. Roughly what percentage of your time on any assignment do you devote to research, composing, and editing? Do you record the time spent on each of these activities separately?

10. Does the firm have a commitment to good writing? If so, how has it made this commitment known?

11. Describe any bottlenecks in the copy flow.

12. What do you think your writing problems are? What have you been told your writing problems are?

13. What writing reference books do you keep at your desk (e.g., dictionary, thesaurus, *Blue Book*, stylebook, usage book)?

CHAPTER 7

Writing in Law Practice II: Lawyers as Publishers: Words Are Their Product

A TYPICAL ISSUE of the *New Yorker* contains enough words to fill 300 typed 8½- by 11-inch pages. An average issue of the *Wall Street Journal*, not counting stock tables, has about the same number of words. This book contains 400 typescript pages. *Gone with the Wind* contains four times as many. But the firm we visited—by no means the largest in the West—churned out between 5700 and 7500 pages per day. Because that total measures work leaving printers scattered around the office, not paper leaving the firm, it is somewhat misleading. Some documents are being counted twice or perhaps more. Still, the volume of the firm's paper is staggering. Each day, this one medium-sized law firm produces typed copy equaling 12 books or 20 newspapers or 750 ten-page newsletters.

One might hazard the supposition that the average lawyer in the course of a lifetime does more writing than a novelist.

WILLIAM PROSSER, 1939

Law firms resemble publishers of magazines, newspapers, and books: They "publish" (that is, distribute to outside readers) a large and continuous stream of typed and printed material. Therefore, the editorial and management principles of these publishing enterprises might sensibly be applied to the writing process at firms.

Every law firm with lawyers who write—and that includes most firms—has a counterpart in the publishing world. A single practitioner or small firm resembles a free-lance writer or a newsletter publisher who relies on desktop publishing. Appellate lawyers often have plenty of lead time and can think of themselves as magazine writers. A big firm with lots of takeover business is closer to a major metropolitan newspaper. In these firms, lawyers generate the typed material overnight, or within hours, just as do journalists who work for daily newspapers.

Even if all lawyers wrote seamless prose when they graduated from law school—and few do—the exigencies of modern law practice conspire against good writing. Lawyers live by the clock. They bill their time in units of six minutes. Despite their deeply held belief in the money value of time, they foolishly waste it. Not even Lewis Carroll could have created a crazier system of writing than lawyers themselves have devised. Those whose time is worth the most must spend unnecessary hours editing those who are paid the least.

This is how it works in many firms: Junior members of a firm write long and carelessly, often checking their writing only for spelling and typographical errors. The piece then moves along to a more senior member of the firm whose hourly rates are much higher. The senior lawyer then edits, rewrites, and polishes, say, a twenty-page, rather than a ten-page, document.

A senior partner at the firm we visited told us that after reviewing a first draft, he proceeds in one of two ways: "If time permits, the associate does a draft, which I edit. If time does not permit, I do the major rewrite myself." No lawyer should be ensnared in such a trap. Few top editors at a newspaper or magazine would perform radical surgery on a story close to deadline. Journalists build in time for editing—the most crucial stage of the writing process. Just like senior partners, top editors are paid for their judgment, and they hire assistant editors to carry out their wishes.

Moreover, law firms are surprisingly inefficient at a mechanical level. Many discourage their associates from using typewriters, much less word processors, often on the pretext that it is "unprofessional" for lawyers to type. So offices with highly efficient terminals and computer networks often wait on associates who are penning their briefs longhand onto yellow notepads or dictating onto tapes that will be transcribed when a secretary is available.

While other specialists may write about complex topics with equal precision as the good lawyer, words do not perform as critical a function in the work of others. It is ironic, then, lawyers are generally such bad writers.

ROBERT PECK, *1987*

Lawyers approach writing differently, of course, depending on their individual quirks, the size and type of their practice, and the importance and complexity of the documents that they produce. Some lawyers break from the mold and seem to use their time wisely. Some who sit atop the pyramid touch only the most important documents and only at the most pivotal stages. Like first-rate editors, they multiply their effectiveness and can attend to many written matters at once. Marvin E. Frankel described to us how he writes: "In briefs for which I am responsible, I will often write a sketchy document with many blanks in order to show junior colleagues the major headings and the order of argument as I conceive it. My most competent colleagues—like many law clerks of another era—take liberties and make significant improvements, produce a reasonably polished product for me to edit and revise." Similarly, Justin A. Stanley sets "out the basic ideas. Various people help fill in and may also contribute their own thoughts. Usually I produce the first draft. Then we start to write. I do not do much supplementary research."

But Stanley's approach is the exception, not the norm. It is counterproductive for senior-level lawyers to revise heavily the work of their juniors, as many of our respondents said they did. It is also a mistake for lawyers stubbornly to reject having fresh eyes look at a product that they themselves think is finished. "I keep tight control of the master and do not let others 'polish' my work," said one senior partner at a major New York firm. Such pride of authorship has no place in the lawyer's world.

It is the lawyer's business to master words; the risk that the law runs is that they may master him.

JUSTICE WALTER V. SCHAEFER, *1958*

The central missing function in law firms is that of a clearly defined editor. Lawyers should edit their own work. But they also need an outsider—beyond the closed loop of the associate who researches and writes the first draft and the partner who supervises—to edit a nearly finished document. Some lawyers would erect the attorney-client privilege as an obstacle to hiring professional editors. But that is wrong. Many people at a firm, including secretaries and proofreaders, read confidential matters although they are not lawyers. Some lawyers—especially those away from the large law factories—do rely informally on a second pair of eyes. Robert M. Goldberg, who runs a small office in Anchorage, Alaska, says he often shows a document to his wife, "who is a wonderful editor." That is a shrewd practice, and large firms should institutionalize such ideas.

A first-rate copy editor at a large newspaper earns between $50,000 and $60,000, an annual salary less than that of most first-year associates at major metropolitan law firms. Skilled copy editors would return their investment in a short period; vastly improved documents would be the daily dividend. Here, we distinguish between proofreading and copy editing. Proofreaders take care of the mechanics—checking for misspellings, dropped lines, and other typographical errors. Many firms already employ proofreaders. Copy editors are quite different. They read for sense, meaning, consistency, and style. With their fresh perspective, they can take the place of the audience—be it judge, client, or opposing counsel—for whom the document is intended. Since many firms are now so large that no single lawyer can review all the writing that goes out the door, it is important that some individual editor (or a small cadre of capable editors) scrub and polish those documents.

That is how newspapers, magazines and publishing houses work. Individual copy editors look at every piece. Their job is to improve copy (and most writers, even those with large egos, bow to this function), to challenge the writer as appropriate, and, equally important, to leave a piece of clean copy alone.

Different approaches to editing abound since different publications have vastly different philosophies. At most book publishing houses, the top editors do little or no detailed editing. They spend their time acquiring manuscripts and looking for trends. Sometimes editors read for major gaps. Copy editors, often free-lancers paid for piecework, review completed manuscripts line by line.

The pace at newsweeklies and newspapers is quicker. A handful of these are "writers' " periodicals that place the emphasis on hiring and pleasing talented writers, who are given wide latitude. The budget is allocated mostly to writers, not editors, because it is presumed star writers require minimal editing. Writers' publications are relatively rare. (Fame for journalists is fleeting—as a quick test, see if you can name more than a half-dozen newspaper or magazine journalists other than those who regularly appear as guests on public affairs television shows.)

I am the last one to suppose that a piece about the law could be made to read like a juicy sex novel or a detective story, but I can not see why it has to resemble a cross between a nineteenth century sermon and a treatise on higher mathematics.

FRED RODELL, *1936*

Most publications emphasize editing. At *Time* and *Newsweek*, often the drafts of dozens of writers and reporters are homogenized by squads of editors. Researchers gather background materials; reporters in the field put their observations and interviews into a file. A writer based in New York City then blends the materials unearthed by the researchers and filed by reporters from different locations into a single story that will be subjected to several stages of editing. Because so many people contributed to stories, until the late 1970s the newsweeklies carried no bylines. Now the names of reporters and writers are listed as contributors to their stories.

At newspapers, as at law firms, important writing projects, in contrast to "spot" news stories, are rarely completed overnight. Skilled reporters may have worked weeks or months on page-one stories. Still, they might be extensively edited or even largely rewritten before the public reads them. Stories that end up on page one in the *Los Angeles Times*, the *Washington Post*, the *New York Times*, and other first-rate papers receive special editing care, but only rarely will they be totally rewritten. At the *Wall Street Journal*, front-page stories go through a special desk of editors who often heavily rewrite pieces that staff reporters have turned in as "finished." On most other sizable papers, reporters turn in stories to different "desks." A financial story is edited by editors who specialize in business news; a local story is given to a metropolitan desk. Supervising editors make sure that copy flows smoothly throughout the day and decide which stories from the different desks are the most important.

The torrent of words that flows each day at newspapers is too great for top editors to read everything that is published. (In contrast, at magazines, where the pace is slightly more leisurely, an editor may read every word before it appears in print—sometimes more than once. That editor reads for tone, checks for conflicts among different stories, and sees that stories have no major gaps.) At law firms, too much happens at the last minute, under tight deadlines. Firms should recognize that lawyers are not fungible and that, like journalists, they have different skills. Those with a knack for research should be assigned to research. An imaginative writer, not just any associate, ought to do most of the early drafting of an important brief. By adopting some of the conventions of publishing and journalism, the written product of law firms will inevitably improve.

No publishing enterprise can serve in its entirety as a model for law firms. Lawyers can pick the features most congenial to their organization and working style. In general, though, senior partners should act as editors in chief, delegating editing functions to a new department—the copy desk. The flow of paper can be managed as it is at newspapers and magazines.

A smoothly functioning copy desk, overseen by an office editor, would be responsible for reviewing all or a specifically designated portion of the office's output. The desk would help set and monitor deadlines, oversee the typing and proofreading staffs, and edit all copy that came through it on the way to senior partners for final approval. Law offices that now work feverishly up to deadline would have to reorganize their timetables for researching, composing, and editing. However painful in the short run, the long-run effects of this rescheduling could only be beneficial.

In the third year of law school, they ought to teach English as a Second Language.

STEPHEN WERMIEL, *1987*

Many associates (and one or two partners) we interviewed favored using a general editor, but they doubted they would use the services of a copy desk *before* an assignment was complete. An editor can be most helpful in the early stages, however, offering suggestions and helping to rewrite very important documents when time allows. Of course, in exceptional circumstances deadlines will preclude advance editing. But the editor can still read documents afterward to assess the writing being distributed under the firm's name. On finding repetitive, stylistic, or other difficulties, the editor can call these problems to the attention of the writers and the firm.

In the short term, the editor could run an office newsletter on writing that would force lawyers to reflect occasionally on the importance of clarity and style. In the middle term, a full-time editor could contribute greatly to recruiting by assessing applicants' writing and by training those who are hired. In the long term, the editor could materially enhance the firm's written work and its image: The documents it issued would be improved and the very presence of an editor would clearly signal that the firm cared about writing.

PART III

Making Your Prose Serviceable

CHAPTER 8

Writing the Lead

K ENNETH A. PLEVAN, a litigator in the New York headquarters of Skadden, Arps, Slate, Meagher & Flom, faced an emergency. He had a day to fend off a temporary restraining order against his client, a toy importer. The plaintiff had gone to federal court in Manhattan, charging trademark infringement. Only Plevan's brief could convince the judge to allow the toy importer to sell its inventory.

As he tells the story, Plevan began drafting in the routine way, rehearsing in a paragraph or two the procedural posture of the case. But as he started to write, he realized that he would surely lose his most important reader—the judge.

In writing seminars at the Skadden firm, we had suggested that lawyers borrow standard techniques from journalism: Instead of reciting facts chronologically, or opening with the narrower points and concluding with the broad proposition, they should adopt the "inverted-pyramid" approach. The most important ideas of the story appear at the top and the least important at the bottom where, if the story runs too long, they can be lopped off. Above all, we had urged lawyers at the firm to pay close attention to the lead—the first paragraph or two of a document. That is where the writer needs to grab the reader, and crisp, cogent leads are as useful for lawyers as they are for journalists. Their purpose is the same: To structure the writing so that the reader is never in doubt about why the writer is writing or whether to continue reading.

The lead is a signpost, a means of orienting the reader to the path to be taken. It might consist of an anecdote or a story. It might suggest points of interest along the way, or it might simply state the destination. Well-constructed leads will tell readers how to make sense of what follows.

Ken Plevan tore up his original paragraphs and crafted a trenchant lead. In the lawsuit, Hasbro, the large toy maker, accused Skadden's client, Four Star International Trading Company, of stealing the design of its rubber dinosaurs. Plevan wanted the judge's attention immediately. He did not wait until page three to put forth an argument, as so often happens when lawyers succumb to the temptation to list a chronology or recite the procedural path of the case. He came right to the point, and graphically so:

> Hasbro opens its memorandum by stating that its "enormously successful 'THE TRANSFORMERS' series of toys has predictably spawned knock-offs." What is equally predictable is that Hasbro, with $300,000,000 in sales riding on this successful line of toys, will go to any length to defend its business. As we show below, however, Hasbro cannot arrogate to itself a monopoly in dinosaur converting figures. It was, after all, the Lord, and not Hasbro, that brought the Tricerotops and Brontosaurus to this earth, several hundred million years ago.

The most important reader of Plevan's brief turned out to be not the judge but the opposing counsel. So stark was the point, and so clearly made, that Hasbro backed off and settled the case on favorable terms within days.

Not all leads can be as direct as Plevan's. No immutable rules govern leads. Anecdotal leads, which have been mastered by writers at the *Wall Street Journal*, work best when the subject is sufficiently complicated that the reader must first be alerted to why the phenomenon matters. Other leads are quite straightforward, with the Five *W*'s (who, what, when, where, and why) and the *H* (how)—the catechism that beginning journalists have memorized for generations. Good leads can accomplish many things:

- Deliver information
- Summarize

• Pique the reader's interest

• Clarify a problem or a circumstance

A few years ago, a group of journalists collected their thoughts on leads for a project sponsored by the Associated Press Managing Editors. They concluded that leads should deliver facts interestingly, quickly, clearly, honestly, gracefully, logically, and in good taste. If your lead succeeds, it can induce busy readers to forsake other activities and follow through to your conclusion.

Now compare Plevan's lead with this vertiginous opening paragraph to the *Washington Monthly*'s "memo of the month."* This is how the brief, which was submitted to the U.S. Court of Appeals for the Fifth Circuit in New Orleans, begins:

> Appellee initially filed a Motion to Strike Appendices to Brief for Appellant on July 22, 1983. Appellant filed a brief in response, which Appellee replied to. Appellant has subsequently filed another brief on this motion, Appellant's Reply to Appellee's reply to Appellant's Brief in Response to Appellee's Motion to Strike Appendices to brief for Appellant (Appellant's most recent brief), to which the Appellee herein responds.

As muddled and uninstructive as this lead is, it is no aberration. Here is the beginning of a brief that Justice William Bablitch of the Wisconsin Supreme Court recites in speeches to illustrate how poorly lawyers write:

> The state's argument is the same as the statement of the court. That is to say, that is what the court did, and that is what the court does, then the court does what the court does; and if that is what the court does, it is all right, because that is what the court does.

---

*The *Washington Monthly*, a provocative magazine that needles the bureaucracy, is edited by Charles Peters, who was trained as a lawyer and launched the magazine with no experience as a journalist. In his recent autobiography, *Tilting at Windmills*, he attributes his effectiveness as an editor, in part, to his legal training, which taught him how to interview, to investigate, and to search for flaws in arguments.

It takes no special learning to see that Plevan's lead does not belong in a grouping with these two mind benders. Plevan's is short, to the point, and contains vivid imagery. You do not have to read it twice to get the meaning. You can read the others over and over without enlightenment.

Good writing, especially good persuasive writing, pulls the reader in. Most legal writing is, by contrast, repulsive.

NEIL SKENE, *1987*

One of the most highly regarded contemporary legal writers and thinkers is Laurence H. Tribe, a professor at Harvard Law School. When, in our survey, we asked lawyers, professors, and judges whose legal writing they most admired, Tribe ranked higher than any other living lawyer. In one of the many cases he has successfully argued before the Supreme Court, he represented Grendel's Den, a Harvard Square restaurant that was seeking a liquor license. This is how he began the brief he submitted:

> At issue in this case is the validity of Massachusetts General Laws c.138, §16C (Section 16C), Brief of State Appellants (State Br.) 2a–3a, which delegates to certain churches and synagogues— those that, in the statute's terms, are "dedicated to divine worship," id. 2a—an ad hoc and absolute veto power over the approval of each liquor license within a 500-foot radius of the church or synagogue. Because it is providently located near the intersection of Mt. Auburn and Boylston Streets in Cambridge, and is invested by the State with an unreviewable veto power under Section 16C, the Holy Cross Armenian Catholic Parish church (Holy Cross Church) can and does exercise absolute regulatory authority over the acquisition of liquor licenses in virtually the entire Harvard Square area.

This thicket of confusing citations and unnecessary definitions could have been avoided and the lead measurably strengthened had Tribe incorporated the much more lively imagery that he buried, in a slightly different context, in a footnote a few pages later:

. . . Virtually every major commercial and entertainment area in Massachusetts is within 500 feet of *some* church. At all events, the gist of Grendel's challenge to Section 16C is that it entrusts governmental power to churches. The particular *radius* of the sphere of influence thereby ceded to religious bodies—whether ten feet or ten miles—is constitutionally immaterial: the First and Fourteenth Amendments were not, after all, written with straight-edge and compass.

Many journalists spend half their writing time on the lead. Some lawyers, such as Jay Topkis, agonize over leads. "Usually I do the first paragraph of a brief many times," says Topkis. If you are like most lawyers, however, you probably spend not much more time on the beginning of a document than on the middle or end. You ought to consider spending far more time on it. The proper lead can dramatically ease your burden of organizing; a tight, well-chosen lead can practically structure —or, if written afterwards, restructure—a document for you.

The part of the first part hereinafter known as Jack, and the part of the second part hereinafter known as Jill, ascended or caused to be ascended an elevation of undetermined height and degree of slope, hereinafter referred to as "hill."

20TH CENTURY PARODY

In composing a lead, you should avoid what Professor Marjorie Rombauer of the University of Washington at Seattle calls "mystery-style writing"—conclusions stated last, rather than first. This common failing often shows up in weak or fuzzy verbs, as though the writer were afraid to tell the reader right away the precise nature of the problem. Consider this sentence, the first in a long opening paragraph from a law firm associate to a partner:

One aspect of the proposed sale of Arizona Charter Guaranty & Trust Company ("Arizona Charter") to Fidelity Life Company concerns the contract between the MAC Fund, a money market fund, and its registered investment adviser, Equitable Money Management, Inc. ("EMM"), a wholly owned subsidiary of Eq-

uitable Financial Services, Inc. ("EFS"), 80 percent of which is
in turn owned by Arizona Charter.

The lead is empty. It tells the reader who has waded unnecessarily through
the chain of ownership that an "aspect" of a sale "concerns" a contract.
The writer has wasted the opportunity to say immediately how the contract
affects the sale, forcing the reader instead to puzzle out a slew of connections between these corporate entities, which may or may not be
relevant.

The chronological style can be equally empty. As Robert Kasanof,
a New York City litigator, observes: "I remain astounded at the de-
pendence of much litigation writing on chronological organization which
is often most difficult for the reader, coming new to the subject, to follow.
Trite though it may be, I believe that a summary introduction gives the
reader a gestalt which makes the arguments flow and adds persuasiveness
to them. . . . A reader of legal writing is likely to be suffering from
severe overload; therefore it is very worthwhile to ease the physical and
logical task of following your argument."

---

*Pyramids would make nice paperweights for lawyers' desks and would
also serve as a gentle reminder that alternative structural forms exist in
writing.*

NEWTON LAMSON, 1987

The chronological lead is commonly used by lawyers who have either
not thought through their problem or not revised their wording once they
have solved it. Here is an example of a typical chronological, fact-stuffed
lead, followed by our suggested revision.

Chronological Lead

On November 8, 1984, Congress passed the Hazardous and Solid
Waste Amendment of 1984, modifying and augmenting the Resource Conservation and Recovery Act (RCRA). Among the several changes wrought by the 1984 amendments is a new Federal
regulatory system governing the installation and operation of underground storage tanks, commonly called the LUST program

(for Leaking Underground Storage Tanks). The final form of this regulatory framework will be fleshed out by the EPA over the next three years as it conducts further research and institutes rule-making procedures. It is the purpose of this Memorandum to inform the client of what sorts of regulations they might expect will ultimately govern their use of underground storage tanks, and when those regulations may take effect. While perfect prediction of an agency's action is impossible, this Memorandum should allow present management to conduct informed decision-making concerning underground storage facilities.

Suggested Revision

A new federal regulatory system will govern those who operate underground storage tanks. No one can confidently predict the substance of the final regulations, but companies must begin to plan now for EPA rule making under the HSWA, an amendment to RCRA.

In his critique of lawyers' writing, Justice Bablitch understands what many of the best journalists know: You must always engage your audience. "Effective brief writing," says the judge, "requires that you constantly remind yourself for whom it is you are writing. You are not writing for your client, nor to impress your client with the depth of your intellect. You are writing for the judge. He or she is your sole audience."

Leon Friedman, a professor at Hofstra Law School and a civil rights litigator, adopts this approach: "The secret is directness: Let the judge know immediately what your position is. Recognize the time limitations that judges suffer under. If you can give him the means to decide the case in the first two minutes of reading he will appreciate your approach."

Neil Skene, who trained as a lawyer, worked as a reporter and editor in Florida, and now is executive editor of *Congressional Quarterly*, says: "The writer should realize the importance of giving the reader a map before setting off for the destination: State the point, then lead the reader through the logic and explanation and back to that point. The reader is more willing to accompany you on this intellectual journey if he has a good understanding of where you are going."

We are not suggesting that lawyers go to journalism school. But

lawyers can master good writing more quickly if they think as journalists do.

---

*The best writers among lawyers are self-confident. They do not have to
fall back on opaque flapdoodle to dazzle non-lawyers.*

FRED GRAHAM, 1987

In his response to our survey, Robert M. Goldberg of Anchorage
recalled that he was greatly influenced by a leading journalist a quarter
century ago: "The late Eddie Lahey, the Pulitzer-prize winning reporter
for the *Chicago Daily News*, told us as college journalists (Amherst
Student Banquet, March 1963) that a good reporter must be able to tell
a story quickly and directly. 'He should be able to cover the Second
Coming of Christ in under 1,000 words!' said Lahey.* His comments,
fueled by a month with Judge Henry Edgerton, a year with Judge David
Bazelon, and 20 years on my own, have convinced me of that fundamental
truth: Tell your story directly, put it in context, make it simple but
interesting, and then practice what my father, former U.S. Supreme Court
Justice Arthur Goldberg, calls the First Rule of Advocacy: 'Sit down!' "

The lead is a sales job, to lure the reader into the story. Many adopt
a conversational approach. Consider these inviting leads, which we have
culled from newspapers in recent years:

- A couple of years ago, it was so quiet here you could almost hear
  the marijuana grow. (From a 1985 *Wall Street Journal* profile of
  a curmudgeonly country editor in northern California.)

- It's after a rainfall, when the earth smells so rich and damp and
  flavorful, that Fannie Glass says she most misses having some
  dirt to eat. (From a 1984 *New York Times* article on a custom still
  practiced in Mississippi and other southern states.)

---

*Lahey is credited with writing one of the best-known leads of his generation. Nathan
Leopold and Richard Loeb were teenage prodigies in 1924 at the University of Chicago
when they killed Bobby Franks in an attempt to commit the perfect crime. Loeb was killed
in prison in 1936 after making a homosexual advance toward another prisoner. Lahey's
lead: "Richard Loeb, the well-known student of English, yesterday ended a sentence with
a proposition."

- Roll call, the teachers agree, is the most difficult part of the day: Ho Suk Ping He, Yana Katzap, Tkkun Amongi, Azaria Badebr, Rotcheild Boruchov, Eduordo Yun. (From a 1986 *New York Times* article on a polyglot school in Queens.)

- Thanks to the elders of the Collinsville Church of Christ, Marion Guinn never needed to sew a scarlet letter to the front of her crisp white nurse's uniform. (From a 1984 *Miami Herald* story on what happened to a woman in a small Oklahoma town who had been found to be a "fornicatrix.")

What distinguishes these leads is how they irresistibly lure busy readers into reading on. Rene J. Cappon, an editor of the Associated Press, advises his readers in *The Word* to think of leads "as though they cost you 10 bucks per word, each word to be engraved on stainless steel while you're sitting on a hot stove. Think economy." The lead is no place for secondary detail, abstract language, or vagueness. Cramming all Five *W*'s and *H* into the first paragraph creates congestion. Avoid "cardiac arrest" in leads, says Cappon, by leaving out inconsequential detail.

Compare these two journalistic leads, which are especially germane to lawyers.

Lead I. WASHINGTON—The U.S. Court of Appeals agreed Wednesday to review a lower court order that found the Nuclear Regulatory Commission in contempt of court for violating an order to hold open budget meetings.

Lead II. WASHINGTON—The U.S. Court of Appeals agreed Wednesday to review a contempt finding against the Nuclear Regulatory Commission for holding a closed meeting.

Louis Boccardi, president and general manager of the Associated Press, calls the first lead "tennis ball writing." In his bulletin, *Prose and Cons*, Boccardi commented: "The problem here is that we treat the reader's mind like a tennis ball to be whacked back and forth across the net. Agreed to review. Bam! Contempt of court. Bam! For violating an order. Bam! To hold open meetings. Bam! You can almost see the ball flying back and forth. It's just too much. You cure it by just stepping back and asking yourself, 'What really happened here?' "

We are encountering more pleadings that appear to be drafted with the eye to their eventual publication in the media.

RICHARD E. CHENEY, 1987

Specifics can be included deeper in the document. That advice applies with equal force to lawyers' writing. Lawyers' prose rarely is deathless, but it should not be deadly. No matter how complicated the facts, one reading should do. And it can be done, as this final example by Judge Learned Hand shows:

> The suit is to enjoin the performance of the picture play, "Letty Lynton," as an infringement of the plaintiffs' copyrighted play, "Dishonored Lady." The plaintiffs' title is conceded, so too the validity of the copyright; the only issue is infringement. The defendants say that they did not use the play in any way to produce the picture; the plaintiffs discredit this denial because of the negotiations between the parties for the purchase of rights in the play, and because the similarities between the two are too specific and detailed to have resulted from chance. The judge thought that, so far as the defendants had used the play, they had taken only what the law allowed, that is, those general themes, motives, or ideas in which there could be no copyright. Therefore he dismissed the bill.

In five sentences, Hand sets out the purpose of the suit, the facts, the issues, and the lower court's decision. No one can doubt what the case is about, and this single paragraph guides the reader through the seven pages that follow. One reading will do. No more can be asked of a lead.

CHAPTER 9

"By the Way, I Forgot to Mention . . ." Form, Structure, and Organization

Suppose you are helping your child assemble a toy giraffe, just removed from the gift box. Out comes a longish neck and backbone, in three pieces; a head, in one; four legs, in twelve; a tail, in two. Unlike the man from Mars, who has never seen even a drawing of a giraffe and never contemplated the concept of a vertebrate, you should have an easy time of it. In the first place, you have a cultural awareness of how a giraffe should look—you do not have to create the form from scratch—so you can probably connect each piece to its mate lickety-split. In the second place, you can stare at the picture on the box. The structure, in other words, is given to you. And if by chance you falter, your junior critic will pipe up quickly: "But Mommy, the head belongs on the neck."

Like a living organism, a piece of prose has a complex structure. Its largest components are easy to spot, but its finer points are often invisible, and to dissect them is often to kill them. Like all creatures, giraffes are not contrived piece by piece; they grow outward from a single cell. Your writing must unfold this way too. Composing a sentence or paragraph is more than putting pieces of a puzzle together.

Like a living organism, too, a piece of writing has different structures. Meaning depends on context, and context depends on location. Words alone are not enough. They must be grouped in phrases and clauses, and these clauses and phrases in sentences. How they are grouped is not an

95

arbitrary matter: The structure depends on grammar and semantics—the rules of construction and the rules of meaning. Sentences in turn must be grouped within paragraphs, and paragraphs must be linked throughout the whole document. A document likewise is divided into units—a head, known as the lead; a torso containing the heart of the argument; and limbs going off in various directions that permit refinements and subtleties.

This is what the writer must create. But the writer has an easier time of it than nature. The living organism gestates but once, and if an unfortunate chemical accident attaches the foot to the neck, nothing apart from surgery can set the matter right. Prose composition, in contrast, can have many gestations. If a document is not structured properly at first, the writer has the luxury—and the duty—to put the head and feet and middle where they belong.

Order and Disorder

The principle of sound organization is this: *Join those elements that belong together.* It is more easily stated than interpreted or obeyed. Elements belong together for one of two reasons: (1) They are part of the same specific topic (witnesses' observations of the color of the traffic light; exceptions to the statute of limitations relevant to the case at hand) or (2) they are related topics (descriptions of the transactions establishing that the defendant violated the insider trading regulations; the international law doctrines that preclude Iran from suing the United States). The signal that the writer has deviated from this principle of organization is the admission, expressed or not, that "by the way, I forgot to mention . . ."

When composing, you will always forget to mention something. Few of us can match the mental power of the nineteenth-century American historian William H. Prescott, whose impaired eyesight forced him to memorize: "He frequently kept about sixty pages in his memory for several days, and went over the whole mass five or six times, molding and remolding the sentences at each successive turn." When you do remember, especially if you are writing rapidly, you are likely to toss the thought on the page just as it comes: "By the way . . ." That's fine. The trick is to recognize, upon rereading, when the foot is on the neck, how to snip it off, and where to sew it back on.

Let's work through an example from a student brief to test the principle of organization. Here is the instructor's description of the factual setting:

> Niles Nasty, a supervisor, continually propositioned Mary Sweetly, his new executive assistant: For months he suggested at least two or three times a week that they dine, that he visit at her home on the weekends to review assignments, and that she stay late at the office to discuss "developments." She politely turned down his every overture. In the eleventh month of a one-year probationary period, Niles told Mary that she would be promoted and given a raise, and he suggested that they go to a cocktail lounge to celebrate. She declined. He grew quite angry and told her that he carried a gun "for broads like you." Mary complained to the company's personnel director, who refused to accept her charges, saying that it would be better to keep the matter quiet. So Mary filed a criminal complaint, and she was immediately transferred to a dead-end secretarial job, three days before the end of her probationary period. Mary's three predecessors had suffered a similar fate. Mary was told that the transfer was temporary and that her old job would be restored when the court issued an order of protection. After the court issued it, Mary was told that her previous position had been filled and that she could not be re-evaluated for a new position until she had stayed twelve full months in any one position. Charging sexual harassment, Mary sued the company for injuries stemming from the hostile work environment, job discrimination, and the retaliatory transfer. The lower court dismissed her complaint. Mary appeals.

What follows is a portion of a student brief:

ARGUMENT

MARY SWEETLY STATES A VALID SEXUAL HARASSMENT CLAIM BE-CAUSE NILES NASTY'S OFFENSIVE AND UNWELCOME BEHAVIOR CREATED A HOSTILE AND INTIMIDATING WORKING ENVIRONMENT AND TANGIBLE JOB DETRIMENT FOR WHICH THE COMPANY SHOULD BE HELD LIABLE.

1. Nasty's intertwining of his invitations with references to Mary's job suggests that Mary's submission to Nasty's advances was a condition of her employment. The modern trend within the

circuit courts has been adoption of the policy of holding employers strictly liable for actions of sexual harassment by supervisors when the sexual harassment centers around threats of tangible job benefits. *Horn v. Duke Homes*, 755 F.2d 599 (7th Cir. 1985) (court stated that whatever the result under the common law of agency, Title VII [of the Civil Rights Act of 1964] demands that employers be held strictly liable in sexually harassing situations). This position of strict liability is founded upon traditional notions of agency, which mandate employer liability when the supervisor acts in an agency capacity. A strict liability rule is intended to eviscerate tangible job detriment in that it ensures compensation for victims and creates an incentive for the employer to take the strongest possible affirmative measures to prevent the hiring and retention of sexist supervisors.

2. The corporation's actions reasonably led Mary to believe that Nasty had the authority to evaluate her performance and recommend her for promotion. The Supreme Court's recent decision in *Meritor Savings Bank v. Vinson*, 106 S.Ct. 2399 (1986), suggests that employers would be strictly liable for sexual harassment under the agency principle. Nasty was acting as an agent for the corporation while simultaneously placing conditions on Mary's economic future. A jury could reasonably find that Nasty's acts were part and parcel of his supervision of Mary, *Davis v. United States Steel Corp.*, 779 F.2d 209, 213 (4th Cir. 1985), (majority of the court held that the employee could present a case under the doctrine of respondeat superior once the offending supervisor's harassing conduct had been observed without reaction by his supervisor). Therefore, the corporation must be held liable for Nasty's threatening actions against Mary's tangible job benefits.

3. Had Nasty been a coworker rather than a supervisor, Mary could have thwarted his propositions without the risk of tangible job detriment. In *Scott v. Sears, Roebuck & Co.*, 798 F.2d 210 (7th Cir. 1986), (the court dismissed a sexual harassment claim against a coworker) the plaintiff admitted that the allegedly harassing coworker was a friend and that he had asked her out only once. The isolated threat posed to Scott's working environment and tangible job benefits by a coworker warranted the dismissal of her claim. Mary, on the other hand, was victimized by a

patterned and pervasive practice of sexual harassment by a supervisor.

4. Upon the establishment of Mary's claim it is now evident that the corporation had constructive, if not actual, knowledge of the existence of the sexually hostile workplace created by Nasty, and that it took no prompt action to rectify that environment. Liability should be assessed against the corporation for the sexual harassment committed by its supervisor Nasty, *Henson v. City of Dundee,* 682 F.2d 897, 905 (11th Cir. 1982) (employer is strictly liable for actions of its supervisors that amount to sexual discrimination or sexual harassment resulting in tangible job detriment to subordinate employee). Mary's three immediate predecessors were all transferred from the department while it was under Nasty's control. Someone from the corporation's personnel department had to transfer these women. Upon that fact alone, the corporation had to have, or at the very least should have known of the offensive environment created by Nasty. Yet with that situation before it the corporation did little or nothing to remove or dissuade Nasty. The corporation could have negated its liability but chose to ignore it through three prior similar instances. The simultaneous observations and inaction on the part of the corporation satisfies the criteria for constructive knowledge as defined by the federal courts, as well as the E.E.O.C Guidelines.

If this passage mystifies you, your confusion is due not only to the grammatical and syntactical errors, infelicities, redundancies, and verbosities but also to the unexplained mixing of topical elements from paragraph to paragraph. Let's stab at the principal points of each paragraph, sentence by sentence:

Paragraph 1. (a) *Nature of act*: Mary's submission or failure to submit was a condition of employment. (b) *Rule of liability*: Employers are strictly liable for sexual harassment by supervisors. (c) *Origin of rule*: The principal of strict liability stems from concepts of agency. (d) *Purpose of rule*: The rule is intended to force employers to banish harassment.

Paragraph 2. (a) *Creation of agency authority*: Mary reasonably believed Niles had authority to act. (b) *Rule of liability*: Employers are strictly liable for sexual harassment by supervisors. (c) *Creation of agency*: Niles was an agent and had authority to act. (d) *Standing to sue*: An employee may sue if the company failed to react to supervisor's actions. (e) *Rule of liability*: An employer is strictly liable if it fails to react to a supervisor's actions. (f) *Legal conclusion*: The corporation is liable.

Paragraph 3. (a) *Extent of liability*: The corporation is liable only for supervisors' harassment, not that of a coworker. (b) *Precedent*: A court dismissed a claim premised on harassment by coworker. (c) *What happened to Mary*: Mary was harassed by her supervisor.

Paragraph 4. (a) *Notice*: The company had notice. (b) *Failure to mitigate*: The company failed to rectify. (c) *Legal conclusion*: The company should be held liable. (d) *Rule of liability*: The company is strictly liable for actions of harassing supervisors. (e) *Notice*: The company, through its agents, must have known of the harassment. (f) *Failure to mitigate*: The company failed to rectify. (g) *Notice*: The company's activities demonstrate it had notice.

Scan this list of main points. No logical order suggests itself. In these four paragraphs, the student has jumbled many different issues: (1) whether Niles was a supervisor, (2) whether supervisors are liable, (3) whether corporations need notice, (4) how they get notice, (5) whether corporations are liable, (6) whether this corporation is liable, (7) what the standard of liability is, (8) whether an employee has standing to sue, and more.

Good writers avoid pseudoscholarship, get to the heart of the matter, and have mastered the ability intelligently to exclude *material that is unimportant. Many legal writers confuse case citations with the scholarship; cases are worth citing only if they truly add to an understanding of the subject at hand.*

JUSTICE RICHARD NEELY, 1987

This mishmash of ideas is hopeless. Readers expect order. When you give directions to friends who propose to visit your home, you start with the street nearest them, explain where to turn next, and so on, in tidy sequence, to your doorstep. You do not say, "Well, forget about the middle roads for the moment, first let me describe a street three-quarters of the way here that may interest you; then there's a street back near you . . ." A rational sequence of thought is not a whim; many writers who reflect on their craft make the same point. Sir Winston Churchill, winner of the Nobel Prize for Literature in 1953, recalled: "I began to see that writing, especially narrative, was not only an affair of sentences, but of paragraphs. Indeed I thought the paragraph no less important than the sentence. . . . Just as the sentence contains one idea in all its fullness, so the paragraph should embrace a distinct episode; and as sentences should follow one another in harmonious sequence, so the paragraphs must fit on to one another like the automatic couplings of railway carriages."

Topic Sentences and Topic Flow

Your topics must be not only sensibly arranged but also sensibly expressed so that your readers can understand right now, right here, why you are talking about a particular point. A topic sentence is to a paragraph what a lead is to the whole document. It directs the reader's attention and gives significance to what comes next. Consider the following string of topic sentences taken from a seventeen-paragraph law review article by David M. Balabanian, a San Francisco practitioner, eulogizing Justice Matthew Tobriner of the California Supreme Court.

The best way to get a laugh out of a law review is to take a couple of drinks and then read an article, any article, aloud. That can be really funny.

FRED RODELL, *1936*

---

1. California lawyers have long played in a colorful local rite: Explaining the Law of California to the World.

2. Lately, the frequency of such conversations has seemed to diminish.

3. Many of the ideas identified with our courts which seemed remarkable, even visionary, twenty, ten or five years ago, now seem commonplace, even essential.

4. More of California's contributions to the national jurisprudence than is generally realized (even in well-informed legal circles) came from a quiet, humble man who spent much of his long judicial career in relative public obscurity.

5. The scope of his work defies quick summarization.

6. Though time alone can adjudicate the durability and worth of his many ideas, two themes stand out:

7. The importance of individuality and the need to defend it against the organizational imperatives of both government and private institutions.

8. The substitution of reasonable expectation for fictitious agreement.

9. The form of his opinions was as characteristic as their content.

10. Another Tobriner hallmark was the absence of the passive voice.

11. He liked good metaphors.

12. Though earnest in defense of the values he held dear, he shunned the self-righteous moralizing which disfigures much liberal advocacy.

13. His great output required great industry.

14. Ever gracious and self-effacing, he resisted all temptation to adopt the eccentricities of manner or displays of choler sometimes mistaken for judicial greatness.

15. There are, of course, many sincere people who heartily deplore his work.

16. Whether, given the stasis of our legislative institutions, they ultimately could or would have struck balances more durable or popular than the courts' is unclear.

17. What is clear is that conflicts unresolved by the legislature have been settled by our judges in ways that once appeared

unremarkable and now seem commonplace, and that one of these judges was a quiet, gentle man who sought neither controversy nor glory, got more of the former and less of the latter than he deserved, and profoundly changed the lives of us all.

From the topic sentences alone, the reader gleans the substance of the article. Each is a summary, paving the way for the illustrations built into every paragraph. Each progresses, moreover, building an argument from an initial premise.

Inexperienced writers, and writers who have never thought much about the structure of paragraphs, should use topic sentences as first sentences until they master the structure of an argument or essay. With control comes variation. Topic sentences need not always lead the paragraph; they can come second or even at the end, where they can lend dramatic emphasis to the examples that precede them. Following is an example of a paragraph that begins with a transition sentence that leads into the topic sentence:

Writing is not merely a matter of words and phrases. Much more important, writing is a process by which we think our way to a solution of the problem that lies before us.

Topic sentences alone are not sufficient to provide clear, flowing paragraphs. The writer must also connect the topics from sentence to sentence in each paragraph: The subjects that each sentence discusses must be the same or closely related. Too great a disparity gives the reader a figurative stiff neck, from turning back and forth while searching for links. Again, an example may clarify the concept. Read the next two paragraphs for sense; note that the topics of each sentence are italicized.

An accredited law school must graduate lawyers before the bar examination is open to them to take. *The bar* will not admit them to practice until they pass the exam. Only then can *they* hang out a shingle. And even then, *the finer points of law practice* will elude them; it will be many years before *they* can practice comfortably. *That experience* is not gained overnight.

Lawyers must graduate from an accredited law school before they may take the bar examination. Not until passing it may *they* be admitted to the bar and hang out a shingle. Even then, it will be many years before *they* can comfortably say they understand the finer points of law practice. *They* cannot gain that experience overnight.

Obviously too much is written. The 1983 circuit court decisions for that year began in 696 F.2d. It is now 1987 and we are at 888 F.2d. By 2000 A.D. we'll be at 2001 F.2d.

                                                          JUDGE JOHN F. KEENAN, 1987

Both paragraphs mean the same thing. But in the first version, the topics of each sentence are disjointed, seemingly unrelated: (1) "accredited law school," (2) "the bar," (3) "they," (4) "the finer points of law practice," (5) "they," and (6) "that experience." The reader glides over each without seeing the connections, which are buried inside the sentences. In the second version, the topics are identical: (1) "lawyers," (2) "they," (3) "they," (4) "they." The substance is the same, but the sentences are glued tightly together; the reader does not pause in going from one to the next. Moreover, a smooth topic flow will usually keep the sentences tighter, shorter, and fewer.

You should recognize that topics are not ready-made, preexisting, universal. You control them. A muddled, disjointed, incoherent topic flow is your fault, not the fault of the material. You should also recognize as a rough generalization that lawyers have five "levels" of topics available to them:

(1) The *party* level: the plaintiff or defendant. "*Mr. Jones* carried the radioactive isotope, contrary to the Montana code, but he failed to receive a warning from Mr. Smith that . . . " or "*Mr. Smith* failed to warn that the radioactive isotope Mr. Jones was carrying . . . "

(2) The *object* or *concept* level: the particular thing or concept that lies at the heart of the matter. "*The radioactive isotope* that Mr. Jones carried, contrary to the Montana code, posed a serious threat."

(3) The level of *principle*: the laws and rules that govern the problem.

"*The Montana code governing the handling* of radioactive isotopes forbids."

(4) The *lawyer* level: the lawyer as writer. "*I* must inform you that the Montana code."

(5) The *audience* level: the client (or judge). "*You* violated the Montana code in carrying the radioactive isotope, but." Which approach you should use will depend on context and purpose. You should be consistent when pitching different topics at the reader. Topics should not wander indiscriminately through the paragraph. Have a reason for what you do and shape your topics to conform to it.

Structure from Strategy and Purpose

Lawyers do not write to amuse themselves but to solve some problem or meet some need. Every document a lawyer writes should reflect the purpose for which it was undertaken, yet too often lawyers seem oblivious of this cardinal principle.

To solve problems, lawyers have a limited set of logical and rhetorical strategies available to them. We suggest that lawyers will ordinarily employ one or more of the following strategies: (1) *defining*, (2) *comparing*, (3) *contrasting*, (4) *classifying*, (5) *evaluating*, and (6) *showing cause and effect* in pursuing one or more of the following purposes: (a) *explaining*, (b) *responding*, (c) *narrating*, and (d) *proving*.

Lawyers who ignore strategies and purpose write muddled documents, like that of the first-year law student who drafts an office memorandum that looks like this:

Lead. Our client is accused of larceny. The definition of larceny is unclear. The courts say different things in different cases.

Body. In Case 1, the court said . . . In Case 2, the court said . . . In Case 3, the court said . . . In Case 4, the court said . . .

Conclusion. Therefore, our client is (or is not) guilty.

Organizing the discussion around discrete cases rarely works, to the chagrin of the typical first-year law student, because the writer cannot connect the facts or law of the cases unearthed to the case at hand. The one-two-three organization precludes a strategy of comparing or contrasting holdings in order to explain the law or to prove the client's innocence.

To structure a document intelligently, you must know what you want to do and how you can go about doing it. Suppose that your goal is to explain the law of larceny in a particular jurisdiction. To explain it, the best strategy is to classify the various definitions that the statutes and the courts have offered. The classification scheme will suggest itself when you have read enough cases. You would not begin by saying, "Look, I've read fifty-two cases, and the first one defines larceny this way, and the second one that way, and the third . . ." Rather, you would begin by telling your reader that the courts have interpreted the larceny statutes in five ways, or whatever the number. You would then define each, naming each set of circumstances according to a classification scheme that you will have developed. Then you would discuss each species in the classification, illustrating the circumstances that give rise to each by referring to the appropriate circumstances of the appropriate cases. Your purpose and strategy thus will dictate how your memorandum must be organized.

That organization might be quite different from the form of a brief in which you are called on to *respond* to your adversary's argument. Then you would probably organize your response around the topics, and in the order set forth, in your adversary's brief. Likewise, your memorandum or brief would be shaped differently if you were required to show how a statutory amendment affected the chances of your client's being acquitted, or if you were asked to narrate the facts, explaining what happened.

If you think out your purpose and strategy first, you should discover that your organizational and conceptual problems will help solve each other.

Format: Flow and Interruptions

Readers falter when they cannot guess what the writer is aiming at, when concepts are disorganized, when the thread of topics winds, and when a document is too long. Readers also lose their way when a document is interrupted by a long quotation, lengthy string citation, or a ponderous footnote.

Lawyers quote too much. There is a talismanic reverence for words that someone else has said that makes law writing particularly dull.

ARTICLES OFFICE, TEXAS LAW REVIEW, *1988*

Quotations. Too many lawyers, showing off their research or hoping to decorate their arguments, load their writing with lengthy or inappropriate passages that someone else wrote. These quotations interrupt the flow of thought, in part because they are never in the same voice or tone and in part because they rarely connect precisely to the point being made. The lawyer who uses long quotations is usually thinking far more about himself than of his audience. Long quotations are often inserted out of laziness or insecurity: The writer is too tired or too uncomprehending to distill the essence of the thought. Rather than undertake that work himself, the writer forces the reader to struggle through someone else's voice. As a consequence, the reader often skips over the passage anyway.

A quotation should be treated as an ornament: to catch the reader's eye and to convey instantly a single thought. Quote other people only when their words sparkle, when they restate the essence of your point in a pithy, epigrammatic way, or when they introduce a vivid metaphor. The apt quotation must be aptly introduced. It must be anchored, not left floating about aimlessly amidst your sentences. Otherwise your point will sink, and your reader with it.

Chiefly I admire legal prose that eschews ostentation and so-called "scholarship." Footnotes and digression poison most legal writing. The older I get, the more I admire succinctness, and the more I despise flash.

MILTON S. GOULD, *1987*

String citations and miscitations. We do not know anyone who reads string citations. Many lawyers suppose they add heft and authority. Too often they are simply stolen from some other document; the lawyer has probably not troubled to read through the cases they name. Shirley Hufstedler, a former federal appeals judge, was one of many sitting or retired judges in our survey who complained of miscitation and misuse of authorities. Salvatore A. Romano, a Washington, D.C., practitioner, views as an increasing problem the "overcitation of case law and other authorities with little or no bearing on the operative facts or issues." Like Judge Richard A. Posner, cite only those cases that you have read. Citations should be confined to the principal cases that support your point; that the courts in dozens of other cases have followed the rule you are advancing may interest the historians but not the readers of your brief.

Footnotes. The biggest interruption to the flow of thought is the lowly footnote. "Encountering [a footnote] is like going downstairs to answer the doorbell while making love," said Noel Coward. Footnotes should be reserved primarily for citations, sparing the eye from the strain of skipping over titles and numbers that disconnect thought. The "scholarly" approach of tackling substantive, sometimes quite subtle, themes and topics in the fine print of footnotes is a fierce distraction. Sometimes, lawyers are so carried away that they even bury their arguments in footnotes, forcing irritated readers to excavate them. Stephen Wermiel, Supreme Court reporter for the *Wall Street Journal*, says, "I'm struck by the frequency with which important qualifying or modifying material is put in footnotes in briefs, court opinions, and law review articles. Often this material is integral to the text and quite obviously doesn't belong in footnotes." If material is germane to your point, you should integrate it in the text. If it is not germane, you should wonder, before your reader does, why you are including it at all.

It is hard to improve on Fred Rodell's acerbic conclusion more than fifty years ago: "If a writer does not really need footnotes and tacks them on just because they look pretty or because it is the thing to do, then he ought to be tried for willful murder of his readers' (all three of them) eyesight and patience."

Helpful formatting. Although long quotations, footnotes, and string citations force the reader onto detours, some formats can illuminate the path of the argument. A series of points can often be obscured by their linear progression in a sentence. Breaking them out, either by numbering each point in an indented line or preceding them with a symbol (usually called a "bullet"), is visually arresting and emphasizes the series. Similarly, subheads serve as signposts that tell your readers where the next paragraphs are taking them. Like all literary devices, special formatting works best when judiciously used.

The Length of a Document

The complexity of a document depends not only on the subject but also on the length. Length determines structure in ways that too few lawyers heed. At one firm we visited, partners told of a young associate who drafted a brief of more than ninety pages, knowing that the court to which it would be submitted would reject briefs longer than thirty-five pages. The cost of this profligacy was measured not solely by the time and energy it took to read. The real bother was reorganizing and cutting fifty-five pages. Just as a mature tree with all its branches and roots is far more complex than a sapling, a ninety-page paper has a structure significantly more complex than a thirty-five-page paper.

Where did lawyers learn that longer is somehow better?
JACK LAHR, *1987*

Yet we have found that lawyers rarely contemplate the length of their documents as they sit down to compose. Dashing headlong down the road without the sketchiest notion of how far you are going is dangerous and foolish. Like runners, writers must learn to pace themselves. Lawyers too often equate bulk with quality; perhaps they suppose they are working harder by making it longer. Paradoxically, quite the reverse is true.

The excessively long document poses many risks:

1. Reacting to long and poorly written briefs, courts are now imposing sharp page limitations.

2. Length antagonizes most readers. Few people have the time or patience to read lengthy documents with care—or even at all.

3. The longer a document, the more likely its structure will be overly complex and difficult to follow. If you restrict your space, however, you will be forced to make your point more concisely and forcefully.

4. Longer documents are harder to edit.

Wordiness is a common disease that afflicts all writers. Once the words begin to flow, it is easier to continue than to stop. It is taxing to focus and limit. That requires discipline. Moreover, from our earliest school days, teachers have ingrained upon us the notion that more is better. The precocious fifth-grader who writes a twenty-page paper is rewarded with an A. As adults, some writers are show-offs eager to display their research and erudition. It is painful to discard research—thus, according to Parkinson, writers will find a way to work it in. And these days, technology indulges this urge.

If any bill, answers, replication, or rejoinder, shall be found of an immoderate length, both the party and the counsel under whose hand it passeth shall be fined.

      SIR FRANCIS BACON, EARLY SEVENTEENTH CENTURY

Lawyers write long for other reasons. One theory, often advanced, is that they fear strategic or legal consequences if they leave any trails unexplored. They may lose their case if the adversary raises a point they have omitted. Or worse, they could be held liable themselves. As Justice Stanley Mosk of the California Supreme Court wrote us: "Lawyers, fearing a later charge of incompetence, and perhaps a lawsuit for legal malpractice, feel an obligation to raise every conceivable point."

Lawyers may justify the length of their written materials as a guard against malpractice, but a more convincing explanation is that lawyers are indoctrinated early on to value thoroughness, even though it is usually a false thoroughness.

That false thoroughness is especially apparent in law review articles, which are used for making tenure decisions in the schools. Being arcane rarely hurts. As Professor John E. Nowak of the University of Illinois Law School argues, "The professorial style of writing, which is meant to impress deans and promotion committees, impedes any professor's ability to explain to the average reader exactly what went on in court cases."

I reject many submissions that would be excellent if anywhere from one-third to two-thirds of the text could be cut.

PHIL TALBERT, U.C.L.A. LAW REVIEW, *1988*

Moreover, academicians are known by their "scholarly apparatus," voluminous and numerous footnotes that wind along often obscure by-ways and are intended to thicken and lengthen every piece. In 1988, in a tongue-in-cheek article on the lawyerly habit of footnoting, the *Wall Street Journal* cited a law review article by Jesse H. Choper, dean of Boalt Hall at the University of California at Berkeley. Choper adorned his article on the Supreme Court with 1611 footnotes. "The numbers aren't very pertinent; it's the quality," Choper deadpanned. Anyway, he said, he "could have had 300 more footnotes" had he not shown restraint.

Some student editors of these law reviews carry with them the lessons of length as they ascend the professional ladder to judicial clerkships. Opinions have been getting longer because of "excessive reliance on and adoption of law clerks' bad habits from law reviews," said Judge Joseph W. Bellacosa of New York's highest court. Shirley Hufstedler concurred: Opinions are longer because "law clerks are doing most of the writing, and even those who are good do not know the difference between a law review note and an opinion."

Law clerks' habits don't exhaust the reasons for lengthy judicial opinions. Judges imagine themselves as scholars. Chief Judge Sol Wachtler of the New York Court of Appeals said, "There seems to be a tendency in some courts to use a legal opinion as a research paper to display the knowledge of the writer." Moreover, judges presented with discursive briefs can demonstrate their scholarship on the cheap. Justice James Leff, a Manhattan trial judge, wrote: "I do hold the opinion that when a news report says, 'In a 76-page opinion, District Court Judge X said . . .' [it means] that he had two briefs with dozens of quotations and that he put his opinion together with scissors and magic tape." Finally, many courts either lack the judgment themselves to exclude what is valueless or else feel compelled to answer every point to show that they are impartial and worthy of the challenge. Justice Mosk says that when inundated with lengthy briefs, "courts must then discuss every conceivable point however meritless."

The consequence is a vicious circle. Long briefs beget long opinions, which beget long briefs. Long opinions provide fodder for professors to chew on in law review articles. Long law review articles provide grist for the brief and opinion writers. The circle is closed.

I [Harlan McCugh, a senior partner with McCugh, McCugh & Moore McCughs] had an instance not long ago where a lawyer for a motion picture studio sent a one-page contract to a screenwriter I was representing. I took one look at it and became furious . . . The studio lawyer apologized and . . . promised to send over the studio's usual 170-page contract right away. As soon as I got it, we started haggling over it for three months, and I was able to charge my client my normal outrageous fee.

ART BUCHWALD, 1983

In response to the deluge of words, courts have begun to cut down their reading load. In some instances, the quality of the writing has improved. For example, the federal district court for the Northern District of California has limited briefs to twenty-five pages. This limitation, reports Patrick D. Mahoney, a San Francisco practitioner, "has forced lawyers to be much more concise, which has led to superior briefs. . . . The effect has been to eliminate repetitive arguments, to sharpen the quality of the arguments that are made, and to eliminate string citations that are of no benefit to anyone."

Page limits are a start. But lawyers in most jurisdictions with such limits circumvent them with impunity. That's unfortunate. Page limitations set outer boundaries; they should not be regarded as minimum lengths or even suggested lengths. Lawyers should learn to stay well within the limits and press the courts to sanction adversaries who exceed them.

The young associate who wrote the ninety-page brief is no longer employed by the law firm that was forced to cut his draft by two-thirds. He might have stayed had he known where to stop before he started. Successful journalists develop a skill in writing to space, often under a tight deadline: They tailor their materials to the inch limitation their editors impose. The most accomplished journalists assess their raw material and *tell* their editors how much space is justified, well before any word is written. Lawyers can as surely develop this skill for their writing.

In the large, the 360-odd volumes of the U.S. Reports have not fared too well in terms of the literary art. A disappointingly small proportion of that enormous output can put forward any claim for recognition as graceful and appealing writing.

CARL MCGOWAN, *1961*

How? Before starting to compose, you must inventory the elements of your document, which by now lie before you. Then set intermediate limits by estimating how many words (or pages) each will require—not rigid limits, but goals. For example, you can oppose summary judgment in a page, by highlighting the facts at issue without extended discussion. You can summarize a case in much less space than your colleagues did in a previous memorandum, by eliminating the irrelevancies and stream-lining your prose. You are not bound to these limits; they are, after all, guesses. But by adhering to them as closely as possible, you will save yourself much time when it counts.

You save this time by not writing extra pages in a draft and also therefore by not having to excise them later. More important, you will be spared the complex task of restructuring the entire document. By their nature, lengthier documents digress more frequently than short ones, giving the former a more tangled structure that requires far more pruning. This is a plea not to omit relevant matters but to keep it short, a plea not for simplemindedness but for simplicity.

Lawyers are paid for judgment, not only in how they select and analyze cases but also in how they explain those cases on their clients' behalf. All too often they fail to exercise that judgment. The lawyer who can learn to be complete while remaining short is the one who will get ahead.

What of the associate who is told: "Tell me everything about the Silver King Mine doctrine"? Suppose after a day's research he locates forty-five cases on the law of eminent domain and ski resorts. The associate who writes a ninety-page document—two pages per case—has not exercised judgment. "Everything" rarely calls for equal treatment of each case. The supervising lawyer is asking for a synthesis, an understanding of doctrine, not a series of case digests. The final brief, whoever writes it, should not contain all forty-five cases.

If you must discuss all forty-five because your boss has ordered you to "write up every case," you should rank them in descending importance. You should know how to cut, or leave instructions for someone who will. Here's one reliable way: Cases of little relevance should be grouped together and marked "first cut." Those of marginal relevance become "second cut," and so on. That way, a hundred-page preliminary memorandum can easily be collapsed into a twenty-five-page brief.

It is implausible that lawyers fail to stop at, say, twenty-five pages because they couldn't charge enough for their work if they did. The view that lawyers write long to run up bills is the nub of the economic argument advanced by Steven Stark and others. That argument overlooks the obvious point that lawyers are no longer paid by the page. It also ignores a less obvious point: For most lawyers, it's harder—and often takes longer—to write short. If lawyers were truly interested in running up bills, they could do so by editing, rewriting, and shrinking their documents. But so far we have come across no evidence that economics are driving lawyers to become crisp writers.

We have, however, encountered some lawyers who say they will not edit because they cannot justify charging their clients even more for editing time, given client skittishness these days over big bills. Our response is that lawyers are professionals and should start acting like professionals. Part of being professional means writing the best possible document within the deadline, just as it means doing sufficient research. Lawyers who are unstinting in research time but sparing in writing and editing fail to do their jobs. Professionals must write polished documents, whether they charge the client for or swallow the time. By writing long, flabby documents rather than short, tight ones, lawyers burden the courts, shortchange their clients, and lower standards across the profession.

CHAPTER 10

Editing I: Wrong Words, Long Sentences, and Other Mister Meaners

FROM CHOOSING the right word to linking several paragraphs in logical sequence, the writer faces a series of choices. Anywhere along the way, a mistake will hinder understanding. Though surely the well-meaning writer commits no error with felonious intent, the cumulative impact on the reader is often fatal. Dorothy Evslin, a professor of English at a community college in Westchester County, New York, told of a student who wrote in an essay: "He was arrested for parking tickets and other mister meaners." That phrase offers an apt name for the writing sins that we discuss in this and the following chapter.

Each offense may be petty in itself, but taken together, they are deadly. They are not sins of the composing process, but of editing. When thinking rapidly, writers should not stop to correct their thoughts on paper, regardless of the clichés, windy phrases, and grammatical and other errors. Faulty grammar and dangling participles are sins only when they are overlooked during editing, for it is during the editing stage that writers must communicate with their audience.

The primary purpose of editing is to make thought intelligible to the writer's audience. The rules that follow are not artificial dictates of some long-forgotten school teacher, but the essentials by which all writers make their thoughts clear.

Readers have too much to read and too little time in which to read it. Writers, therefore, are always competing for the reader's time. If your syntax is tangled, your grammar incorrect, your vocabulary mistaken, and your phrases a thicket, your readers will stumble and lose their way. To find your meaning, they must retrace their steps and begin again. If you force them to reread your prose too often, they will become weary of the journey and quit. When they quit, you lose.

This proposition is not speculation. Psychologists have shown that readers rushing through sentences store the points in a short-term memory register, which has a limited capacity. The longer your sentences and the more ideas they carry, the less likely that your readers will grasp, absorb, or retain your points.

Here's a simple example, from Kenneth Majer, an executive with Siegel & Gale. Look at the row of numerals on the next line for five seconds, then cover it over, and try to list each one.

$$3 \quad 8 \quad 6 \quad 1 \quad 4 \quad 0 \quad 2 \quad 9 \quad 7 \quad 5$$

The odds are high that you missed one or two. The odds are even higher that you could not repeat them all in the order listed. But if you glance at the row of numerals on the next line

$$1 \quad 2 \quad 3 \quad 4 \quad 5 \quad 6 \quad 7 \quad 8 \quad 9$$

You'll know them all instantly and can immediately list them in the correct order. These are the same numerals that appeared above, but now there is a logical order.

Readers come to documents knowing many kinds of structure and expecting to find the appropriate one. One, as we have just seen, is the familiar arithmetical order: If you ask someone to write out the numerals conventionally, you expect them to be listed in the order given in the second row above.

Another, less obvious, structure that readers know and expect is the placement of elements within a sentence. The expected word order is what Donald C. Freeman, professor in the English Department and the Law Center of the University of Southern California, calls the "canonical word order" of a sentence. George Gopen and Joseph Williams call it the "reader expectation." When sentences do not conform to this expectation, the reader falters and meaning is lost.

Here we distinguish between "readers" and "audience." Most instructors and manuals exhort the would-be writer to think about the *audience*: Always have in mind the particular person or group for whom you are writing. That's sound advice, as far as it goes, and we venture farther into the topic in Chapter 12. As part of varied audiences (judges, clients, other lawyers, newspaper subscribers), readers have different backgrounds, knowledge, intelligence, experience, and levels of sophistication. You can never assume that different audiences will react in the same way to a piece of writing. One audience, ignorant of the subject, will expect considerable detail; you may assume that others know the facts. One audience will be puzzled unless you write in plain English; another will be insulted if you don't speak their jargon.

Although you can anticipate that specific audiences will have different expectations, you must not think *reader* expectations also differ. English is a language that depends heavily on word order for meaning. No matter what substantive knowledge they possess, literate readers expect sentences to conform to rules governing structure and usage.

This proposition is easily tested by translating a foreign sentence into English in the same word order. For instance: *Wir sind schnell nach Hause gegangen*. Translated literally: *We have quickly home gone*. This translation from the German is unclear because it violates normal word order in English. The sentence should of course read *We have gone home quickly* or, even more idiomatically, *We went home quickly*.

That readers expect sentences to be structured in certain ways explains why writing instructors talk of clarity and order. Obscure words, helter-skelter prose and faulty order, and sentences crowded with ideas all discourage the reader. In contrast, short sentences meticulously phrased with vivid words and images, along with frequent road maps, help direct a reader from beginning to end.

Transforming a meandering first draft into a clear path is no mystery. The way is clear, if you apply the rules that follow, rules that tell you how to deliver what readers expect.

Two notes about the examples we have chosen:

First, we have culled most of them from our teaching of lawyers and students. Others were sent to us, and still others come from our reading. Occasionally, we have embroidered an example to highlight a mistake. Almost always we have changed names to mask the identities of the workshop participants and their clients.

Second, we have compressed passages to illustrate our points. The worst legal writing is so long and complex that it would be self-defeating to reprint it. We wish to avoid what we call the "Ishtar syndrome," after the 1987 Warren Beatty–Dustin Hoffman movie that bombed because it portrayed two bad songwriters whose bad songs were actually sung in their entireties.

Words

Vocabulary

Referring to *Roe v. Wade*, a student wrote: "Scientists do not yet know whether life begins at contraception." The student didn't mean to be funny, but like many an unwary writer, he was oblivious to the meaning of certain words. Lawyers, writing, must not behave like Lewis Carroll's Humpty Dumpty, who told Alice that "when I use a word, it means just what I choose it to mean—neither more nor less." You need a comprehensive dictionary as your constant ally, and if you still confuse "disinterested" with "uninterested" or "affect" with "effect"—as many lawyers do—you probably should consult one of several books that pinpoint common mistakes in vocabulary. (The glossary discusses the most common mistakes we've found in lawyers' writing.)

Example: George then states that Harry's bad faith in failing to investigate his customers is *exacerbated* with the *ease* with which breaches of the license agreement could be avoided.

Problem: "Exacerbate" means to increase the severity of or to aggravate, to make worse. You can't exacerbate bad faith, and you certainly can't do it with ease.

Solution: George then states that Harry's bad faith in failing to investigate his customers was all the worse because he could so easily have avoided breaches of the license agreement.

Example: The instant case is exactly analogous to S's case.

Problem: The writer misunderstands the meaning of "analogous," which by its nature is never exact. Also, "instant" only clutters.

Solution: This case is analogous to S's case.

Legalese: Latinisms, Pomposities, and Bureaucratese

After three weeks in law school, even the rawest apprentice lawyer realizes that lawyers often write in an odd style that mixes archaic words, Latinisms, jargon, and pomposities. David Mellinkoff showed that most legal jargon is fuzzy and avoidable. In *Plain English for Lawyers*, Professor Richard C. Wydick of the University of California School of Law at Davis echoed this theme: "Lawyerisms are words like *aforementioned, whereas, res gestae*, and *hereinafter*. They give writing a legal smell, but they carry little or no legal substance. When they are used in writing addressed to nonlawyers, they baffle and annoy. When used in other legal writing, they give a false sense of precision and sometimes obscure a dangerous gap in analysis."

Or they can be just plain misused. Here's a gossip columnist trying to sound formal: "After her marriage Saturday to sportscaster Frank Gifford, 'The Morning Show' co-host Kathie Lee Johnson will heretofore be called Kathie Lee Gifford." In 1977, Alfred E. Kahn, then chairman of the Civil Aeronautics Board, sent out a memo to his staff suggesting that "every time you are tempted to use 'herein,' 'hereinabove,' 'hereinunder,' or similarly, 'therein' and its corresponding variants, try 'here' or 'there' or 'above' or 'below' and see if it doesn't make just as much sense."

Legal argot exists along a spectrum, ranging from stilted usages, such as the irksome and always unnecessary uses of "said" and "such" as adjectives, to impenetrable Latin and other foreign phrases that tempt even the best writers. Several years ago James J. Kilpatrick, the syndicated columnist and usage expert, scolded William H. Rehnquist, then associate justice of the U.S. Supreme Court, for questioning whether "the power of Congress may be thought to *ex proprio vigore* apply to the power." Rehnquist, now Chief Justice, apparently has had difficulty breaking his habit of using foreign phrases, even when writing for a more general audience. In 1987, he wrote *The Supreme Court: How It Was, How It Is*, a book noted favorably in the popular press. In an otherwise flattering review, however, Professor Philip Kurland of the University of Chicago Law School complained of Rehnquist's affinity for the foreign term. For example, Kurland noted, "When Mr. Rehnquist describes oral argument in the Court, he writes that it 'requires controlled enthusiasm and not an impression of *fin de siècle* ennui.' Again: 'Advocacy before our Court is preeminently a *carrière ouverte aux talents* in the very best tradition of that phrase.' Some of us will not have the slightest notion what kind of ennui was peculiar to the *fin de siècle*, or what is the grand tradition of a *carrière ouverte aux talents* he has in mind. It is to be presumed that the Chief Justice was not setting an example to brief writers to indulge in such esoterica."

> **Example:** The pending motion for a preliminary injunction involves a challenge under Delaware law to an antitakeover defense sometimes picturesquely described as a "street sweep." That *sobriquet* is used by *cognoscenti* in the esoteric field of corporate takeovers to refer to a rapid accumulation of a large block of target corporation stock.

Problem: The phrase "street sweep" may be picturesque, but the author, a judge, smudges his prose by packing together words that should rarely be used alone. As H. W. Fowler observed in his *Dictionary of Modern English Usage*, "those who run to long words are mainly the unskillful and tasteless; they confuse pomposity with dignity, flaccidity with ease, and bulk with force."

> **Example:** Sixty days *prior to* expiration of the license . . .

Problem: "Prior to" is one of the most commonly and unnecessarily used lawyer's phrases. It is clunky and almost always a matter of habit that can be unlearned. Use the shorter and simpler "before." With "subsequent to," use "after."

> **Solution:** Sixty days before the license expires . . .

> **Example:** *Under date of* February 29, 1988 . . .
> **Solution:** On February 29, 1988 . . .

Example: *Pursuant to* the terms of the covenant, a payment of $100 must be remitted by you.

Problem: Here we have another clunker, no more precise than the far more accessible "under." Lawyers who routinely use phrases such as "pursuant to" and "prior to" often stuff their writing with other unnecessary and flabby phrases. Note that in this example, "the terms of" is a phrase that adds nothing to the meaning. Moreover, the frost has settled over the main clause, freezing a verb into a noun and making an active verb passive.

Solution: Under the covenant, you must pay $100.

Example: *Pursuant to* his authority as regional manager, plaintiff entered into a general agency contract with himself designating himself a general agent to solicit life insurance applications and memberships in the Elks.

Problem: Comfortable with "pursuant to," this writer unfortunately continues unmindful that his flaccid writing obscures his point.

Solution: As regional manager, the plaintiff designated himself by contract a general agent to solicit life insurance applications and memberships in the Elks.

Example: *Enclosed herewith please find* . . .

Problem: This is one of the most common openings to lawyers' letters and certainly one of the silliest.

Solution: I'm enclosing . . .

A close cousin to legalese, bureaucratese—or gobbledygook, the word coined by Congressman Maury Maverick in the 1940s—is a form of "government-speak" that flattens readers by rolling over them with long phrases, pompous expressions, and polysyllabic words. A simple but classic type is the police report, which speaks of "apprehending the perpetrator." Bureaucratese of this type is intended to impress readers with the author's seriousness, and it often breaks out when a lawyer or other professional staff aide writes the remarks. Here, for example, is John L. Lewis, long-time president of the United Mine Workers:

No action has been taken by this writer or the United Mine Workers of America, as such, which would fall within the purview of the oppressive statute under which you seek to function. Without indulging in analysis, it is a logical assumption that the cavilings of the bar and bench in their attempts to explicate this infamous enactment will consume a tedious time.

Sometimes bureaucratese, like legalese, is simply jargon that the writer has assimilated, forgetting the more obvious alternatives to these obfuscations. A new form of bureaucratese is "tech speak," and its whimsical chronicler, Edward Tenner, provides hilarious examples of how turgid and pompous phrases can replace ordinary words. For example, a dish is a "ceramic nutrient manipulation surface." A cemetery is a "biolysis center." A bartender is an "applied ethanol chemist," and a bookmaker at the racetrack is an "equine concurrent bioenergetic evaluation professional." Tech speak itself is a "postcolloquial discourse module protocol for user status enhancement"—a self-mocking explanation for this kind of pompous jargon.

But bureaucratese, like legalese, has a sinister side. George Orwell warned in *1984* and in his 1946 essay "Politics and the English Language" that English could be corrupted to oppressive political ends. The euphemisms of "doublethink" and "Newspeak"—"War Is Peace"—could anesthetize the citizenry or blind it to the crimes committed in its name. When a company renames elevator operators "vertical transportation corps" and grocery stores call their baggers "career associate scanning professionals," we may laugh or wince. When the courts refer to the retarded committed to institutions as people with "minimally adequate training" or when hospitals refer to someone who died as one who "did not fully achieve his wellness potential," we cringe. But when taxes become "revenue enhancements," when women become "special interests," when a terrible fire at Three Mile Island becomes "rapid oxidation" and explosion "energetic disassembly," the joke is no longer funny.

Usage

Eliminating legalisms is no guarantee of clean prose. Over the centuries, English usage has become a matter of custom, not logic. For example, knowing when to use "who" and when to use "whom" is a sign of literacy. The lawyer who writes "the defendant became angry and often violent with whomever opposed her" violates the conventions of grammar and usage and offends both ear and eye. Usage can change, of course, and books on the subject may differ on particulars, but since many forms of usage have hardened into near rules, lawyers disregard at their peril the consensus of usage experts. Like a competent dictionary, a comprehensive usage book belongs on your shelf. (The most common usage problems are discussed in the glossary.)

> **Example:** Children in congregate care require the treatment setting to be *comprised of* a group of peers to *who* they can relate and with whom they can share basic values.

Problem: Nothing can be "comprised of" anything; that usage is always incorrect. The word "comprise" means include or embrace; for example, "the United States comprises fifty states." Since this sounds awkward to many ears, you should choose instead the words "consist of" or "composed of." The latest *Random House Dictionary of the English Language* (2d edition, 1987) notes that the corrupted form is becoming more common in ordinary speech, so your grandchildren may use "comprised of" with impunity, but you will offend the discerning ear. And note that the writer busy with "comprised of" has overlooked the inaccurate "who."

> **Solution:** Children in congregate care should be placed with a group of peers to whom they can relate and with whom they can share basic values.

> **Example:** These openings occurred *due to* the voluntary departure of two engineers from their positions.

Problem: "Due to" is incorrectly used as an adverbial phrase; the proper construction is "owing to," "resulting from," or "because of." "Due to" as a modifier means "attributable to" and can be used only to modify nouns. Here's a mnemonic: Only if the sentence makes sense when you substitute "attributable to" is your use of "due to" correct. This usage, too, is in flux; a few experts now permit the corrupted usage. But again, the discerning will balk and condemn you as illiterate.

Solution: These positions became available because the two engineers voluntarily departed.

Example: The delay was due to a flat tire.
Solution: This usage is correct. The prepositional phrase "due to" here modifies the subject, "delay," and "attributable to" can correctly be substituted for it.

Example: The Wisconsin Supreme Court has acknowledged that when a dispute exists *as to* the existence of an easement . . .

Problem: For some reason, lawyers perhaps more than other writers stumble over prepositions. Prepositions are connecting words, such as "in," "on," "from," "to," "under." In recent years, probably from the familiarity of "as to" in introductory phrases ("as to Sect. 3"), the unfortunate yoking of "as" and "to" has increasingly, but quite wrongly, displaced conventional prepositions. The result is a growing sterility of expression, as the far more colorful idiomatic English is washed away. For example, we often read of "the clue as to his whereabouts." "As" adds nothing; the proper expression is "clue to." In "question as to whether," eliminate "as to" altogether. We could "wonder as to his whereabouts," but we would be thinking more clearly if we "wondered where he was." Again, the use of prepositional idioms is not logical but customary.

Solution 1: The Wisconsin Supreme Court has acknowledged that when there is a dispute over the existence of an easement . . .

Note that this change eliminates "as to" but introduces the troublesome "there is."

Solution 2: The Wisconsin Supreme Court has acknowledged that when a dispute arises over the existence of . . .
Solution 3: The Wisconsin Supreme Court has acknowledged that when the parties dispute the existence of . . .

Example: If adopted, the amendment would have barred the plaintiff's recovery *where* the plaintiff's negligence was equal to that of the defendant.

Problem: Be wary of "where." Lawyers frequently confuse it with "when," "if," or "that." The word "where" refers to space, location, or geography; "when" can imply a condition or situation, as well as the temporal. In this example, the word should be "when" or "if" or perhaps even "because." "Where" makes the sentence imprecise. A different, unforgivable misuse occurs in such an expression as, "We note where one court said." The writer means "We note that one court said."

Overcaution and Reckless Abandon

Lawyers alternate between extreme caution and wild exaggeration. One moment, they hesitate to commit themselves even when the facts are with them—adding the qualifiers "usually," "often," "sometimes," "almost," "possibly," or "seemingly" when omitting these words would enhance their argument. The next moment, they may blithely, even exuberantly, overstate their case. Chief Justice Edward Douglass White was famous for his overheated style. As Harvard's constitutional law professors noted twenty-five years ago: "What impresses later generations in White's opinions is less their substance than their extraordinary form. He moved portentously across the thinnest ice, confident that a lifeline of adverbs—'inevitably,' 'irresistibly,' 'clearly,' and 'necessarily'—was supporting him in his progress." Few phenomena are truly "remarkable"; fewer legal points are "absolutely clear" or even just plain "clear." Likewise, "as everyone knows," "as we can plainly see," "literally," "undoubtedly," and "certainly" seldom bolster a case that has not already been made. Many lawyers use these words, and many others like them, reflexively—the hedge words because they do not want to be shown wrong, the emphatic words because they are afraid they have failed to persuade the reader. These words enfeeble rather than enhance the prose.

> **Example:** The situation in this case is *substantially* analogous to that in *Utah Coal and Lumber* . . .

> **Problem:** The situation is either analogous, meaning similar, or identical. Omit "substantially."

> **Example:** When addressing factual situations similar to that present in this case, courts in other jurisdictions have been *virtually* unanimous in holding . . .

Problem: The sentence is ambiguous. It could mean that most courts which so held did so unanimously, that all courts have so held by close-to-unanimous votes, or simply that most courts have so held. Most likely, the writer meant "most courts in other jurisdictions have held," though the reader strains to reach that meaning. One imprecise word can gum up a thought.

Example: *It would seem that* the options are basically three . . .

Problem: Phrases such as "it would seem that" and "it would appear that" are among the most common (and worst) forms of lawyerly timidity. Geraldine A. Ferraro, in a letter to the *New York Times* in 1988 about her candidacy for vice president four years earlier, wrote that cynics had dismissed her designation by Walter A. Mondale as "strictly a political move playing to the gender gap. I would agree . . . he removed gender as a disqualification for national office." That makes her sound tentative. What she means is "I agree." Ruthlessly suppress your penchant for these phrases.

Solution: You have three options.

Example: Under Illinois law, tape-recording a telephone conversation without the consent of the other parties to the conversation *may constitute a criminal violation.*

Problem: Can the statute be so ambiguous that the average lawyer will mistake what the legislature thinks about taping without consent? That is unlikely—what other purpose can the statute serve? The lawyer is being timid and stuffy.

Solution 1: Under Illinois law, tape-recording a telephone conversation without the consent of the other parties is a crime.
Solution 2: Under Illinois law, it is a crime to record a telephone conversation unless the other parties consent.

Example: Since many of plaintiff's allegations of *alleged* illegal activity . . .

Problem: "Alleged" is a legitimate word often overused and sometimes misused. In this example, the writer, overly cautious, is being redundant. Eliminate "alleged."

Example: Plaintiff's failure to state the basis of her claims that Kuhn Inc. is an *alleged* criminal enterprise illustrates her lack of good faith in making this allegation.

Problem: No need to hedge. By referring to the plaintiff's claim, the writer is not assenting to the proposition that Kuhn is a criminal enterprise and so is not conceding his adversary's position—the usual fear that prompts lawyers to overuse "alleged." The assertion here is entirely the plaintiff's. She is not claiming that Kuhn is an "alleged" criminal enterprise but that it is an actual criminal enterprise.

Solution: By failing to state the basis of her claims, the plaintiff shows her lack of good faith in alleging that Kuhn is a criminal enterprise.

Example: It is truly remarkable, but not surprising . . .
Example: Amazingly, the G memorandum, once again, . . .

Problem: Enough!

Obviousness

Another writing difficulty born of fear, conceptually sandwiched between the overly cautious and the recklessly exaggerated, is the tautology—or obviousness. Not every tautology is bad—showing that the defendant's stock sales fit squarely within the definition of insider trading is a useful, and often difficult, proposition for a prosecutor to make. But the lawyer who reminds the reader that the client wishes "to live by the statute and not break the law" is saying twice what needs to be said only once. Say what you must say, but avoid the obvious details.

Example: If the client does not commence litigation, it gambles that the opponents will or will not do so.

Problem: That's not much of a gamble: The proposition is a certainty. The writer probably meant to say that if the client does not sue, it risks being sued.

Example: *Suffice it to say,* Section 7 expressly states . . .

Problem: A cousin of "needless to say" (if it is needless, why say it?), "suffice it to say" means nothing more than "this is all I want to say about the matter right now" or "when I say what I'm about to say, you'll understand what I'm saying." Rarely necessary and overworked. Purge.

Example: The law is *obvious* . . .

Problem: Then why do we need lawyers?

Clichés

A cliché is an overworked expression that broadcasts the writer's laziness or fatuousness. A cliché may communicate, but it does so at the risk of sending the reader to dreamland. The cliché suggests that the writer lacks the King's English; it certainly won't knock the reader's socks off, and sometimes it will just draw a blank. Most of us speak in clichés because we learned them when we were knee high to a grasshopper, and at first blush we just grin and bear it. But in writing they tend to come a cropper. So let's get down to brass tacks, and with both feet on the ground, face the music and turn over a new leaf: Gird up your loins at these wolves in sheep's clothing, give clichés the short shrift, and from now on, avoid them like the plague.

That said, clichés can sometimes be useful, precisely because they are familiar. Sparingly used, the proper cliché can make your point most clearly. In any event, you should prefer the well-worn cliché to a ludicrous attempt to avoid one by refashioning it. Better to say that your client was speaking "tongue in cheek" than to assert that he was speaking with "tongue rolled in mouth." Better to attribute his motive to "sour grapes" than "tart grapes." Better to say he's "squeaky clean" than "whiny clean." In the hands of a good writer, a cliché can be turned to considerable effect. Consider Henry Thoreau's play on "spur of the moment": "I feel the spur of the moment thrust deep into my side. The present is an inexorable rider."

Example: In RICO's first decade *on the books* . . .

Problem: The clause is both tautological and cliché-ridden. By definition, a statute is "on the books."

Solution: In RICO's first decade . . .

Slang

A relative of the cliché, slang ordinarily sets too low a tone for writing by lawyers.

> **Example:** York has *no problem* with fair competition.

Problem: Not only is "no problem" slang, it is ambiguous. In what way is it "no problem"?

> **Solution:** York favors [or welcomes] fair competition.

> **Example:** In refusing to compel disclosure, the court stated *flat out* that the work product exemption . . .

Problem: The author meant "stated explicitly" or "went directly to the point."

> **Solution:** In refusing to compel disclosure, the court flatly [unequivocally] stated . . .

Throat Clearing

Wise as it is to provide the reader with a road map, some introductory phrases serve only to let the writer rev up while composing. Use them to get going, but they need not be embedded in the draft. When you edit, delete them; they have no proper place in a final version.

> **Example:** *It is interesting to note that* the declaration of Miller's spy, Mr. Arthur, fails to indicate when movement of inventory from Deer Valley was observed.

Problem: To whom is it interesting? Why? If your point is inherently interesting, your readers will recognize it. Moreover, this sentence is inverted and padded so that even if it is interesting, the thought is so submerged that the reader is lost. For example, does "declaration" mean anything more than the failure to indicate?

Solution 1: The declaration of Miller's spy, Mr. Arthur, fails to indicate when he saw the movement of inventory from Deer Valley.

Solution 2: Miller's spy, Mr. Arthur, failed to say when he saw inventory being moved from Deer Valley.

Example: *You are undoubtedly well aware of* Sect. X of the Utah statutes and the *general* position of the Utah courts regarding employee covenants not to compete, and *I do not intend to burden you with a lengthy dissertation on the subject.*

Solution: I will briefly recap Sect. X of the Utah statutes and how Utah courts regard employee covenants not to compete.

Example: *At the outset, it is critically important* to define and clarify *terminology with respect* to fraudulent inducement.

Solution: First, we must define fraudulent inducement.

Wordiness

Fuzzy Phrases

Lawyers tend to use many words when one will do. They say "on the grounds that" or "for the reason that" when they could say "because." They say "in the event that" or "under circumstances in which" when "if" is fine. They say "with regard to" or "concerning the matter of" when "about" is preferable. They say "has the opportunity to" or "is able to" when the reader will get the point more clearly if the writer had said "can." Look for these fuzzy phrases in your writing and eliminate them. When one word works, use it.

Example: The court's criticism of the jury charge focused *on the fact that* the trial court instructed the jury that it could consider . . .

Problem: A sentence including "the fact that" is almost always faulty. All usage books pounce on this construction. Strunk and White call it "especially debilitating" and advise that it "be revised out of every sentence in which it occurs."

Solution 1: The court's criticism of the jury charge focused on the trial court's instruction that the jury could consider . .
Solution 2: The court criticized the jury charge, focusing on the trial court's instruction . . .

Example: In addition, *in light of* plaintiff's failure to make disclosure of the existence of the covenant not to sue or to abide by it . . .
Solution: Also, because plaintiff failed to disclose or abide by the covenant not to sue . . .

Example: The defendant was *in a paying nexus with* the plaintiff.

Problem: Fuzziness coupled to bureaucratese.

Solution: The defendant paid the plaintiff.

Noun Compounding

The Germans do it legitimately: Their language permits words to be constructed by crunching together shorter words—for example, *Untergrundbahnhofeingang* (underground railway station entrance). Imitating the German logic but ignoring the linguistic difference, writers with tin ears often pack nouns tightly together in impenetrable phrases.

Example: We had a *company staff size analysis determination.*

Problem: No aversion to verbs can excuse a sentence like this one. We are not sure, but possibly it means:

Solution: Our company analyzed the size of its staff.

Example: Several courts have recently been confronted with alleged interested director transactions.
Solution: Several courts have recently heard cases involving directors accused of having personal interests in company transactions.

Negatives

George Orwell said it should be "possible to laugh the *not un-* formation out of existence." The cure, he suggested, is to memorize this sentence: "A not unblack dog was chasing a not unsmall rabbit across a not ungreen field." It is not unlikely that Orwell was overly optimistic. Thirty-five years later, Secretary of State Alexander M. Haig, the dean of bureaucratese, remarked: "This is not an experience I haven't been through before." In their desire to hedge, lawyers, too, persist in their love of double negatives, one more element of unnecessary complexity employed in the false belief that it lends weight or elegance to an otherwise dismal style.

> **Example:** We are *not unmindful* that litigation in a foreign jurisdiction is a burdensome inconvenience for any company.
> **Solution:** We are aware that . . .

> **Example:** This argument *would not be without* some support under Iowa case law.
> **Solution 1:** This argument has some support under Iowa case law.
> **Solution 2:** Iowa case law supports this argument somewhat.

> **Example:** The vast majority of the contracts *contain no provision* for refund of unearned premiums to the borrower in the event of cancellation of the insurance policy engendered by prepayment of all or part of the loan.

Problem: Troublesome negatives can creep into sentences without signaling their presence as clearly as in the "not un-" doublet. Negative writing slows down the reader, confounding the usual expectation of a proposition affirmatively stated. The reader is also slowed down because the writer has used windy phrases and heavy nouns instead of verbs.

> **Solution:** Few contracts provided for refund of unearned premiums to the borrower if the insurance policy was canceled because all or part of the loan was prepaid.

> **Example:** The witness said that although he once knew, he *no longer remembered* the killer's identity.

Problem: Often, you can avoid the negative by searching for an affirmative word that strengthens the point. For example, "few" instead of "not many"; "rejected" instead of "did not accept"; "too young" instead of "not old enough"; "left" instead of "did not remain."

> **Solution:** The witness said that although he once knew, he had since forgotten the killer's identity.

Redundancies

Lawyers tend toward redundancy because their technical language is richly endowed with repetitive phrases that once had legal consequences—"cease and desist," "rest, residue, and remainder," "null and void," and "give and grant." Many of these doublets and triplets were adopted during the Middle Ages when law language became an amalgam of English, Latin, and French. Whether these legal redundancies should continue to be used in drafting is not our concern. What makes us unhappy is that this way of thinking has seeped into ordinary writing. Some Watergate witnesses repeatedly lost their memories "at this point in time." They could have drained their prose of this muck and said simply "now" or "at this point" or "at this time." Simple redundancies are easily spotted and excised: "bedraggled" rather than "bedraggled in appearance," "green" rather than "green in color." Likewise, never speak of "consensus of opinion" or a "free gift" or "final outcomes" or "completely finished."

> **Example:** On September 16, 1988, at *the hour of 10 a.m. in the morning* . . .
> **Solution:** On September 16, 1988, at 10 a.m. . . . .

> **Example:** After C's death, the *remaining balance* of the trust . . .
> **Solution:** After C's death, the balance of the trust . . .

> **Example:** In addition, there are *no facts whatsoever* to indicate . . .
> **Solution:** No facts support . . .

> **Example:** The *subject matter area* of the discussion . . .
> **Solution:** The subject of the discussion . . .

Example: Dolly has asked us to describe the legal *consequences which would result* if she were to unilaterally terminate her service contracts with the hospitals.

Problem: A consequence *is* a result.

Solution 1: Dolly has asked us to describe the legal consequences if she were to terminate unilaterally her service contracts with the hospitals.
Solution 2: Dolly has asked us to describe the legal consequences of breaking her service contracts with the hospitals.

Example: The *logical corollary* of her argument . . .

Problem: By definition, corollaries are always logical.

Solution: The corollary of her argument . . .

Example: By encouraging spurious class *action lawsuits* . . .

Problem: An "action" is a lawsuit. Omit "lawsuits."

Example: The *difficulty* of attracting such individuals is magnified by the *difficult* task this board *has faced in the past* and *will have to face in the future.*
Solution: Attracting such individuals is made all the more difficult by the sizable task this board continues to face.

Verbosity

Lawyers have always been verbose. Combat this tendency by pretending that you will be paid inversely to the number of words—or that *you* must pay for the words you use. Cut, cut, cut.

Example: During *the course of* our phone conversations . . .

Problem: A conversation, by its nature, has a course.

Solution: During our phone conversations . . .

Example: The *facts of Deer Creek* are *apposite to the instant motion in that* Heber has disputed . . .

Solution: Just as in *Deer Creek,* Heber has disputed . . .

Example: In *Shrager,* the *plaintiff commenced an action claiming* that it had . . .

Problem: No "plaintiff" exists until an action has been commenced; no action without a claim, so shorten this.

Solution: In *Shrager,* the plaintiff claimed that it had . . .

Example: When the bulldozer *became engaged as a result of the jump start,* it rolled over the decedent *causing her death.*

Problem: Between being started and killing the decedent, the bulldozer necessarily was engaged. And why not use her name?

Solution: After the bulldozer was jump-started, it rolled over and killed Mrs. Fields.

Example: Despite plaintiff's *claims to the contrary,* since plaintiff has failed to provide *any factual information at all concerning the terms of* the *alleged* oral contracts, the *contract claims* are so uncertain that defendants are unable to respond.

Problem: One clue to verbosity: clumps of repeated words.

Solution: Because the plaintiff has failed to state the terms of the (alleged) oral contracts, the defendants are unable to respond to his claims.

Example: *As hereinafter indicated,* we *presently believe* it *would be in your best interests* to enter into a permanent agreement to opt out of the Act, although this is a subject we should discuss in some detail.

Problem: Breaking a sentence apart often clarifies thought and may shrink the total number of words.

Solution: You should enter into a permanent agreement to opt out of the Act. Doing so is something we should discuss at length.

Example: *In order* to sustain an allegation of fraudulent concealment, the plaintiff must *successfully allege* (1) that defendants wrongfully concealed the conspiracy, (2) that plaintiff did not discover the existence of the conspiracy, and (3) *that plaintiff failed to discover the conspiracy* despite the exercise of due diligence.

Problem: The writer is splitting too many hairs at the end, after being merely foolish at the beginning.

Solution: To sustain an allegation of fraudulent concealment, the plaintiff must prove that (1) defendants wrongfully concealed the conspiracy and (2) plaintiffs did not discover the conspiracy even though they exercised due diligence.

Example: Her heirs, whom she predeceased and who survived her, . . .

Problem: Why split heirs? If she predeceased them, they survived her.

Solution: Her surviving heirs . . .

Strings of Prepositions

Too many prepositional phrases obscure the point of the sentence or force the reader to absorb too many points. Not every qualification of the principal point must be jammed into the sentence where first made.

Example: *In* rejecting the argument that a large increase *in* senior securities entitled *to* dividend and liquidation priorities resulted *in* an alteration *of* the "special rights" *of* a class *of* junior securities entitling such class *of* junior securities *to* a class vote, the Delaware Supreme Court in *Erickson* stated. . . .

Problem: The reader must hurdle nine prepositional phrases, including four consecutive phrases beginning with "of," before reaching the subject. That's too much to ask.

Solution: In *Erickson*, the Delaware Supreme Court held that a class of junior securities was entitled to a class vote despite a large increase in the number of senior securities. The senior securities had priorities to dividend and preference in liquidation. The Court stated . . .

The rule once was that a preposition was something you should never end a sentence with. If you can avoid doing so, without sounding stuffy, do it. We could have said, "The rule once was that you should never end a sentence with a preposition." Sometimes, however, the effort to avoid prepositional endings sounds stilted or pompous; that's because English has so many verbs that change meaning with the prepositions linked to them.

Example: That is the sort of thing the judge said he would look into.

Problem: To move the preposition from the end leaves you with a sentence like this: "That is the sort of thing into which the judge said he would look." One solution is to look for a different verb.

Solution: That is the sort of thing the judge said he would examine.

Verbs

The verb should carry the load of every sentence. The verb contains the action. It tells what the subject is doing. In longer sentences, the verb provides the link between the agent of the action and the thing to which the action is done. The verb is the key to the sentence: The stronger and sharper the verb, the clearer your meaning. Good writers avoid strings of sentences with only such verbs as "is" and "has" to prop them up.

Nominalizations

Sentences that submerge the action in nouns, stripping the verbs of their function, usually collapse of their own weight. Without active verbs, a sentence lumbers. Freezing the action of verbs in nouns is what the grammarians call *nominalization.* Don Freeman, an English professor who for many years served as the director of training at Shearman & Sterling in New York and at Baker & McKenzie offices around the world, says that nominalization is bad because it "interrupts canonical word order": It subverts the reader's expectation of locating the agent of the action in the subject of the sentence. The reader expects the verb to contain the action of the sentence and the subject to constitute the person or thing doing the action. When the doer is not in the subject, normal word order is interrupted. Moreover, the writer often must add prepositions and other phrases to sort out meaning, giving the sentence a choppy effect. Freeman gives this example:

> At the time of Abco's cashing of the check, there plainly was a dispute between the parties as to the amount owing Abco under paragraph 4(d) of the Security Agreement.

This sentence nominalizes its two actions—cashing and disputing—and puts the agents into prepositional phrases. The subjects of the two clauses should be the doers—"Abco" and "the parties." Instead, the subjects become the actions, and the agents, the people about whom the sentence is written, are subordinated. Rewritten and denominalized, the sentence loses many of its prepositions and is shorter and clearer:

> When Abco cashed the check, the parties plainly disputed the amount owed Abco under paragraph 4(d) of the Security Agreement.

Nominalizing is one of the most serious afflictions of legal prose, draining a sentence of vitality. Fortunately, nominalizations are easy to spot and easy (sometimes even fun) to transform into vigorous English. Common nominalizations include "determination," "commencement," "investigation," "reliance," "failure," "formulation," and "analysis." Nominalizations can also freeze the action of verbs in adjectives —"supportive" and "violative."

Example: Before the *commencement* of the federal bankruptcy case . . .
Solution: Before the bankruptcy case begins . . .

Example: We carried out an *analysis* of the blood samples.

Problem: Note that this sentence has a verb, but a weak, empty one. Weak verbs such as "conduct," "make," "is," and "has" signal that the main action lies elsewhere in the sentence.

Solution: We analyzed the blood samples.

Example: . . . *termination* of the audit within seven hours after its *commencement.*
Solution: . . . ended the audit seven hours after it began.

Example: Plaintiff's *reliance* on *Jeremy Ranch* for its *contention* that a marketing plan or system need not be explicit is misplaced.
Solution: Plaintiff mistakenly relies on *Jeremy Ranch* to argue that a marketing plan or system need not be explicit.

Example: . . . that certain practices of that company were *in violation of* the California labor laws.
Solution: . . . that certain practices of that company violated the California labor laws.

Example: Courts and scholars have articulated numerous *formulations* of the business judgment rule.

Problem: The overused verb ''articulated'' vanishes when we eliminate the nominalization.

Solution: Courts and scholars have formulated the business judgment rule in many ways.

Example: The plaintiff suffered the *loss* of his right hand when it was pulled in by his *operation* of a meat grinder.
Solution: The plaintiff lost his right hand when it was sucked into a meat grinder he was operating.

Example: The decisions in those shopping center cases granting specific performance have placed *emphasis* on combinations of the following factors.
Solution: The decisions granting specific performance in shopping centers emphasize combinations of the following factors.

Example: The court displayed no *reluctance* in awarding to the lender its substantial damages.

Problem: This sentence does not technically nominalize. But by rewriting, we can still put the emphasis in the verb.

Solution 1: The court did not hesitate to award the lender substantial damages.
Solution 2: The court readily awarded the lender substantial damages.

Useful Nominalizations

The sentences we have just edited were wrenched out of context to illustrate principles of denominalizing. Of course sentences never occur in isolation: They are always linked to other sentences. Therefore, remember another principle of good writing: Links between thoughts and sentences must be tight. Nouns that describe or sum up the action of a previous sentence often can serve as a tidy bridge between the two. Beyond their use as a bridge, some nominalizations have become so standard that it would be awkward to transform them into verbs. Nominalizations can also help you avoid the awkward "the fact that."

> **Example:** Judge Bangerter *heard* argument last week. At the *session in which the lawyers argued,* he said . . .
> **Solution:** Judge Bangerter heard argument last week. At the hearing . . .

> **Example:** The defendant *denied* that he was in the room when the *murder* was committed. The jury looked astounded *when he denied being there.*
> **Solution:** The defendant denied that he was in the room when the victim was murdered. His denial astounded the jury.

> **Example:** No taxation without representation.

> *Problem:* Better left unchanged than to say: "Don't tax us unless we can vote for our representatives."

> **Example:** *The fact that the cars collided* was the top news story.
> **Solution:** The collision was the top news story.

The Passive Voice

Often mistakenly referred to as a "tense," the passive voice is a construction that permits the writer to avoid naming or referring to the person or thing that takes the action. In the sentence "The lease was broken," no one can say who broke the lease. The action is passive; it is done to the thing that is the subject of the sentence. In the active voice, the writer must tell us who is doing the breaking: "The landlord broke the lease." Lawyers overuse the passive voice, sometimes because they know no better, sometimes to avoid assigning responsibility. Chiding lawyers who use the passive, Judge Patricia M. Wald said in her 1988 commencement address at New York Law School that the passive voice "sanitizes and institutionalizes [lawyers'] writing and often anesthetizes the reader: all views are attributable to an unknowable 'it.' 'It is said,' 'it is reported,' 'it is argued.' "

The passive voice is easy to spot: The verb is always in the participial form ("broken," instead of "broke") and always follows a form of the verb "be" ("is," "was," "being," "been")—*was broken, is being broken, has been broken*. The passive verb is often followed by a "by" clause, just as in this sentence—"broken *by the landlord*." Even if not, you can always mentally insert a "by" clause in the sentence.

> **Example:** The appointment of Noela Snowflower as trustee of the debtor *was made* by stipulation between Jan Albertson, counsel for the debtor, and Deborah Redford, counsel for the creditor.

> **Problem:** This sentence couples passives and nominalizations. Although readily understandable as written, it bespeaks bad habits that will clog later sentences.

> **Solution:** Albertson and Redford stipulated to the appointment of Snowflower as trustee of the debtor.

> **Example:** Plaintiff's second effort to bring before this court a six-year-old dispute by a disappointed borrower against his former lender-bank *should be dismissed* with prejudice.
> **Solution:** This court should dismiss with prejudice the plaintiff's second effort to bring before it a six-year-old dispute by a disappointed borrower against his former lender-bank.

Example: Chancery Rule 19 tracks exactly Rule 19 of the Federal Rules of Civil Procedure. Accordingly, interpretations of the federal rules by the federal judiciary *are given* great weight by Delaware courts concerning the interpretation of their own parallel rules.

Problem: The first verb we encounter is vivid but imprecise. The second sentence links nominalizations to passives, unnecessarily creating a winding trail of prepositional phrases.

Solution: Chancery court Rule 19 is identical to Rule 19 of the Federal Rules of Civil Procedure. Therefore, Delaware courts have given great weight to interpretations of the federal rules by federal courts.

Sentences routinely written in the passive make writing dull and listless. But the passive voice does have important purposes, and correctly used, it clarifies rather than obscures. Use the passive when:

(1) The agent of the action is unknown or irrelevant.

Example: More than fifty arsonists *were convicted* in this city last year.

Note: The reader does not want to know *who* convicted the arsonists, and to find out, you would have to inquire whether they were all convicted by a judge, several judges, or juries.

(2) The subject of a series of sentences is the object of the action expressed in the verb.

Example: The *lease* is a type of contract that for centuries has been interpreted to favor landlords. *It* is usually drawn by lawyers who specialize in real property, and *it* often consists of boilerplate that has been threshed out over decades or even longer. *Leases* should not be signed unless you read them carefully.

Note: That paragraph focuses on the lease. To transform the sentences into the active voice, you must find subjects, and they would vary from sentence to sentence, disrupting the flow of thought. Thus: ''For centuries *courts* have interpreted leases to favor landlords. *Lawyers who specialize in real property* draw them up, and *courts and lawyers* have often threshed out their boilerplate language over decades or even longer. *You* should not sign a lease without reading it carefully.''

> *(3) The sentence would be top-heavy without the passive.*

Example: Judges, lawyers, professors, people who have served on juries, bailiffs, clerks, and others involved in the judicial system know the difficulty.

Solution: The difficulty is known to judges, lawyers, professors, jurors, bailiffs, clerks, and others in the judicial system.

> *(4) Adjacent sentences can be better connected with a passive construction.* Sentences should not be random collections of thoughts; they should link in some reasonable way so that the reader can follow each point as it arises. One important principle, discussed on pp. 155–156, is that newer information should generally be placed at the end of the sentence, older information at the start. Since the older information usually refers to something discussed in the preceding sentence, the link is tighter. To put the older information there, the passive can be a useful tool.

Example: The police sought the murder weapons by *dragging* the river in a Coast Guard launch. Classes on seamanship and navigation *teach* cadets every fall the *techniques of dragging*. By the time they graduate, they know the river intimately.

Solution: The police sought the murder weapons by dragging the river in a Coast Guard launch. *Dragging techniques are taught* to cadets every fall in classes on seamanship and navigation. By the time the cadets graduate, they know the river intimately.

"There Is"

If your sentences are liberally sprinkled with ''there is's,'' ''there are's'' and ''there have been's,'' your writing lacks sharpness. This construction obscures the action in a phrase that, repeated frequently, is numbing. Although ''there is'' can sometimes be appropriate, the alternative is almost always preferable. If you find yourself opening sentences with "there is" more than once or twice in a document, go back and edit.

Example: *There is* no case law *which* specifically addresses the question presented.
Solution: No case law specifically addresses the question.

Example: *There is* no cure for sloppy thinking but to rethink.

Problem: To recast, denominalize, and find a new subject.

Solution: The only cure for sloppy thinking is rethinking.

Subject-Verb Agreement

Literacy requires that subjects and verbs agree—a singular subject takes a singular verb and a plural subject a plural verb. The only trick is knowing when a subject is plural.

Example: Neither the tennis players nor Nancy *are* coming over for dinner.

Problem: In "or" and "nor" constructions, the verb must agree with the subject immediately before it. Here, "Nancy" is singular, and so the verb should be "is." In contrast, if subjects are connected by "and," the verb should always be plural: "The tennis players and Nancy are coming over for dinner."

Example: Mere recitations of the legal issue presented to the court *does* not constitute sufficient pleading.

Problem: The subject is "recitations," a plural, not "issue," the singular object of the prepositional phrase; the verb must track the subject.

Solution: Mere recitations of the legal issue presented to the court *do* not constitute sufficient pleading.

Example: Both the format and the design of the data base as well as the selection of information included within it *is* solely attributable to counsel for Leroy.

Problem: The writer was fooled by the singular "selection"; the subject, though, is plural. Also, "within it" is surplusage.

Solution: Both the format and the design of the data base as well as the selection of information included *are* solely attributable to counsel for Leroy.

Example: The format of the data base, together with the selection of information, *are* solely attributable to counsel for Leroy.

Problem: Clauses beginning with "as well as," "together with," "along with," and "in addition to," are not conjunctive—they are not the equivalent of "and." Therefore, the verb must be singular if the subject outside the clause is singular, as it is in the sentence just given.

Solution: The format of the data base, together with the selection of information, *is* solely attributable to counsel for Leroy.

Split Infinitive

When a modifier is placed immediately after the "to" in the infinitive form of the verb—for example, "to rapidly walk"—the writer has split the infinitive. A rule prohibiting split infinitives was once immutable; today, however, writers should regard it as a principle to be followed when possible. If unsplitting the infinitive creates a choppy sentence, then by all means split it. But be aware that a few remaining purists abhor every instance of the split infinitive and will think the less of you if they find any.

Example: By demurring, defendants are only exercising their right *to vigorously litigate* their claims.
Solution: By demurring, defendants are only exercising their right to litigate their claims vigorously.

Pronouns and Sexism

Using "I"

Lawyers turn somersaults to avoid using the first person. They write convoluted sentences that only an acrobat can extricate himself from: "In my opinion, it is not an unjustifiable assumption" should be "I think." Some lawyers believe that writing in the first person is too informal for a court and follow that feeling in all their writing. But says Chief Judge Patricia M. Wald: "Too many young lawyers today are afraid to show strong feelings of any kind: the jargon in which they write illustrates all too graphically their insecurity about stating what they believe in. They rarely use a straight declarative sentence or the pronoun 'I.' "

> **Example:** Enclosed for your consideration is a copy of a proposed trust which *has been prepared* pursuant to our conference of Oct. 2.

> **Problem:** To avoid using "I," the writer must often invoke the passive.

> **Solution:** I enclose a copy of a proposed trust I prepared after our Oct. 2 conference.

Pronoun Antecedent

The reader will lose the thought if a pronoun can refer to more than one object or person in the sentence. The problem of the obscure antecedent crops up often with the overused "it" and also in the lazy construction in which the writer substitutes the word "this" for a concept expressed in an earlier sentence. This difficulty also occurs in the misuse of "which."

> **Example:** Plaintiff does not know that Sam knew that it was *his* thirty-fifth wedding anniversary.

> **Problem:** Whose anniversary? The reader will never know.

> **Example:** Thus, even assuming *arguendo* that punching out of a part of the label had the net effect of making it resemble another label used on women's jeans, *this* cannot constitute a copying of a "registered" mark.

Problem: Aside from the redundant Latinism, the unnecessary "had the net effect," and the dangling modifier, the sentence is obscure because it is not clear what the word "this" refers to. Fix the antecedent problem by attaching "this" to a noun that sums up what has gone before, thus strengthening the reader's understanding. Never force the reader to reread your sentence to figure out what you were trying to say.

Solution: Thus, even if we assume that punching out part of the label made it resemble another label used on women's jeans, *this alteration* cannot constitute a copying of a "registered" mark.

Example: Each company is precluded from expanding its production capacity by covenants with its creditor banks *which* prevent borrowing for capital expansion until at least 1991.

Problem: Does the "which" refer to creditor banks or to the covenants? Although the sense becomes clear after studying the sentence, you don't want to force your reader to do so.

Solution: Covenants with creditor banks preclude each company from expanding production capacity because they prevent borrowing for capital expansion until at least 1991.

Example: The defendant looked wildly about the room, *which* was evident to all the jurors.

Problem: What does "which" refer to? The syntax suggests it refers to the room, but the sense is rather to the action in the preceding clause as a whole. Although in some simple sentences the missing antecedent can be deduced, such constructions should be avoided.

Solution 1: The defendant looked wildly about the room. His wild motions were evident to all the jurors.
Solution 2: The defendant looked wildly about the room, a gesture that was evident to all the jurors.

Confusion of "That" and "Which"

Among lawyers, the appropriate choice of "that" or "which" as a relative pronoun is discussed more than it should be. The distinction between "that" and "which" is no longer an absolute rule, just as the prohibition against split infinitives is no longer rigid. Again, however, because so many purists are adamant on this topic, it is worth knowing and using the rule as it once existed. Simply stated, "that" introduces a clause that is meant to define the noun it follows. A comma never precedes "that" when used in this way. "Which," always preceded by a comma, introduces subsidiary information. For example, "This is my house, which Jack built" expresses the thought that this is *my* house. Jack's role is secondary. "This is my house that Jack built" suggests that of the many houses I own, this is the one built by Jack. In recent decades, several usage experts have noted the tendency to use "which" in both sentences. However, "that" is a word of many meanings and uses, and the writer would err to suppose that "which" can always substitute for it.

Example: Recently we received information *which* you were interested in our publication . . .

Problem: This sentence was in a letter to one of the authors from a leading legal publisher; even the professional word people suffer their lapses. The construction is illiterate because it substitutes "which" for "that," serving here as a conjunction, not as a relative pronoun.

Solution 1: Recently we received information *that* you were interested in our publication . . .
Solution 2: Recently you told us you were interested . . .

Fused Participle

Dear Reader: Do you mind *us* reciting all these examples? The preceding question does not convey the meaning we intended. Although it is a grammatical sentence, it asks whether you object to *us* rather than someone else. We intended to ask whether you objected to the recitation itself. We should have said: "Do you mind *our* reciting all these examples?" The problem for the writer in all such sentences is to locate the object of the sentence. In the sentence that carries our intended meaning, the object is the clause "reciting some examples." The pronoun that modifies the clause must be in its possessive form—"our" rather than "us." In 1906, H. W. Fowler, a leading grammarian of his day, coined the term "fused participle" for this problem, and unfortunately the name has stuck.

Example: Wall Street law firms should be concerned about *professors exhorting* their students to work elsewhere.

Problem: The firms need not be concerned about the professors, only about the exhortation.

Solution: Wall Street law firms should be concerned about *professors' exhorting* their students to work elsewhere.

Example: What the Justice feared was the *Constitution* of the United States *becoming* a shield for the criminal.

Problem: The Justice feared the "becoming," not the Constitution. But in the sentence as it stands, it is impossible to put "Constitution" in the possessive form, because of the clause that follows. Some grammarians insist, therefore, that the sentence is proper as it stands.

Solution 1: What the Justice feared was the *Constitution's* becoming a shield for the criminal.
Solution 2: What the Justice feared was that the Constitution of the United States would become a shield for the criminal.

Sexist Language

Sexism in language is an evolving concern, and no standard usage or formula eliminates it. English lacks a generic singular pronoun encompassing "he" and "she." Resorting to pronouns such as "each," "anyone," "everybody," and "everyone" frequently causes as many problems as it solves. For example, in the sentence "Anyone who fails the bar will lose *their* job," the writer avoids the singular possessive "his" at the cost of grammatical accuracy. "Anyone" is a singular pronoun, and it must take a singular verb and singular referent. Similarly, when referring to a unnamed person—for example, "if a *client* complains, *send him* to the bar association"—the latter pronoun must be singular to agree with its antecedent noun.

Sexism often can be eliminated by rephrasing sentences to avoid the singular pronoun. The easiest way is to pluralize the subject. For example, "if *clients* complain, send *them* to the bar association." Another way is to write in the second person, as we generally do throughout this book, in the first person plural, in the neutral third person ("one"), or with the relative pronoun "who." Or eliminate the pronoun altogether.

> **Example:** If a lawyer wants to write clearly, *he* should avoid fancy words.
> **Solution 1:** As a lawyer trying to write clearly, *you* should avoid fancy words.
> **Solution 2:** As lawyers trying to write clearly, *we* should . . .
> **Solution 3:** As a lawyer trying to write clearly, *one* should . . .
> **Solution 4:** A lawyer *who* wants to write clearly should . . .
> **Solution 5:** When trying to write clearly, *a lawyer* should . . .

Other, though less preferable, methods include recasting the sentence in the passive voice and using a relative clause: "A client who complains should be sent to the bar association."

As a last resort, use both the masculine and feminine singular pronouns—"he or she." Usage books increasingly accept the use of both pronouns. Casey Miller and Kate Swift in the *Handbook of Nonsexist Writing* write: "Despite the charge of clumsiness, double-hyphen pronoun constructions have made a comeback, apparently on the reasonable grounds that words should reflect reality." In the manual of style appended to the second edition of the *Random House Dictionary of the English Language* (1987), the editors say that using both the masculine and feminine singular pronouns is the approach "most likely to produce awkwardness." But, they add, "if the pronouns do not need to be repeated too often, it may in some cases be the most satisfactory solution available."

Unacceptable approaches are the attempts to create portmanteau pronouns or noun blends: "s/he," "he/she," "wo/man." These barbaric constructions have no place in any kind of writing. Another unacceptable approach is to alternate the feminine and masculine pronouns; it is confusing and artificial, sacrificing clarity to politics. We disagree with the approach that Professor Richard H. Weisberg takes in *When Lawyers Write*, a 1987 book about legal writing: "The perceptive reader will quickly note that I have chosen to use masculine nouns and pronouns in odd-numbered chapters and feminine equivalents in even-numbered chapters. This convention spares my reader the cumbersome devices proposed by writers these days to prove their good will.'' The devices we recommend are less cumbersome and contrived.

A final point on sexism. Whenever possible, use gender-neutral terms to describe occupations, status, or positions. For example, "workers' compensation," not "workman's compensation"; "firefighter," not "fireman"; "business executive," "manager," "retailer," but not "businessman"; "drafter," not "draftsman." In all events, avoid language that calls attention to the sex of an individual when sex is irrelevant. Instead of "man-made fiber," use "synthetic fiber."

Arranging the Components of a Sentence

We have been concerned with the building blocks of a sentence. Next we consider how they should be arranged so that the sentence conveys its meaning most clearly.

The Dangling Participle

Lawyers often lose their way in a sentence, forgetting that a participial clause refers to the subject that follows. These clauses dangle when they are not attached to the appropriate subject. The mistake is commonly enough made, even by the best writers. For example, Emily Brontë wrote in *Wuthering Heights*: "On ascending to Isabella's room, my suspicions were confirmed." But suspicions did not ascend to the room; Nelly did. The sentence could have read: "On ascending to Isabella's room, I confirmed my suspicions."

Example: Before *addressing the specific paragraphs in the complaint,* some general comments are in order.

Problem: The participial clause is "addressing the specific paragraphs in the complaint." The subject of the sentence is "some general comments." The sentence begins to say, therefore, that "before the comments address the paragraphs." This is, of course, utter nonsense. To remedy the dangling modifier, replace the subject of the sentence with a more appropriate one, or rewrite the participial clause with a subject and an active verb.

> **Solution 1:** Before addressing the specific paragraphs in the complaint, I offer these general comments.
> **Solution 2:** Before I address the specific paragraphs in the complaint, some general comments are in order.

> **Example:** *Assuming* the governor signs the bill, *you* can purchase the extra shares.

Problem: Technically, the clause dangles, because "you" are not doing the assuming. But many grammarians say that a sentence such as this one is acceptable because every reader will understand that it is the writer doing the assuming, just as the writer might begin, "Summing up." That said, the sentence can still be tightened.

> **Solution:** If the governor signs the bill, you can buy the extra shares.

Misplaced Modifiers and Clauses

A modifier or clause wrongly placed can lead to ambiguity.

> **Example:** The court emphasized that unjust enrichment was involved so that whatever was taken *wrongfully* constituted the fund.

Problem: The writer could be saying that something was "taken wrongfully" or that something "wrongfully constituted the fund." Move the modifier.

> **Solution:** The court emphasized that whatever was wrongfully taken constituted the fund.

> **Example:** Likewise, defendants' assertion that injunctive relief is *only* to be granted where trade secrets are involved is simply not the law.

Problem: Of the general problem of misplaced adverbs, "only" looms the largest and most vexing, in part because "only" sometimes must be placed idiomatically and other times logically. The one sure error is to plunk down an "only" without thinking; its placement can dramatically alter meaning. Consider this sentence referred to by Theodore M. Bernstein: "I hit him in the eye yesterday." "Only" can be put in eight different positions, and every placement means something different. Try it.

> **Solution 1:** Likewise, defendants are legally wrong in asserting that injunctive relief is to be granted only when trade secrets are involved.
> **Solution 2:** Likewise, defendants legally err in asserting that injunctive relief is to be granted only when trade secrets are at stake.

> **Example:** Justice White abruptly announces that the interest in "liberty" that is implicated by a decision not to bear a child *that is made a few days after conception* is *less* fundamental than a comparable decision made before conception.
> **Solution 1:** Justice White abruptly announces that the interest in "liberty" implicated by a decision made a few days after conception not to bear a child is *less* fundamental than a comparable decision made before conception.
> **Solution 2:** Justice White abruptly announces that the interest in "liberty" is less fundamental if a decision not to bear a child is made a few days after rather than before conception.

Putting Sentence Elements in Order

Readers expect the subject, verb, and object of a sentence to be closely linked. No rule dictates how tight the link, and good writers certainly vary the rhythm of their sentences. But a sentence can become impenetrable if these major elements stray too far apart.

> **Example:** Thus contrary to plaintiffs' assertions, this court in *Rubell* clearly ruled that any investigation of the circumstances upon which a suit is being presently litigated is based is privileged.

Problem: In the clause beginning with "that," the link between the subject "investigation" and the verb "is privileged" has been lost, and the sentence is further confused by the two other uses of "is." No one can catch the meaning in one reading.

Solution: This court in *Rubell* held privileged any investigation of circumstances upon which a pending suit is based.

Example: Nancy Reagan, in order to exert in a more direct way her power over the President's schedule, in 1982 began in a carefully hidden manner, to determine the most propitious days on which he could travel, a series of consultations with a San Francisco astrologer, according to Donald Regan in his new book. (This sentence is fifty-three words long.)

Problem: Note the disconnections:

> *Subject-verb: Nancy Reagan* [in order to exert a more direct power over the President's schedule, in 1982] *began*

> *Verb-object: began* [in a carefully hidden manner, to determine the most propitious days on which he could travel,] *a series of consultations*

> *Verb-object: exert* [in a more direct way] *her power*

Solution 1: According to Donald Regan's new book, in 1982, in order to exert a more direct power over the President's schedule, Nancy Reagan began a carefully hidden series of consultations with a San Francisco astrologer to determine the most propitious days for traveling. [Forty-two words]
Solution 2: According to Donald Regan's new book, to exert more power over the President's schedule, in 1982 Nancy Reagan began secretly to consult a San Francisco astrologer to determine when he might travel most propitiously. [Thirty-four words]
Solution 3: In 1982, Nancy Reagan began secretly to consult a San Francisco astrologer to control more directly the President's schedule. This revelation appears in Donald Regan's new book. The astrologer determined when the President might travel most propitiously. [Thirty-seven words]

Now look at the connections:

Verb-object: exert [more directly] *her power*; or *control* [more directly] *the President's schedule*

Subject-verb: Nancy Reagan began

Verb-object: began secretly to consult a San Francisco astrologer

Parallelism

Parallelism is a principle requiring equivalent elements of a sentence to be constructed in an equivalent way. If you put two relative clauses in the predicate, and one begins with "that," so should the other. If one clause uses a verb in the present tense and active voice, the other should not use a passive or the verbal form ending in "-ing."

> **Example:** However, as a practical matter, committees usually *make* recommendations to the full board rather than *taking* official actions of their own.
> **Solution:** However, as a practical matter, committees usually make recommendations to the full board rather than take official actions of their own.

> **Example:** Although the objective of the government remains legitimate, whether this method is *rationally related* to advancing this legitimate objective, or a *punishment* for carrying the AIDS virus is arguable.
> **Solution:** . . . it is arguable whether this method rationally relates to advancing this legitimate objective or punishes people for carrying the AIDS virus.

Emphasis within a Sentence

In *Style*, Joseph M. Williams sets out two rules for achieving proper emphasis within a sentence:

(1) Move from old to new: "Whenever possible, express at the beginning of a sentence ideas already stated, referred to, implied, safely

assumed, familiar, predictable, less important, readily accessible. . . . Express at the end of a sentence the least predictable, the newest, the most important, the most significant information, the information you almost certainly want to emphasize.''

(2) Move from short to long: A long subject makes it hard to find the verb. Put the longer elements at the end of a sentence.

Example: It was worthwhile paying every penny that we did for this information.

Problem: ''This information'' suggests that in a previous sentence the writer has introduced us to the information in question. Hence it is an idea already stated or referred to; that we had to pay for it is new. Turning the sentence around will make it more emphatic and will link it more tightly to the preceding one.

Solution: This information was worth every penny we paid for it.

Example: Judges who live among the people, who understand their hopes and fears and predilections, assuming that they are learned, fearless, and upright, are who we want to serve.

Problem: The sentence is top-heavy; its subject is so long that we lose our way before we come to the predicate. Flip it around.

Solution: We want learned, fearless, and upright judges who live among the people and who understand their hopes and fears and predilections.

Letting Your Sentence Tell the Story

The errors we have discussed in this chapter obscure the meaning of the sentences in which they are committed. If you sense that your sentence is hazy, without knowing quite how, you often can repair it simply by asking where the real story is and recasting it to reflect the central point. Recall the discussion of topics (pp. 101–105). Put your central point in the topic of the sentence, and put the elements of the sentence in appropriate order. Here's an example that Don Freeman gives:

Any Product received by A from C pursuant to the terms of the Agreement which fails to meet the Standards of Specifications or is damaged, defective, or not of merchantable quality, in the view of A, acting reasonably, entitles A to receive a full credit from C for such Defective Product.

This sentence is difficult because the reader starts out thinking that it is about a "Product" and ends up learning that it is really about A's entitlement to a refund. It should be recast to reflect its true topic:

A is entitled to a full credit for any Defective Product received from C whenever it fails to meet the Standards of Specifications under the Agreement, or is damaged, defective, or in A's reasonable view, not of merchantable quality.

This principle, that a sentence or a series of sentences should fashion topics into subjects, applies even to the most abstruse sentences. George Gopen has applied this principle to rewrite major portions of the Uniform Commercial Code. Here is an original passage, which he then edits:

§1-102(3): The effect of provisions of this Act may be varied by agreement, except as otherwise provided in this Act and except that the obligations of good faith, diligence, reasonableness and care prescribed by this Act may not be disclaimed by agreement but the parties may by agreement determine the standards by which the performance of such obligations is to be measured if such standards are not manifestly unreasonable.

As drafted, the passage buries the actors—namely, the parties—and chops up the sentence with many prepositional phrases. By focusing on what the parties may or may not do, Professor Gopen makes it easy to follow the point:

§1-102(3) [redrafted]: Parties are free to agree to vary the effects of the provisions of this Act except

(a) when this Act explicitly provides otherwise, and
(b) when this Act prescribes obligations of good faith, diligence, reasonableness, and care.

When the obligations listed in §1-102(3)(b) are involved, parties may agree to determine the standards by which the performance of the obligations is to be measured, as long as those standards are not manifestly unreasonable.

If on rereading you find your sentences unclear, or if you are criticized for muddling your thought, look hard at your subjects and ask whether the ones you have chosen are appropriate. Check to see whether the true topics of your sentence are buried later on in the sentence (or the paragraph). If so, exhume them, put them where they belong, and let them resuscitate your sentence.

Transitions

Transitions are words or phrases that link sentences. Transitions are not necessary between every pair of sentences, because the logic of your thought, and the relation of your topics, should be strong enough to get the reader from one to the next. But, as in this sentence, occasionally you help the reader along by pointing out certain types of connections; here *opposition* (other terms that demonstrate opposing concepts are *nevertheless, however, on the other hand, although*). *Next*, as here, you can *sequence* your thoughts (*first, finally, in conclusion*). *Furthermore*, as here, you can show how one sentence *adds* to the next (*moreover, also, in addition*). That's not all. You can stress your point. *As a matter of fact*, this sentence does just that (as will *indeed, in fact*, and *even*). Or you can illustrate a point. *For example* as this sentence does, you can show how the point of a sentence *exemplifies* the point of the preceding one (*for instance, to illustrate*). *Finally*, you can show how one thought logically or causally follows from another by *concluding (therefore, so, consequently, as a result)*.

Transitions are not window dressing, to be displayed just to catch your reader's eye. Each term has meaning, and that meaning must make sense in the context of your sentences. Otherwise, the reader will be lost.

Example: The brief is due in court in three hours. *However*, we might get the judge to give us an extension.

Problem: "However" expresses opposition, but where are the opposing thoughts here? The sentences imply but do not state a difficulty.

Solution 1: The brief is due in court in three hours. However, we do not have time to finish it.
Solution 2: We have only three hours left to complete the brief and six hours' work remaining. However, we might get the judge to give us an extension.

Sentence Length

Even if your sentence is grammatically and syntactically sound, it still may confound the reader if it is too long. For years, journalists, grammarians, and writing analysts have debated just how long is too long. Into the 1960s, tabloid newspapers would not permit sentences with more than seventeen words. Many of today's newspaper editors frown on sentences exceeding twenty-five words. Rudolf Flesch, a life-long critic of writing problems, developed what he termed a "readability formula" that measures the average sentence length in words and the average word length in syllables. Applying his formula to different kinds of writing, he determined their "readability." Under his formula, "John loves Mary" scores high, meaning that the sentence is easy to read. A much more difficult sentence, under the Flesch formula: "Even though John is not given to a display of his deeper emotions, he allegedly has developed a profound affection for Mary, as compared to the more equable feelings he seems to have for Lucy, Fran, and, to an extent, Sue."

Flesch's formula has been widely adopted. For his adherents, a sentence should contain no more than twenty words, averaging a syllable and a half, to qualify as "plain English."

Common sense suggests that Flesch's formula and similar ones are unnecessarily confining. Appropriate sentence length depends on the number of thoughts and their complexity. A reader can wend through dozens of words in a sentence with a relatively simple thought and not lose the thread. Consider, for example, this sparkling hundred-word sentence, the last in Lewis Carroll's *Alice in Wonderland*:

Lastly, she pictured to herself how this same little sister of hers would, in the aftertime, be herself a grown woman; and how she would keep, through all her riper years, the simple and loving heart of her childhood; and how she would gather about her other little children, and make *their* eyes bright and eager with many a strange tale, perhaps even with her dream of Wonderland of long ago; and how she would feel with all their simple sorrows, and find a pleasure in all their simple joys, remembering her own child life, and the happy summer days.

But a sentence expressing even a single complex concept must be far shorter for the meaning to emerge. A sentence, Justice Cardozo warned, "may be so overloaded with all its possible qualifications that it will tumble down of its own weight." Even the maxim "one thought per sentence" may not apply if the thought is too complex. Then one thought may require two or three sentences. Under no circumstances should more than one complex thought be included in a single sentence, as so many lawyers, victims of the "headnote disease," feel driven to do.

These reflections are rooted in the reader's psychology. In 1922, Urban A. Lavery wrote:

The sentence is the natural unit of thought, words are the artificial units. Thought operates not by words but by ideas, that is by sentences. In reading, the eye picks up one word after another until the idea is conceived and born in the mind; then the mind forgets the separate words and only the idea remains. Or, to put the matter another way, the words are the chaff out of which the mind must winnow and save the grain, which is the thought. As we read a page of print the thought passes into the memory in the form of an idea and not as a group of words. . . . The mind will readily turn back into the words the precise meaning of what has been read; but not into the same words unless they have been laboriously learned by heart. . . . The reason for short sentences in the work of a lawyer becomes at once obvious. . . . The reader is forced to break the [long] sentence up into fragments—to camp by the way, so to speak—while the mind catches up with the eye; or perhaps while it tries to catch up but fails and gives up the chase. Of course, such delay—and more particularly such failure—works disaster on the real meaning of the author.

Example: Issuers, directors, underwriters, signatories of the registration statement, and professionals, whose reports or evaluations are used in connection with the registration statement, may all be found liable for these misstatements or omissions, subject to detailed affirmative defenses of due diligence contained in 11b.

Problem: At least two thoughts here. Split the sentence.

Solution: Those who may be found liable for these misstatements or omissions include: . . . Their liability is subject to detailed . . .

Example: In *Chiarella*, the Supreme Court reversed the conviction under Sect. 10(b) of the Exchange Act of an employee of a financial printer who had purchased the stock of companies that were about to become the targets of tender offers after learning of the proposed tender offers from documents that the acquiring companies had submitted for printing.

Problem: This writer was suffering from a fever induced by the headnote disease. Every possible thought and qualification, the panicked mind believes, must be included. Not so.

Solution: In *Chiarella*, the Supreme Court reversed the conviction of an employee of a financial printer under Sect. 10(b) of the Exchange Act. The employee had purchased the stock of companies that were about to become targets of tender offers. He bought the stocks after learning of the proposed tender offers from documents that the acquiring companies had submitted for printing.

Example: Appellant's failure to make an affirmative showing of injury means that he cannot prevail either on his claim that the amount of summation time he was granted was in itself inadequate or on his other allegation that the trial court's distribution of summation time between plaintiff and defendants was in some sense unfair.

Solution 1: Because he failed to make an affirmative showing of injury, appellant cannot prevail on either of his claims—that he was not given enough time to present his summation or that the trial judge unfairly allocated the time to make summations.

Solution 2: Because he failed affirmatively to show an injury, appellant must lose on both his claims: (1) He was not given enough time to present his summation and (2) the trial judge unfairly allocated the time to make summations.

Overly long sentences come from hurried writing and meager editing. Under the best of circumstances, lawyers are allergic to periods. At times, they forgo periods altogether. They inhale deeply, spit out word after word after word, and never pause for breath. Consider this 161-word written harangue, all packaged in one sentence, from a justice of the Utah Supreme Court:

> However, this does not mean that the Constitution of the United States, which in no uncertain terms says the states are supreme in this country and superior to the philosophy of federal protagonists who deign to suggest that a coterie of 3 or 5 or even 9 federal persons immune from public intolerance, by use of a pair of scissors and the whorl of a 10 cent ball-point pen, and a false sense of last-minute confessional importance, can in one fell swoop, shakily clip phrases out of the Constitution, substitute their manufactured voids with Scotch-taped rhetoric, and thus reverse hundreds of cases dimmed only by time and nature, but whose impressions indestructibly already indelibly had been linotyped on the minds of kids and grandkids who vowed and now would or will vow to defend, not only the institution of marriage and motherhood, but to reserve to the states a full budget of legitimate, time-tested mores incident to that doctorate.

Enough said.

CHAPTER 11

Editing II: Revising Your Prose

Finished a draft of that brief you've been researching the past month? Good show. Have a swell dinner. Take in a movie. Lounge in your hot tub. Get some sleep. But don't gloat. You're only half done. Maybe not even.

Writing is like building a house. Working with a plan, you put up the superstructure—you dig a foundation, pour in concrete, erect the walls, lay the beams that carry the stress, and finally nail down the roof. Your neighbors can see the framework of your dwelling. If you're careful (and lucky), you will have anticipated unevenness in the soil and measured the boards to a sixteenth of an inch so that they mesh. If you haven't been quite so meticulous, you'll saw off the ends of boards that stick out. But you would not yet invite your neighbors to tea. Much remains to be done: sanding, plastering, papering, painting—and you'll need running water, electricity, windows, and doors. Structure is important, but the details make your house livable.

There's no such thing as good writing—there's only good rewriting.
LOUIS D. BRANDEIS

In writing it is the editing that gives coherence to the structure of your thoughts. By the time you've completed a draft, you have "solved" the conceptual problem, but that solution is not likely cast in the form in which it will communicate your points most sharply and effectively to your audience. The shaping work—the editing that will take your structure and make it talk to others—lies before you.

Editing should not be an afterthought. It is not a cursory inspection to ensure that you've spelled the names of your client and the judge properly. The paragraphs may seem to make sense to your exhausted eye, but you have much to do before you can be certain that you are seeing what others will see the first time they read it. That certainty comes from editing. Editing is as crucial to the final product as the draft itself, and you need to spend as much time editing as you did composing.

I am glad to note that it has been some years since I have seen the expression in a brief "it's incredulous."

JUSTICE LEONARD H. SANDLER, 1987

How you edit is important. There is an order to editing, just as there is an order to finishing your house. You cannot do it all at once or wildly out of sequence. You would not paint your house before you sanded it, and if you hope to show off your handiwork, you should apply a primer and several coats of high-gloss paint. Of course, you don't have to go to all this trouble to live in your house—*you* can live in an unfinished structure. If a portion of a wall protrudes, you can learn to walk around it, even laugh about it, tell your neighbors you like the eccentricity. But you can take no such comfort in your unfinished writing. You do not write only for yourself. Others will live in, or die by, your words.

Seductive as your own words on paper may be, you must resist the feelings that your finished draft arouses in you. Abandon sentimentality; the joy will come from scraping, sanding, and burnishing, not from papering over the beam that doesn't fit.

In the memoirs of professional writers who reflect on their craft, the loudest theme is revision. Raymond Carver, the American short story writer, regularly wrote twenty to thirty drafts of each story. Philip Roth says he once spent six months of eight-hour days and emerged with one page: "I often have to write 100 pages or more before there's a paragraph that's alive. Okay, I say to myself, that's your beginning, start there; that's the first paragraph of the book. I'll go over the first six months of work and underline in red a paragraph, a sentence, sometimes no more than a phrase, that has some life in it.'' Ernest Hemingway always rewrote what he had written the day before, only then adding his daily allotment of 400 or 500 new words.

These are professional writers, you protest—that's all they do. True, you may not have the luxury of their more relaxed deadlines, but you should take your work no less seriously. Many busy professionals do, and it shows.

As far as grammar, style, and use of jargon go, however, I don't think lawyers are worse than other specialists and maybe better than many. If you want to read really terrible writing, try the social scientists.

ELIZABETH SACKSTEDER, ARTICLES EDITOR, YALE LAW JOURNAL, *1988*

John Kenneth Galbraith has said that the air of spontaneity in his writing begins to appear only around the fifth or sixth revision. Judge Richard Posner, one of the most widely admired legal writers in the country, wrote us: ''I do much self-editing, sometimes going through as many as twenty drafts (though ten is the most in all but a tiny handful of cases) until I am satisfied. Much of the editing is designed to simplify the product and give it a casual, colloquial, and spontaneous appearance. I admit to hypocrisy in working so hard to give the appearance of effortlessness!''

Editing is difficult, and it takes time. Lawyers who assert that they are so squeezed for time that they must routinely file a document minutes after it is drafted are shortchanging their clients, irritating the judges, and deceiving themselves. If you can honestly say you have no time to edit, then you misunderstand the writing process.

Even if you are on a tight schedule, a relatively painless way to open up time for editing is to impose a false deadline. Plan to finish your draft some hours, days, or weeks before you must submit the document. For example, if on Monday you are assigned a brief due Friday afternoon, plan to complete your draft no later than Wednesday afternoon. Put it aside until Thursday morning, and then begin to edit.

Editing should not begin the instant you have completed the draft. To read your own words dispassionately, you must distance yourself to forget what you thought you meant by them. In editing, you must stand outside yourself and read from the perspective of a stranger. That means you should lay the draft aside at least overnight and even, if you have planned well, a day or two.

A smooth document emerges from discrete edits. As with every other aspect of writing, the sequence of editing is not rigid. Each writer must find a suitable way. Regardless of the sequence, however, every document should be edited for structure, length, clarity, and continuity and for proofreading errors.

Editing for Structure

Experienced writers generally begin by reviewing the structure of the draft. Read through the entire document once or twice. Then reread the first and last paragraphs. Ask these questions:

1. Have you written a lead?

2. If your lead provides a road map, does your concluding paragraph show that you've reached your destination?

3. Does every paragraph have a single point?

4. Is a single concept discussed in a single place in the draft or is the discussion scattered?

5. Do transitions work—are your different points well connected?

You can answer these questions readily enough by writing in the margin what topics each paragraph discusses (see the Niles Nasty exercise, pp. 97–100). Use only a word or two. You will quickly discover whether your paragraphs wander and how well they are connected. If a topic is split among several unconnected paragraphs, it is time to restructure. Bring each piece of the topic together and rewrite. If the transition between topics is too abrupt, find a way to connect them. For instance, if your transition is "in an unrelated development" or "moving along now to the next point," that's a sure sign that you are not connecting well. Ask yourself why one point ought to follow another, and then tell your reader.

> *For all the criticism about attorneys and their writing, they have nothing to be ashamed of in comparison to environmental consultants.*
>
> HARRY G. MEYER, *1987*

Even though you may have rewritten the lead in your first draft several times, you are never guaranteed that it carries the load it should until you have rethought its relation to the rest of the document. And if you have hastily written out one draft, without having rewritten as you progressed, this editing step is imperative. Your original vision of how your argument would unfold may have been mistaken—it often is. Not until you have finished the entire document—that is, solved your problem—can you clearly see the entire course, from start to finish. Only then can you have the confidence and perspective to rewrite the lead in a form and style that will serve the reader best.

Editing for Length

Once assured that the structure is sound, you must trim ruthlessly. Most drafts are too long, for two very different reasons: (1) They exceed a court-mandated page limitation or (2) wanting to be as comprehensive as possible, you left nothing out. The length of your draft should never be a guide to the length of your final effort. You can surely shed more than a quarter of your words without destroying the substantive sense.

Cutting takes time. Most of us have been taught, perhaps subliminally, that length equals effort: The lengthier paper, we falsely assume, takes more time to write than the short one. In fact, it is harder work to cut —while preserving all salient points—than it is to write long initially. "It takes enormous amounts of time to make legal writing short, simple, concise, and clear," says Richard Emery, a New York City lawyer whose words and phrases are frequently quoted in local newspapers. "Long briefs are generally the result of not enough work on the finished product."

Cutting must be done in two steps—in the loose jargon of our age, the editor must take a "macro" chop and a "micro" slice. The macro chopping excises unnecessary substantive discussion. The micro slice removes clutter, verbiage, obviousness, windy phrases, and redundancies. Does every case you cite require a forty-line description of the facts?

Can you more concisely summarize the holdings in your principal body of cases? Must you list every precedent governing the conditions for ruling in your favor? Judge Joseph W. Bellacosa of the New York Court of Appeals complains of string citations and "cut-and-paste quotation montages posing as briefs or legal writing."

Brevity is a virtue twice over. A short paper saves the busy reader time. A short work also dramatically enhances your prospects of being understood. Robert Kasanof of New York says: "Ordinary legal writing is often so choked with the desire not to leave out anything which comes to the writer's mind that the objective of the writing is often lost."

Editing for Clarity

From the last chapter, you should be familiar with the principles of micro cutting (even though we did not call it that). Draw up an editor's checklist, using the guidelines laid down there. Now apply these principles to your editing, one category at a time.

My pet peeve is lawyers who are under the mistaken impression that they know the "rules of grammar" or that, since their writing "gets the idea across," the rules they don't know aren't important. Punctuation rules are particularly susceptible to this view.

RANDAL R. CRAFT JR., *1988*

For instance, read through your document once, looking just for nominalizations. Wear blinders to every other problem. After you check for and remove nominalizations in one or two documents, you will discover that you can spot and remedy them quickly—in far less time than had you been trying to correct every mistake in every sentence on a single pass. Then go on to root out unnecessary passives, then flabby phrases, then throat-clearing openings or transitions, then excessive use of "there is," then dangling and misplaced modifiers, and so on through the checklist. To guard against sentences that are too long, check to see whether periods are generally occurring every three lines or less. If not, your sentences are probably too long, so split them up, rewriting as you do.

A long-term benefit of micro editing is that over time it will become increasingly less necessary. As you become adept at correcting your mistakes, you will become less likely to commit them while you're writing.

The mechanics of the editing process depend on what you feel comfortable with. Some people want a clean copy after each pass. Others mark in different colors. Many use arrows, some scissors. Increasingly, writers are making changes on a screen, often leaving the editing trail invisible. But however you choose to edit, you must have a clean copy before going on to edit for continuity.

Editing for Continuity

By now you will have read through the document many times. It may not look much like the first draft. You have rewritten your sentences, shifted paragraphs, and condensed or omitted arguments. Now read through the document once again as a whole, this time looking for continuity. Ask yourself whether the transitions make sense, whether first references fully identify a case or person, and whether sentences and paragraphs have been logically reordered. Because you have recast your original organization, you need to be sure that this much changed version is strongly structured.

Proofreading

Only at the end will you undertake to proofread—a task that many lawyers mistakenly regard as the primary purpose of editing. Proofreading comprises three distinct tasks: checking for misspellings and "typos," fixing punctuation, and ensuring consistency in capitalization and other matters of style. Proofing is essential—you do not go to court with your shirttails hanging out, and your final copy should be just as well dressed as you are.

Exactness in the use of words is the basis of all serious thinking. . . . Words are clumsy tools, and it is very easy to cut one's fingers with them, and they need the closest attention and handling: But they are the only tools we have, and imagination itself cannot work without them.

FELIX FRANKFURTER, *1947*

Checking for Spelling and Typographical Errors

In 1987, a group of New York lawyers protesting an action of a bar association committee began a letter this way: "The Executive Committee of the Association of the Bar of the City of New York, again implementing its own recently adopted procedure, has authorized a special committee to review and evaluate the qualifications of Judge Douglas Ginsberg for appointment to the United States Supreme Court." Although the issue became moot when Judge Ginsburg withdrew from consideration, he did not withdraw the "u" from his name.

Bad spelling was the excuse that almost cost Daniel Manion a spot on the U.S. Court of Appeals for the Seventh Circuit in Chicago in 1986. A 1973 graduate of Indiana University School of Law, Manion had difficulty with words like "defiately" (definitely?), "verbatum" (verbatim), and "comperable" (comparable). His secretary eventually took responsibility for mistakes that, she said, "happen at the end of a very demanding day." In an editorial, the *Wall Street Journal* suggested Manion buy his overworked secretary a spell-checker for her word processor. But his secretary's chivalry hardly exonerates Manion, who was responsible for briefs that he signed and who could easily have proofread them before submitting them in court.

The row over Manion prompted Daniel Seligson, *Fortune Magazine*'s "contrarian," to point out spelling mistakes he had spotted in opinions of the Supreme Court. In one of then–Chief Justice Warren Burger's opinions "resistant" came out "resistent." Justice Brennan recently rendered "chastise" as "chastize." "Defendants" often become "defendents." A vast number of lawyers misspell "accommodate." That group includes Wallace Stevens, who was trained as a lawyer and spent a double career as poet and insurance executive.

Many people, not just lawyers, say they just can't spell, never could, and aren't likely so deep into their careers to master the admittedly illogical system of English spelling. They shrug, or they buy spell-checking programs for their word processors. As a check against true "typos"—typographical errors introduced by tired fingers—a competent spell-checker is a handy device. It will flag the most obvious errors, such as inversions of letters ("hte" for "the") and extra letters ("pleeadings"). It will also catch hopelessly muddled words, like Manion's. But spell-checkers have sharp limitations: They will not spot words wrongly used, such as the commonly confused "there," "their," and "they're." Nor do they have any sense of context or syntax, and so they will never find a dropped word or line, words typed out of order, verbs in the wrong tense, or inverted dates and numbers. If you cannot spell, you must hire someone who can, someone who will patiently read proof for all the other typos that can sandbag an otherwise well-crafted document.

Checking for Bad Punctuation

Like spelling, punctuation seems to many lawyers a niggling afterthought, scarcely worth the effort of understanding and much less that of an extra reading. In rare instances, that attitude can be legally fatal. Theodore Bernstein recalled the Michigan Constitution, which some years ago legalized slavery by misplacing a comma. Section 8 of Article 2 said: "Neither slavery nor involuntary servitude, unless for the punishment of crime, shall ever be tolerated in this state." That sentence says that criminals may be punished by making them slaves. The mistake discovered, the comma was moved from its position after "servitude" to its appropriate place after "slavery."

The courts should feel obliged to make themselves intelligible to the men on the street or the subway.

JEROME FRANK

In most instances, punctuation can mean the difference between a graceful document and a clumsy one. But somehow the pernicious notion arose that punctuation does not count in the law, that, as a nineteenth-century Massachusetts judge put it in a phrase adopted by the Supreme Court, "punctuation is no part of the statute." Mellinkoff rightly calls this dictum a "snatch of concise nonsense."

Punctuation can make all the difference, as the fight over the 1984 Republican platform nicely illustrated. The original draft spoke out against "any attempts to increase taxes which would harm the recovery." That was a position against some but not all taxes—against only those taxes that would be harmful. The Republican right wing, insisting on holding President Reagan to his vow never to raise taxes, protested and won a comma: "any attempts to increase taxes, which would harm the recovery." Thus it was asserted that *all* taxes would damage economic recovery.

Punctuation rules are found in many treatises and usage books (see p. 255); here we catalogue only the most prevalent errors and difficulties.

THE COMMA

After appositives. Use commas before and after appositives, clauses parenthetical to the main thought. Too many lawyers will throw in a comma at the beginning and omit one at the end.

Example: The Supreme Court, in a fit of pique at the rising number of Fair Labor Standard cases said yesterday that . . .

Problem: The clause "in a fit of pique . . . cases" is appositive, and must have commas at both ends.

Solution: The Supreme Court, in a fit of pique at the rising number of Fair Labor Standard cases, said yesterday that . . .

Serial comma. We are of two minds about the serial comma, used to distinguish between the final two items within a series of elements named in a sentence. One of us, who insists that his way is clearer and more logical, stoutly urges that the comma be used before the last item in the series: "She took her umbrella, newspaper, suntan lotion, and high spirits to the beach." The other insists that his way saves space (a valuable commodity in magazines and newspapers) and is no less logical (because a comma substitutes for "and") and just as stoutly urges that the final comma be dropped: "She took her umbrella, newspaper, suntan lotion and high spirits to the beach." We refused to settle the issue with a coin toss and agreed to air our difference. Whichever choice you make, be consistent.

After most opening phrases and some dependent clauses. Under this heading, we could spin out lots of variations, but we won't. As in the preceding sentence (and this one too!), separate the adverbial phrase that begins the sentence from the main body. Also separate the parts of a sentence connected by conjunctions and disjunctions (*and, but, or, neither, nor, so*). But do not set off conjunctions and disjunctions by themselves when they start a sentence. Do set off dependent clauses that follow the main clause if they add parenthetical information. In the last sentence, "if they add parenthetical information" is not parenthetical; it is, in the technical language, a restrictive dependent clause, necessary to the thought, and takes no comma. A nonrestrictive dependent clause occurs in the next sentence and requires a comma: These rules really are very simple, even though they may take some time to learn.

After dates and states. It is wrong to omit the comma after the year if you are giving the full date: "On August 1, 1988, we finished the manuscript." Likewise, you must follow a state with a comma if you precede it with the city: "We got to Park City, Utah, in time for the big parade."

To avoid run-on sentences and comma splices. A run-on sentence is simply two sentences packed into one without any punctuation. A comma splice is a form of the run-on, in which two independent sentences are wrongly joined by a comma.

Example: Maritime jurisdiction under the Suits in Admiralty Act is exclusive the Federal Tort Claims Act is not applicable to this action.

Problem: Two sentences here: One ends after "exclusive" and the other begins with "the Federal." A run-on sentence is always wrong. Fix this sentence with a semicolon or a period.

Solution: Maritime jurisdiction under the Suits in Admiralty Act is exclusive; the Federal Tort Claims Act is not applicable to this action.
Solution 2: Maritime jurisdiction under the Suits in Admiralty Act is exclusive. The Federal Tort Claims Act is not applicable to this action.

Example: The ITA in all cases to date has determined that the PRC has a state economy, however, it has in some cases determined that Yugoslavia has a state-controlled economy but not in others.

Problem: A comma splice. Again, the writer has joined two sentences through faulty punctuation surrounding the "however," an all-too-common mistake. Note in the Option below you may start a sentence with "however." It is wrong, however, to surround "however" with commas when it is separating two complete sentences. Note also that in the example the last four words are redundant.

> **Solution 1:** The ITA in all cases to date has determined that the PRC has a state economy; however, it has in some cases determined that Yugoslavia has a state-controlled economy.
> **Solution 2:** The ITA in all cases to date has determined that the PRC has a state economy. However, it has in some cases determined that Yugoslavia has a state-controlled economy.

Quotation Marks

In American usage, the punctuation at the end of a sentence almost always goes inside the final quotation mark. The most common misuse of quotation marks in lawyers' writing occurs in the indented quotation. When you indent a long quotation to set it off from the text, *omit* the quotation marks. The indenting signals that it is a quotation; the marks are redundant.

Colons

Setting off a series or announcing a connected thought, the colon usually is simple enough to use: Words, phrases, or entire sentences can follow the colon. But in setting up a series preceded by a verb, you should not use the colon after "is," "was," or "were." For example, omit the colon in "The major components were: fire, earth, air, and water." Use it, however, in the next sentence: "He rattled off the places they had visited: Beijing, Paris, Durban, Caracas, and Carbondale."

APOSTROPHES

More and more, apostrophes are less and less. Students and young lawyers all seem to have missed the same day in sixth grade when the apostrophe was handed out. Strunk and White start out with rules about apostrophes, apparently to no avail. The possessive form of nouns must contain an apostrophe: John's coat, Mary's lamb, the town's regret, for pity's sake, the court's ruling, the next move was Sophie's. The plural possessive sometimes gives pause. Strunk and White entreat you to add an "s" to possessive singular words ending in "-s"; thus, James's. But you can't be literal about this rule: who ever heard of "Illinois's?" Plural nouns do not take an extra "-s": the birds' flight.

Apostrophes are not confined to showing possession. They are also used in contractions: hadn't, won't, isn't, it's. The last is often stupidly confused with the possessive pronoun "its." Possessive pronouns do not take apostrophes: The day was hers; it was his game. "It's" means "it is" or "it has" and nothing else.

Checking for Consistency in Style

Finally, when editing you should check for consistency in style. Style is a matter of custom or preference, not logic. Some firms, offices, and courts impose a stylebook—the *Blue Book*, for example. Some use more general works: *The United States Government Printing Office Style Manual, The New York Times Manual of Style and Usage*, or *The Chicago Manual of Style*. These are all quite useful for their particular purposes (although the *Times*'s stylebook is now fifteen years old and a bit out of date—for example, the book says to use "Ms." only in quoted matter; the *Times* adopted the general use of "Ms." in 1986). But a law office will find only parts of these general references tailored to the lawyer's needs.

For the sake of consistency, an office should have a set of general rules governing such matters as capitalization, use of honorifics, abbreviations, spelling out of numbers, and citation forms. We have a memorandum from a senior partner of a law firm who chastised associates who capitalized "court." He told them to capitalize only when referring to the Supreme Court or the court for whom the document is being written.

When memoranda circulate in firms about such niggling points, it is time the office recognize the need for a comprehensive stylebook.

A stylebook should focus on matters relevant to your daily practice. Too often, legal stylebooks wander, providing all sorts of obscure information with which most lawyers will never concern themselves and which, in any event, can be found more easily in dictionaries or usage books. For example, *The Texas Law Review Manual on Style*, used in some offices, lists as a spelling aid 300 words ending in "-ible" or "-able." Some are not even listed in ordinary dictionaries. These include such words as "coctible," "marcesible," and "thurible."*

The sensible office should borrow the best suggestions and most relevant items from existing stylebooks and publish its own, just as it publishes a telephone directory. No longer would partners need to circulate condescending memos a few items at a time, and secretaries, typists, and proofreaders could enforce a firmwide consistency.

Editing in Steps

The diligent writer has now completed editing, having checked for appropriate structure and length, rewritten for clarity and continuity, and proofread for errors in spelling, punctuation, and capitalization.

To illustrate the principles discussed in this chapter, we offer four passages that we edit in a series of steps. In a full-length document, chances are that each editing pass will reveal the types of errors we've described. Because these are short excerpts, not every type of mistake is present.

Example: On Friday, September 5, Judge Earp entered a temporary restraining order against defendants to prevent them from "chopping down the tree" before this matter could be heard by this court and after his characterization of certain "self-help" "brute force" conduct in which defendants had engaged—spe-

---

*We had to look these words up. "Coctible," which we found only in the unabridged *Oxford English Dictionary*, is an obsolete term for "may be cooked." "Marcesible," again listed only in the Oxford, means "liable to wither or fade." "Thurible" is listed in American dictionaries; it means "censer," a container for burning incense. These words don't belong in stylebooks, and they don't belong in your briefs.

cifically, unilaterally seizing what plaintiff's counsel conceded was corporate property as security for an alleged indebtedness from plaintiff—as "law of the jungle."

Edit 1: On Friday, September 5, Judge Earp entered a temporary restraining order against defendants to prevent them from "chopping down the tree" before this matter could be heard by this court. The judge did so after his characterization of certain "self-help" "brute force" conduct in which defendants had engaged as "law of the jungle." He was referring to the unilateral seizing of what plaintiff's counsel conceded was corporate property as security for an alleged indebtedness from plaintiff.

Commentary: The original sentence is too long and requires several readings to interpret—primarily because clauses are misplaced. First step: Break it apart and rearrange the clauses.

Edit 2: On Friday, September 5, Judge Earp entered a temporary restraining order to prevent defendants from "chopping down the tree" before this court could hear the matter. He characterized as "law of the jungle" defendants' "self-help" "brute force" conduct. Judge Earp was referring to defendants' seizing of what plaintiff's counsel conceded was corporate property as security for a debt they claimed plaintiff owed them.

Commentary: Edit 2 illustrates a verb check. In sentence 1, we converted the passive "could be heard by this court" to the active voice. Also, we eliminated the redundant "against defendants to prevent them" by placing the object ("defendants") of the infinitive ("to prevent") where it belongs. In sentence 2, we denominalized "characterization," put a strong verb in its place, and moved the critical clause "law of the jungle" directly next to the verb it modifies. In sentence 3, we again denominalized the flat "alleged indebtedness," adding verbs ("claimed," "owed") to strengthen the point. We then could eliminate the overworked "alleged" without conceding that the debt was owed.

Edit 3: On Friday, September 5, Judge Earp temporarily restrained the defendants from "chopping down the tree" before this court could hear argument. He characterized their conduct as "law of the jungle." Judge Earp was referring to defendants' seizing of corporate property as security for a debt they claimed the plaintiff owed them.

Commentary: This pass is "fine tuning." In sentence i, we have eliminated the nominalization, even though we recognize "temporary restraining order" as a term of art; nothing is lost in being direct. Also, "the matter" is less precise than "argument," which is what the court actually will hear. For the sake of idiom, we added "the" before "defendants" and "plaintiff."

In rereading sentence 2, we discovered that the structure was awkward and the sense redundant. Once having said that Judge Earp found the defendants behaving under the "law of the jungle," the writer dilutes the point with extra descriptions, which pale in comparison, and are merely aspects of Judge Earp's broader characterization. Because the sentence is now so much shorter, we can eliminate the second use of the word "defendants" and substitute "their."

In sentence 3, we removed as irrelevant the counsel's concession. (A possible refinement: "Judge Earp was referring to defendants' seizing of corporate property as security for a debt claimed to be owed." The passive here shortens the sentence, although in so doing we may be exchanging clarity for brevity—still, who else could be claiming that a debt is owed but the defendants?)

Example: Paragraph 51(2) of the stipulation implies that religion is not an important facet of a child's life and that in-religion placement will not result in any higher quality care. Yet this is contrary to the Legislature's determination that the placement of a child with an authorized agency under the control of persons of the same religious faith as that of the child is the best method of instilling in that child a moral and ethical value system in accordance with that child's religious heritage when the State is acting *in loco parentis.*

Edit 1: Paragraph 51(2) of the stipulation implies that religion is not an important facet of a child's life and that the child will not benefit from being placed in a religious family. Yet this is contrary to law. The Legislature has determined that placing a child with an authorized agency under the control of persons of the child's religious faith will best instill in that child a moral and ethical value system that accords with that child's religious heritage.

Edit 2: Paragraph 51(2) of the stipulation undervalues the importance of religion in a child's life and implies that the child will not benefit from being placed in a religious family. The stipulation ignores the law. The Legislature has determined that a child should be placed with an authorized agency run by persons of the child's religion. Those persons will best instill ethics and morals that conform to the child's heritage.

Option 2: . . . The Legislature has determined that to best instill ethics and morals that conform to a child's heritage, the child should be placed with an authorized agency run by persons of the child's religion.

Commentary: The original passage is overly long, opaque, and redundant. Our editing strategy was to break the sentences into simpler parts, denominalize, find more precise verbs, and eliminate vacuous phrases; for example, "ethical and moral value system." Note that in context the state must be acting *in loco parentis*; the state cannot otherwise place children, so we eliminated that clause as obvious.

Example: Here is the text of an April 1988 fund-raising letter to members of the Harvard Law School class of 1980:

Dear Classmate:
What impact do you have on the Harvard Law School?

- You make it financially possible for one of the 1,273 students who need financial aid to attend the Law School.

- You guarantee that the Law School expends the highest quality clinical education program, while other schools cut back their clinical education programs due to costs.

- You continue innovations in legal education, including smaller and multifaculty classes for first-year students.

It is true that current students benefit every day from alumni support. We also benefitted from the support of alumni when we were students. Tuition, $11,400 this year, covers only 60% of the cost of educating current students.

Your gift does make a difference to the Law School. I hope that you will join me in making sure that we can continue to make it possible for every qualified student to attend the Law School, without regard to financial circumstances. I hope you will help us maintain the Law School's reputation for advances in legal education.

Please send your gift by June 15th to assure that it is credited in this fiscal year. Please accept my thanks for your gift to the Law School.

Commentary: The letter is stuffed with redundancies, stray words, pompous phrases, and it sounds as if it had been dictated from a telephone booth. No editor's pencil ever scratched its surface. The blue pencil first searches out redundancies: "financially possible" and "financial aid"; "highest quality clinical education program" and "clinical education program"; "students benefit" and "we also benefitted"; "making sure that we can continue to make it possible." Next the pencil deletes throat-clearing phrases: "It is true that." Then wrong words and phrases: "guarantee," "expends," "continue innovations," "due to costs," and "maintain reputation for advances." Then a little collapsing, and rewording, and the letter, by the second edit or so, now reads like this:

Solution:

Dear Classmate:

How do your contributions help the Harvard Law School?

- You enable one of 1273 financially needy students to attend.

- You help the Law School retain its high-quality clinical education program, while other schools without funds cut theirs back.

- You sustain innovation in legal education, including for first-year students smaller and team-taught classes.

Students benefit every day from alumni support, just as we did when we were students. Tuition, $11,400 this year, covers only 60 percent of the cost of educating each student.

Your gift makes a difference to the Law School. I hope you will join me to assure a place for every qualified student, regardless of financial need. Help us maintain the Law School's lead in legal education.

Please send your gift by June 15 so that it can be credited in this fiscal year. Thanks.

Example: The following passage is an excerpt from Chief Justice Burger's 1974 opinion in *United States v. Nixon.* In that case, the Supreme Court by a vote of 8-0 held that President Nixon must surrender his Watergate tapes to the United States special prosecutor. The case was heard and decided in extraordinary circumstances; the Court issued its opinion sixteen days after hearing argument.

This presumptive privilege [executive privilege] must be considered in light of our historic commitment to the rule of law. This is nowhere more profoundly manifest than in our view that "the twofold aim [of criminal justice] is that guilt shall not escape or innocence suffer." We have elected to employ an adversary system of criminal justice in which the parties contest all issues before a court of law. The need to develop all relevant facts in the adversary system is both fundamental and comprehensive. The ends of criminal justice would be defeated if judgments were to be founded on a partial or speculative presentation of the facts. The very integrity of the judicial system and public confidence in the system depend on full disclosure of all the facts, within the framework of the rules of evidence. To ensure that justice is done, it is imperative to the function of courts that compulsory process be available for the production of evidence needed either by the prosecution or by the defense.

In this case we must weigh the importance of the general privilege of confidentiality of presidential communications in performance of his responsibilities against the inroads of such a privilege on the fair administration of criminal justice. The interest in preserving confidentiality is weighty indeed and entitled to great respect. However, we cannot conclude that advisers will be moved to temper the candor of their remarks by the infrequent occasions of disclosure because of the possibility that such conversations will be called for in the context of a criminal prosecution. On the other hand, the allowance of the privilege to withhold evidence that is demonstrably relevant in a criminal trial would cut deeply into the guarantees of due process of law and gravely impair the basic function of the courts. A President's acknowledged need for confidentiality in the communications of his office is general in nature, whereas the constitutional need for production of relevant evidence in a criminal proceeding is specific and central to the fair adjudication of a particular criminal case in the administration of justice. Without access to specific facts a criminal case may be totally frustrated. The President's broad interest in confidentiality of communications will not be vitiated by disclosure of a limited number of conversations preliminarily shown to have some bearing on the pending criminal cases. . . . The generalized assertion of privilege must yield to the demonstrated, specific need for evidence in a pending criminal trial.

Edit 1: This presumptive privilege must be considered in light of our historic commitment to the rule of law, a commitment most profoundly manifest in our view that "the twofold aim [of criminal justice] is that guilt shall not escape or innocence suffer." In our adversary system of criminal justice the parties must develop all relevant facts and contest all issues before a court of law. If courts were to reach judgment without all the facts, the ends of criminal justice would be defeated. Integrity of the judicial system and public confidence in it depend on the fullest disclosure of facts consistent with the rules of evidence. To ensure that justice is done, courts must be able to compel witnesses to produce evidence needed by either the prosecution or the defense.

In this case we must balance an interest in ensuring that presidential communications remain private against the court's need for disclosure. We must choose between a policy of disclosure that could imperil the President's capacity to carry out his responsibilities of office and a policy of preserving confidentiality that could impair the court's ability to reach sound judgment.

The interest in preserving confidentiality is entitled to great respect. However, we cannot conclude that the President's advisers will become less candid because in a criminal prosecution a court might infrequently require them to testify about their conversations. And were we to bar such evidence in criminal trials in which it is demonstrably relevant, we would undercut the guarantee of due process of law and gravely impair the courts' basic function. A President's acknowledged need for confidentiality in the communications of his office is general, whereas the court's need for relevant evidence in a criminal proceeding is specific. If the parties do not have access to specific facts, the case may be totally frustrated. When a limited number of conversations have been shown preliminarily to have some bearing on a criminal case, their disclosure will not vitiate the President's broad interest in keeping his communications confidential. . . . The generalized assertion of privilege must yield to the demonstrated, specific need for evidence in a pending criminal trial.

Edit 2: The President's claim to an absolute executive privilege depends on the strength of our historic commitment to "the rule of law," a commitment most profoundly shown in our view that "the twofold aim [of criminal justice] is that guilt shall not escape or innocence suffer." In our system, adversaries must develop all relevant facts and contest all issues. If courts reached judgments without all the facts, criminal justice would be defeated. Integrity of the judicial system and public confidence in it depend on the fullest disclosure of facts consistent with the rules of evidence. Justice requires that courts be empowered to compel witnesses to produce evidence needed by either party.

In this case we must balance two interests: privacy of presidential communications and the court's need for disclosure. We must choose between a policy of disclosure that could imperil the President's capacity to carry out his responsibilities and a policy of preserving confidentiality that could hinder a court from reaching a sound judgment.

We respect the strong interest in preserving confidentiality. However, we cannot conclude that the President's advisers will become more reticent because a court might infrequently require them to testify in a prosecution about their conversations. And barring such demonstrably relevant evidence in criminal trials would undercut the guarantee of due process of law and gravely impair the courts' function. A President's need for confidentiality is general, whereas the court's need for relevant evidence in a prosecution is specific. Without access to specifics, the parties may be totally frustrated and justice thwarted. When preliminarily a few conversations have been shown to bear on a prosecution, their disclosure will not jeopardize the President's general claim of confidentiality. . . . The generalized assertion of privilege must yield to the demonstrated, specific need for evidence in a pending criminal trial.

Commentary: From the original to Edit 2, we sheared off more than 25 percent of the words (from 405 to 297). To do so, we hunted down redundant and windy phrases—for example, "our adversary system of criminal justice," "court of law," "in the communications of his office." We added more precise verbs: "jeopardize" for "vitiate," "respect" for "is entitled to respect." In Edit 1 we untangled sentences but left most of the surplusage undisturbed. After we let some time elapse, we then attacked the verbiage. These edits took time (we spent about an hour getting to Edit 2). For all the changes that are apparent on p. 183, we discussed and discarded as many more changes. In both edits, we strove to preserve the court's tone. Had we chosen to alter the tone and sharply simplify the passage, it would read like this summary (now boiled down to seventy-eight words, a little more than one-sixth of the original):

Summary: The President asserts that his advisers will be circumspect if it is even barely possible that conversations may be disclosed in court. His position is entitled to respect. But his claim is general and cannot outweigh a court's need for specific information that, at least preliminarily, has been shown to be relevant to the pending prosecution. Without all the facts, our adversary system of criminal justice could not work. Public confidence and judicial integrity depend on full disclosure.

Neither Edit 2 nor the summary is the last word on this passage. Only the clock can tell us when to stop, but you should keep editing until time runs out. "We must check our writing right up to the moment of deadline," says James J. Kilpatrick, offering advice that he calls "perhaps the most important of all." We endorse his call for rigorous copyediting and proofreading, as we do so much else in his admirable book *The Writer's Art*. But just a few pages later, referring to a book by Theodore Bernstein on outmoded rules of English usage, Kilpatrick mistakes its title, calling it *Miss Throttlebottom's Hobgoblins*. In fact, the book is titled *Miss Thistlebottom's Hobgoblins*. Bernstein said he gave the book this peculiar name in part because he believed "that a title so hard to pronounce and so hard to remember will be difficult to forget." Kilpatrick's mistake serves as a reminder that no matter how diligently we edit, errors, like stubborn weeds in a garden, infest our prose.

The remedy: Edit again. (For an editing checklist, see p. 225.)

PART IV

Making Your Prose Memorable

CHAPTER 12

Making Your Writing Memorable

Uɴᴛɪʟ ɴᴏᴡ, we have shown how to write acceptable prose—prose more serviceable than that of most lawyers. Apply our principles and you will produce sturdy prose. For most purposes, sustained clarity is sufficient; you will be considered an able writer. But writing is more than clarity and concision. Many would-be painters are adept at drawing; they can draft a cloud or a human form that is technically acceptable. Their finished works, however, are not judged solely by technique but by more subtle considerations of style, feeling, and composition. So tone, voice, and style mark an essay as more than technically proficient. They enable a lawyer to transcend the mundane and make a piece of writing memorable.

I admire Holmes above all legal writers, followed by Robert Jackson and Learned Hand. Of course writing of their quality cannot be taught, but if only lawyers would strive to write clearly and simply, avoiding legal jargon, exaggeration, and polemic, improvement would be vast.

JUDGE RICHARD A. POSNER, 1988

In the twentieth century, a few judges and lawyers have enriched our culture with their words. In writing about free speech, Justice Louis D. Brandeis could have said that "cultures without free speech have reacted negatively to irrational impulses and taken actions that they later, knowing more, might have regretted.'' Instead, he said: ''Men feared witches, and burned women.''

Too often, though, lawyers don't know the difference between prose that soars and prose that sinks. Here is a paragraph lifted from a brief submitted to us as an example of ''good'' lawyerly writing. In this passage, the lawyer is discussing a statute which permits a child's out-of-court statements to be admitted in evidence:

> Despite the facial clarity of the plain words of the above statute, the litigant fares no better than the scholar in searching for a definition of ''corroboration.'' The statute implies that the term is not only susceptible to definition, but indeed, demands that such a definition be expressed in functional operation if the statute is to represent more than precatory words. Absent definition, the statute is a right without a remedy, a tiger without fangs—an osmotic membrane masquerading as a shield for abused children.

The tangled images alone are enough to trip the reader. To show that the legislature has botched the statute, the lawyer should be understated, cool, direct, and should not resort to bombast and purple phrases. Garish images are not the obvious alternative to the gray run of legal prose; just because this kind of language differs from the ordinary does not make it effective.

''Even good writers become infected with the bug of ostentation when they write for courts,'' says Milton Gould, a New York trial lawyer and noted storyteller. ''The older I get, the more I admire succinctness, and the more I despise flash.'' Scott F. Turow, a lawyer and best-selling novelist, counsels the legal writer to strive for ''lucidity and quiet persuasiveness.''

Evan Thomas, Washington bureau chief of *Newsweek*, who spent a summer in the 1970s as an associate at a large law firm in New York, recalls: ''The young lawyers wrote this dense, turgid, overanalyzed convoluted stuff, while many of the older lawyers wrote so simply and clearly that their prose could go on a sports page. For all their verbiage, the young lawyers never got to the point, while the old guys zeroed right in.''

Lawyers are so immersed in the plodding prose of the workaday world that they often confuse an ornate, oily, and overdone tone with good writing. Or they are beguiled by simple or nonlegal expressions and think

> *I have yet to find a poor lawyer who is a good writer. There are some cases of good lawyers who are bad writers, but not many.*
>
> ARTHUR ROVINE, *1987*

that even the pedestrian phrase shines. At one firm we visited, a young associate told us breathlessly that a partner had coined a perfectly marvelous phrase that was, unfortunately, now being rather overused in the firm's brief—it was that good. The phrase: "strikingly similar."

The stuffy tone is not limited to the formal memorandum or brief. Accustomed to flab, the lawyer often finds it difficult to lighten up. Here is the first paragraph of a 1982 fund-raising letter to 30,000 Harvard Law School alumni:

> In preparation for Year 33 of the Annual Giving campaign of the Harvard Law School Fund serious consideration was given as to the amount that should be set for this year's goal. Last year contributions to the Fund from alumni and friends were $3,524,600, a new record amount both overall and in alumni gifts, yet we were $75,400 short of our $3.6 million objective. The setting of this year's goal at $4 million, therefore, represents a formidable challenge.

Burdened by heavy nouns, we slog through the anonymity of the passive construction to find unsociable sentences. That is a strange way to induce people to part with their money, a lot of money, a redundant amount of money, a "new record amount"! This opening paragraph wholly misses its audience; it dwells on the woes of the fund's officers, not on the concerns of the potential givers.

In a more serious matter, a Wisconsin lawyer misjudged his audience in writing a snide open letter to the judges of the state court of appeals, who had affirmed a decision to commit his client to a mental institution. Here's how he began:

> You are probably quite smug about your decision in this case. You were presented with an issue which was admittedly not clear cut and which had a potential impact on a fairly large segment of persons who had been committed under the Wisconsin insanity law. So what did you do? You *think* you managed to avoid de-

ciding the case altogether. Sorry I can't congratulate you on this clever evasion of a precedential statutory interpretation. This may come as something of a shock, but you *didn't* avoid an interpretation of the insanity law with a major impact on this state.

This lawyer misconstrued the meaning of informality. A respectful, colloquial tone might have caught the judges' sympathy; instead, this snide, taunting tone irritated the Wisconsin Supreme Court, which dismissed his petition and noted:

> At a minimum, defense counsel violated a cardinal rule of effective appellate legal writing. The rule is: *"Avoid disparaging lower courts or opposing parties."* At a maximum, some language in the petition may have gone beyond the realm of permissibly zealous advocacy.

Similarly, when judges depart from their pedestrian tone, they often lose control of their language and write opinions memorable only for their silliness, immaturity, or hyperbole. In 1930, Judge M. M. Logan of the Kentucky Court of Appeals dissented from a majority opinion that upheld the dominion of a surface owner over caves that lay beneath his land:

> Let us give thought to the petitioner Edwards, his rights and his predicament, if that is done to him which the circuit judge has directed to be done. Edwards owns this cave through right of discovery, exploration, development, advertising, exhibition, and conquest. Men fought their way through eternal darkness, into the mysterious and abysmal depths of the bowels of a groaning world to discover the theretofore unseen splendors of unknown natural scenic wonders. They were conquerors of fear, although now and then one of them, as did Floyd Collins, paid with his life, for his hardihood in adventuring into the regions where Charon with his boat had never before seen any but the spirits of the departed. They let themselves down by flimsy ropes into pits that seemed bottomless; they clung to scanty handholds as they skirted the brinks of precipices while the flickering flare of their flaming flambeaux disclosed no bottom to the yawning gulf beneath them; they waded through rushing torrents, not knowing what awaited

them on the farther side; they climbed slippery steeps to find other levels; they wounded their bodies on stalagmites and stalactites and other curious and weird formations; they found chambers, star-studded and filled with scintillating light reflected by a phantasmagoria revealing phantoms, and tapestry woven by the toiling gods in the dominion of Erebus. . . . They knew nothing, and cared less, of who owned the surface above; they were in another world where no law forbade their footsteps. They created an underground kingdom where Gulliver's people may have lived or where Ayesha may have found the revolving column of fire in which to bathe meant eternal youth.

And that's not all; Judge Logan was only warming up.

Lest anyone suppose his grand flourishes belonged to an age past, consider two more opinions, both written in the mid-1980s. First, an opinion by Justice Bruce Wright of the Supreme Court in Manhattan, concerning a property dispute. The characters in this drama are a dentist and an assistant who became his lover and then jilted him for another man. This is how Justice Wright begins:

Two young people, cohabiting without the ceremony of a wedding, lived for a time in blissful harmony and trust, confident in the fragile balustrade of an imagined future and its longevity. They plighted a troth without ritual. Wrapped in the drama of their mutual pulse, they were ill-starred. Passionate pilgrims, they had no seer to caution their fall from the grace of doomed affection, or warn that love places its victims on emotional welfare rolls.

Now the prose begins to gallop:

As with the Trojan War, where the heroes of Homer squabbled, some of the symmetry of tragedy crept into the relationship of the parties. Ill-starred lovers have from time immemorial stumbled gloriously among the snares of their own drums. Troilus sighed for the infidelity of Cressida. Pyramus and Thisbe had their midsummer night's mésalliance, as did Othello and Desdemona. There are precedents a-plenty for bitterness and the scathed spirit. . . . Palinurus, wounded by betrayal, wept that, "The object of loving is to end love." Savaged by the treason of uxorial cuckoldry, he

felt, in the words of a poet that "Life goes on, but I don't remember why."

And then, in an abrupt order, Justice Wright denied a motion for a
preliminary injunction, allowing the case to proceed to trial. That's a lot
of erudition to waste on a preliminary motion.

In Chicago, Judge Richard Curry of the Cook County Circuit Court
ruled on the Chicago Cubs' request to install lights in Wrigley Field:

> Baseball, "the national pastime"—the thing of which young boys
> dream and old boys fantasize—the subject of songs, poems, satire,
> ballads and verse—the occupation of heroes and bums—the grist
> for the columnist and the gambler—the avocation of the bystander
> and the theatre for the grandstander—the ballast for the summer
> months and the leaven for the winter months—the theme which
> accommodates both nostalgia and expectation—a game that can
> be played as work, witnessed as fun and memorialized as
> history—a diversion which has developed its own lexicon with
> words such as "bush"; "choke", "whiff"; "balk" (and in Chi-
> cago) Hey! Hey!. . . . In as much as this case is in the domain
> of "everybody's business" its issue should be deliberately stated
> in a manner most likely to attract and hold maximum attention.
> Perhaps something like this:
>
>> Do those who schedule play time for the games of our national
>> pastime have the right to interfere with bedtime by starting the
>> game at nighttime, instead of the customary daytime?

Blithely misspelling his way through sixty-two pages of a little law and
a lot of lore, Judge Curry winds up:

". . . YOU'RE OUT!"

Yes, you're out. O . . . U . . . T. The Cubs are out. The inning
is over. The contest is lost. Now it's time for the box score,
summary and the wrap up. Have you ever heard a postmortem
on a sporting event when some "intangible" wasn't cited as an
element in the victory or the defeat? Well we have one in this
case also. The Cubs lost, of course, for all of the reasons stated
above but, in addition thereto, they should have had a better

scouting report before coming to Court. Everyone around the courthouse is familiar with ''Justice'' with her robes flowing, her blindfold and her scales. What the Cubs' ''book'' on her failed to note is that she is a southpaw. *Justice is a Southpaw* and the Cubs just don't hit lefties!!!

''. . . AT THE OLD BALLGAME''.

Judge Curry's opinion is so overspiced (or overcooked) and his sarcasm so heavy-handed that the plaintiff could justifiably cry foul. (See what happens when you read too much overheated prose?)

Judge Curry evidently meant to be funny. But self-conscious humor by those who cannot control it is puerile. As Justice Benjamin N. Cardozo said in 1925 in his famous essay ''Law and Literature'': ''Flashes of humor are not unknown, yet the form of opinion which aims at humor from beginning to end is a perilous adventure, which can be justified only by success, and even then is likely to find its critics almost as many as its eulogists.'' And as Judge George Rose Smith, of the Arkansas Supreme Court noted in the 1960s: ''Judicial humor is neither judicial nor humorous. A lawsuit is a serious matter to those concerned in it. For a judge to take advantage of his criticism-insulated, retaliation-proof position to display his wit is contemptible, like hitting a man when he's down.''

Probably the worst form of judicial humor is doggerel. In a suit filed by a seaman against a shipowner to recover lost wages, Edward R. Becker, U.S. district judge in Philadelphia, explains why he resorted to verse:

> The motion now before us
> has stirred up a terrible fuss.
> And what is considerably worse,
> it has spawned some preposterous doggerel verse.
>
> Plaintiff's counsel, whose name is Harry Lore,
> read defendant's brief and found it a bore.
> Instead of a reply brief, he acted pretty quick
> and responded with a clever limerick:

> Not to be outdone, the defense took the time
> to reply with their own clever rhyme.
>
> Overwhelmed by this outburst of pure creativity,
> we determined to show an equal proclivity,
> Hence this opinion in the form of verse,
> even if not of the calibre of Saint-John Perse.

A Michigan appeals judge, J. H. Gillis, in upholding a lower-court ruling that denied damages to the owner of a tree rammed by an automobile, began his opinion:

> We thought that we would never see
> A suit to compensate a tree.

It does not take much literary sensibility to see that these opinions are not even good doggerel. Judges Becker and Gillis do damage both to justice and the memories of Joyce Kilmer, Ogden Nash, and other versifiers who controlled the form of their expression. What makes these opinions so demeaning is not so much that they are lighthearted but that they unsuccessfully ape a literary form to which they are unsuited, at the expense of the litigants.

Humor can have its place if it emerges from substance rather than form. A pro se plaintiff sought damages in Judge Gerald J. Weber's court against "Satan and His Staff" for placing "deliberate obstacles in his path." Judge Weber, of the Western District of Pennsylvania, could have dismissed the case peremptorily or responded with a derisive opinion. Instead, he chose to treat the plaintiff with dignity, and the opinion that resulted is dry and understated. Here is a portion of Judge Weber's solution:

> We question whether plaintiff may obtain personal jurisdiction
> over the defendant in this judicial district. The complaint contains
> no allegations of residence in this district. While the official re-
> ports disclose no case where this defendant appeared as defendant
> there is an unofficial account of a trial in New Hampshire where
> this defendant filed an account of mortgage foreclosure as plaintiff.
> The defendant in that action was represented by the preeminent

advocate of that day, and raised the defense that the plaintiff was a foreign prince with no standing to sue in an American Court. This defense was overcome by overwhelming evidence to the contrary. Whether or not this would raise an estoppel in the present case we are unable to determine at this time.

Judge Weber is funny with a straight face. Wry humor is difficult for even the best stand-up comics, who can call on body and facial expressions; it's far more difficult for a writer, especially one writing in the legal tradition. Nevertheless, wit deftly used elevates a passage to make it memorable. Here's Judge Frank R. Easterbrook of the U.S. Court of Appeals for the Seventh Circuit in Chicago, one of the youngest federal appeals judges in the country:

> Morton Goldsmith was the head of a chain of clinics and pharmacies, many flying the banner of Drug Industry Consultants, Inc. (DIC). Between 1981 and 1984 DIC's clinics and pharmacies, and those of associated enterprises, prescribed and sold large quantities of codeine-based cough syrups to addicts. The clinics were selective. To be a patient, you had to have a Medicaid card. Not necessarily yours; anyone's would do. The Medicaid card was the key to DIC's profits.

Self-deprecating wit helped Supreme Court Justice Robert H. Jackson blunt the embarrassment of disavowing a position he had taken as attorney general a few years earlier. In an elegant paragraph into which he skillfully wove quotations, Jackson wrote what has become almost the standard apology for judges who must retract or lawyers who must backtrack:

> I concur in the judgment and opinion of the Court. But since it is contrary to an opinion which, as Attorney General, I rendered in 1940, I owe some word of explanation. I am entitled to say of that opinion what any discriminating reader must think of it— that it was as foggy as the statute the Attorney General was asked to interpret. . . . Precedent, however, is not lacking for ways by which a judge may recede from a prior opinion that has proven untenable and perhaps misled others. See Chief Justice Taney recanting views he had pressed upon the Court as Attorney General of Maryland. Baron Bramwell extricated himself from a somewhat

similar embarrassment by saying, "The matter does not appear to me now as it appears to have appeared to me then." And Mr. Justice Story, accounting for his contradiction of his own former position, quite properly put the matter: "My own error, however, can furnish no ground for its being adopted by this Court. . . ." Perhaps Dr. Johnson really went to the heart of the matter when he explained a blunder in his dictionary—"Ignorance, sir, ignorance." But an escape less self-depreciating was taken by Lord Westbury, who, it is said, rebuffed a barrister's reliance upon an earlier opinion of his Lordship: "I can only say that I am amazed that a man of my intelligence should have been guilty of such an opinion." If there are other ways of gracefully and good naturedly surrendering former views to a better considered position, I invoke them all.

Quoting this paragraph years later to justify his own repudiation of an earlier opinion, California Justice Stanley Mosk appended a memorable line written by Supreme Court Justice Wiley Rutledge, who also had had occasion to change his mind: "Wisdom too often never comes, and so one ought not to reject it merely because it comes late."

Jackson adroitly adapts his tone to solve the problem he faced: how to apologize for errors while retaining his dignity and authority. The reader, after all, might suppose that if he was wrong once, as he admits, he might be wrong even now. Jackson's tone serves to disarm the reader. A man who can publicly concede his sins, without false humility or obsequious servility, is absolved of blame. In invoking great men of the past who had confessed to similar errors in similar ways, in acknowledging the fallibility of mature adults, Jackson is never reduced to sniggering or self-abasement. He manages to amuse the reader without detracting from his solemn underlying message: Trust me now.

Tone is bottled in no formula. An appropriate tone depends on your audience and your sense of self. In choosing a tone, you always have options: reserved or casual, solemn or whimsical, serious or ironic, sober or sarcastic, genuine or sycophantic. But you should not confuse your tone with the seriousness of your purpose, because as a lawyer you are always serious. Mark Twain's tone was always comic, his purpose usually serious. Because a quarrel seems trivial, it need not be dismissed by a joke. Nor does a case with large stakes compel a solemn tone. Look how

U.S. District Judge William C. Conner in Manhattan deflates the pretensions of the litigants:

> The lawsuit represents a major battle in an endless war between two titans of the over-the-counter ("OTC") drug industry, in which each accuses the other of falsity in its advertising claims of efficacy and safety. Small nations have fought for their very survival with less resources and resourcefulness than these antagonists have brought to their epic struggle for commercial primacy in the OTC analgesic field.

Tone is embedded in every piece of writing. Formality and dullness are tones as much as a cool wit or a heart-tugging narrative. You cannot escape tone; you can only hope to strike the proper one for your purposes. The choice lies not simply between the dull and the extravagant. Tone, like style, ranges across a spectrum between these extremes.

The tone of a work should not be confused with its style. Much of this book has been concerned with questions of style: of long sentences or short, of fancy words or plain, of active doers or passive agents, of points made directly or hinted at. The spare style is often identified with Ernest Hemingway, an author who started as a journalist and whom many legal writing specialists suggest emulating. This advice angers others, who say that what Hemingway did is not what lawyers ought to do.

Hemingway deserves better. His name is bandied about, without analysis, to stand for two distinct propositions: (1) Lawyers should (or should not) write in a spare style. (2) Lawyers should (or should not) narrate stories about real people rather than abstractly expound legal concepts. The debate is oversimplified. Proponents and opponents of Hemingway rarely join issue. We advocate a spare style, without at the same time suggesting that lawyers imitate Hemingway. Although lawyers and judges sometimes speak in high levels of abstractions, at other times the circumstances call for a narrative approach. It disserves Hemingway, and lawyers, to suppose that questions of style and storytelling are "either-or" propositions. Too often, lawyers forget that the best way to engage their audience is to tell stories. Reflecting on hundreds of petitions for certiorari that he reads each year, Stephen Wermiel of the *Wall Street Journal* says: "It strikes me that lawyers feel no need to make their cases

sound interesting. And I think that is a serious error. . . . The justices
need to have their interest captured just as much as I do.''

Here's Judge John R. Brown, a widely admired judge of the U.S.
Court of Appeals for the Fifth Circuit, telling a story, as he begins an
opinion about a collision between two vehicles on a navigable waterway:

> It was a dark and stormy night. A patchy, low-lying fog covered
> the murky waters of the river and obscured the banks. Ships,
> passing in the night, were but phantoms, vague outlines disap-
> pearing into the mist. Ships' whistles, echoing across the dark
> expanse, seemed like mournful cries from another world. Then
> suddenly, looming out of the darkness, another ship appeared.
> The distance was too small; time too short; before anyone could
> do more than cry out, the unthinkable occurred. The ships col-
> lided. The tug, helpless, drifted downriver. Floundering like some
> giant behemoth wounded in battle, the tanker came to ground and
> impaled itself on some voracious underwater obstruction. And
> still the whistles, echoing, seemed like cries from another world.*

The style of this passage may be too flamboyant for some tastes, but
compared to a straightforward, abstract beginning—"Two vessels, one
large and one small, were involved in a waterway collision on an evening
of inclement weather"—it leads to fuller understanding of the issues.

Another judge, Donald Burnett, of the Idaho Court of Appeals, affects
the taut style favored by mystery writers. Here he begins in what might
be called an "opinion *noir*" style:

---

*Judge Brown's opening sentence parodies by repeating the famous line that opens Edward
George Earle Bulwer-Lytton's novel *Paul Clifford* (1830). The Bulwer-Lytton sentence is
a literary cliché that has even spawned a contest sponsored by an English professor at San
Jose State University in California. Contestants are asked to submit the worst opening
sentence of a terrible novel, mocking Bulwer-Lytton's imagery. The 1986 winner, Patricia
Presutti, wrote:

> The bone-chilling scream split the warm summer night in two, the first half being
> before the scream when it was fairly balmy and calm and pleasant, the second
> half still balmy and quite pleasant for those who hadn't heard the scream at all,
> but not calm or balmy or even very nice for those who did hear the scream,
> discounting the little period of time during the actual scream itself when your ears
> might have been hearing it but your brain wasn't reacting yet to let you know.

It was a shotgun blast in the early morning that killed Merardo Rodriguez. As he lay on the floor of his house, his wife placed a pillow beneath his head and watched him die.

This direct, matter-of-fact tone is immediate and forceful. The story flows without digression, and no muddy phrases distort the reader's view. The direct tone, used effectively by Judge Burnett, works well in narrative but is not limited to storytelling.

Dissenting from the majority's decision to permit life-support equipment to be turned off, Judge Joseph R. Nolan of the Massachusetts Supreme Judicial Court restrains his anger, letting his understated prose make a compelling point with an economy of words. His points are substantive, not rhetorical; his facts are expressed in nouns and verbs, not adverbs and adjectives:

> In the forum of ethics, despite the opinion's high-blown language to the contrary, the court today has endorsed euthanasia and suicide. Suicide is direct self-destruction and is intrinsically evil. No set of circumstances can make it moral. Paul Brophy will die as a direct result of the cessation of feeding. The ethical principle of double effect is totally inapplicable here. This death by dehydration and starvation has been approved by the court. He will not die from the aneurysm which precipitated loss of consciousness, the surgery which was performed, the brain damage that followed or the insertion of the G-tube. He will die as a direct result of the refusal to feed him. He will starve to death.

As these examples suggest, eloquence comes more from simplicity than from a profusion of lush and overblown words learned once just before you took the college boards. Long words and dandified phrases deaden rather than enlighten. In a remarkable commencement address at Yale Law School in 1979, Professor Leon S. Lipson ended his speech with a four-minute exhortation written and spoken entirely in words of one syllable. Here are some of those remarks:

> On this day, or soon, you will take leave of this yard, these halls, and us. We wish you well. As your Sage for a Day, coaxed to

preach if not to teach, I ought to send you on your way with great store of wise and shrewd saws, short sharp tools that I should put in your hands for you to wield so as to carve a good and full life from the wild lush fields of the law.

But I know that you did not wait to hear this from me, or till now. You made haste to shop for those tools as soon as you came here. In the past three years, or—as it may be—two or one, you have learned some facts and some law; you have made some friends, young and not so young and not so old and old, learned from them and they from you; in class and in your rooms, with your friends or by your own lone selves, you have picked a few books to bits, page by page, case by case, line by line. Your brains are stocked with rules clear or dim, with thoughts keen or dull, some of them your own; you have heard much of rights and wrongs, of courts and boards and jails, of new ways to tax the rich or help the poor or plead to a charge or bust the trusts or split the stock or cut the pie, and why not to; your ears are cocked to catch (if not to heed) the still small voice of truth, and your eyes are strained to spy out a star to steer by.

As you lead your life in the law, we hope you will do good, grow wise, and thrive. In the years to come, think of us now and then. Come back to see us when you can, and more than once if you can. Let us hear from you words of your feats of skill and works of art. . . .

As you grow more and more skilled in *what* you do, and as you ask *why* you do what you do, we trust that on the whole we here shall prove to have meant much more to you: more as the time goes on, and not least when you have no thought of us at all, for, will you nill you, you will bear—all the rest of your life—the stamp, or brand, or blaze, of the Yale Law School.

Professor Lipson's talk is memorable more for its entirety, as a tour de force, than for any single line. But sometimes one memorable line can elevate an otherwise mundane brief. A single sentence in legal discourse can powerfully affect the outcome or recast or transform the debate. A few years ago, for example, Irwin Rochman, a defense lawyer serving as a special state prosecutor in New York, spent several hours composing a single sentence. The name Attica, he wrote, "should be a symbol not only of riot and death, but also of the capacity of our system of criminal justice to redress its own wrong." Rochman had two goals:

to persuade a judge to dismiss the remaining indictments stemming from the prison uprising in 1971 and, secondarily, to have the *New York Times* choose his sentence as its quotation of the day. He was doubly successful.

The power of clear statement is the great power at the bar.

DANIEL WEBSTER, 1849

Every lawyer should strive for one original, memorable sentence in every document, the sentence that the judge will borrow from your brief, perhaps the sentence that will be quoted by journalists who read your brief. This kind of writing is not easy, but if they are to be remembered, sentences must sound as though they were composed effortlessly. Examine these memorable sentences:

Justice Cardozo: "The criminal is to go free because the constable has blundered."

Justice Holmes: "The most stringent expressions of free speech would not protect a man in falsely shouting fire in a theater and causing a panic." (This is one of the most widely quoted and *misquoted* lines of a judge. The word "falsely" is frequently— and perhaps corruptly—omitted, changing Holmes's meaning entirely.)

Justice Thurgood Marshall, addressing the standard of review in equal-protection cases: "A sign that says 'men only' looks very different on a bathroom door than a courthouse door."

The power of these sentences lies in their earthiness. Here are no words of art, no foreign terms, no polysyllabic tongue twisters. The words are plain, homespun, evocative. They paint a picture that encapsulates a truth as the writer perceives it and that makes it easier for the doubters to swallow their doubts. It is not coincidental that these lines were penned by justices who dissented, for in dissent lies freedom to speak one's mind.

Whether or not these judges were born with the capacity to write memorable lines, it is a skill for which all writers can strive. The training required is to be well-read. From what we hear, few lawyers are. Milton S. Gould said: "In my view good writing requires more than mental skills; it requires exposure to the substance of human experience in history and literature and in general science." Speaking of the lawyers his office hires, he said bluntly: "Mostly they are half-educated—literary and historical allusions make no impression because they know nothing about literature or history." David M. Brodsky noted that his firm, Schulte, Roth & Zabel, has a book club "which is our attempt to introduce good literature to persons in the firm, yet sadly, few people attend."

The best way to prepare for the law is to come to the study of law as a well-read person. Thus alone can one acquire the capacity to use the English language on paper and in speech and with the habits of clear thinking which only a truly liberal education can give.

JUSTICE FELIX FRANKFURTER, 1954

We have tested the proposition that lawyers don't read well, or widely, by asking students and lawyers in workshops we have conducted to read several passages from great literature. One of these is a brilliant, evocative paragraph by Loren Eiseley, the finest American science writer of his time. The short excerpt from *Darwin's Century* discusses the discovery of geological time that prepared the way for the theory of evolution:

Like the fabulous western isles the idea [of evolution] would be coasted at first through dangerous intellectual waters. It would be termed a phantom, a figment of man's restless imagination. It would be labeled like a sea monster "blasphemous," "illusory," and "godless." Finally it would lie there under the lifting fog-wisps which had so long obscured the human vision, a country of wraiths and changelings among whom was to be counted man himself. Time such as humanity had never dreamed before lay across that world. It was a land where water wore away the shapes of mountains, and the great bones and carapaces of vanished beasts lay hoar and rime-frosted in deep crevices and canyons.

With only a handful of exceptions, the 500 students and young lawyers whom we have asked to read this paragraph turned up their noses. The most common complaint: It's too abstract! So immersed are these people in their professional literature that they have little capacity to be moved by a style alien to them. Eiseley paints a vivid, image-laden picture about a highly abstract concept; the paragraph is a model of its kind. The distaste of young lawyers for Eiseley's style suggests a hardening of intellectual faculties, a lack of imagination, and a narrow vision of professional responsibilities. Lawyers who do not read, either for pleasure or from duty, are assembly-line mechanics and derelict in their responsibility to minister to human concerns.

[Lawyers possess] a peculiar Cant and Jargon of their own, that no other Mortal can understand.

JONATHAN SWIFT, 1726

Over the years, gifted advocates and judges have set forth great thoughts in single sentences or clusters of sentences. We offer several examples:

Chief Justice John Marshall

We must never forget that it is a *constitution* we are expounding.

The first Justice John Marshall Harlan, dissenting (using a phrase taken from the brief by Albion Tourgee, the losing plaintiff's lawyer):

Our Constitution is color-blind, and neither knows nor tolerates classes among citizens.

Justice Oliver Wendell Holmes

[W]hen men have realized that time has upset many fighting faiths, they may come to believe even more than they believe the very foundations of their own conduct that the ultimate good desired is better reached by free trade in ideas—that the best test of truth is the power of the thought to get itself accepted in the competition of the market, and that truth is the only ground upon which their wishes safely can be carried out.

Every idea is an incitement. . . . Eloquence may set fire to reason.

Justice Benjamin N. Cardozo

Immunities that are valid against the federal government by force of the specific pledges of particular amendments have been found to be implicit in the concept of ordered liberty, and thus, through the Fourteenth Amendment, become valid as against the states.

Judge Learned Hand

Anticipation as such cannot invalidate a copyright. Borrowed the work must indeed not be, for a plagiarist is not himself pro tanto an "author"; but if by some magic a man who had never known it were to compose anew Keats's Ode on a Grecian Urn, he would be an "author," and, if he copyrighted it, others might not copy that poem, though they might of course copy Keats's.

Justice Robert H. Jackson

[If] there is any fixed star in our constitutional constellation, it is that no official, high or petty, can prescribe what shall be orthodox in politics, nationalism, religion, or other matters of opinion or force citizens to confess by word or act their faith therein.

If it is interstate commerce that feels the pinch, it does not matter how local the operation which applies the squeeze.

We are not final because we are infallible, but we are infallible only because we are final.

Chief Justice Earl Warren

Legislators represent people, not trees or acres. Legislators are elected by voters, not farms or cities or economic interests.

Justice William O. Douglas

We deal with a right of privacy older than the Bill of Rights. [Marriage] is a coming together for better or worse, hopefully enduring, and intimate to the degree of being sacred. It is an association that promotes a way of life, not causes; a harmony in living, not political faiths; a bilateral loyalty, not commercial or social projects. Yet it is an association for as noble a purpose as any involved in our prior decisions.

These passages are simply and concisely stated, vivid, and supply fresh ways of looking at commonplace issues. Search the vocabularies of these writers: You will not need a dictionary to understand the thought, nor a thesaurus to sharpen the image. Words are not wasted, nor sentences prolonged. Most illustrate the abstraction with a concrete and unexpected image—what could better evoke irrationality than the belief in witches or the immolation of women; what could better describe the ideals of equality than the homespun picture of a color-blind constitution?

The Great Legal Writers

The passages just quoted are the most memorable words of lawyers who are among the best writers in our legal tradition. Our respondents agreed, naming many of the judges just quoted as their favorite legal writers. Unscientific though our survey might have been, we think the answers are revealing. The top eight were Oliver Wendell Holmes, Jr., Benjamin N. Cardozo, Learned Hand, Robert H. Jackson, Henry J. Friendly, Louis D. Brandeis, the second John Marshall Harlan, and Laurence H. Tribe. Because each has a distinctive voice, the appeal of these writers is not universal. For example, some respondents put Cardozo on a least admired list. Many well-read lawyers explicitly said they could think of *no* admirable legal writers.

Holmes and Brandeis, though, do endure. Anthony Lewis of the *New York Times*, widely regarded as the best contemporary writer about law, puts them at the top of his list. "No one today comes close," he says. He calls Brandeis's concurring opinion in *Whitney v. California* the "greatest single piece of legal writing I know." Read the following central passage from that opinion slowly. Look at the words Brandeis chooses, particularly the verbs. Watch how the topics of each sentence connect. Notice the lengths of sentences, and ask whether even the long ones are difficult

to grasp. Above all, heed the reasonable, measured tone. Justice Brandeis
is not braying, he is persuading:

> Those who won our independence believed that the final end of
> the State was to make men free to develop their faculties; and
> that in its government the deliberative forces should prevail over
> the arbitrary. They valued liberty both as an end and as a means.
> They believed liberty to be the secret of happiness and courage
> to be the secret of liberty. They believed that freedom to think
> as you will and to speak as you think are means indispensable to
> the discovery and spread of political truth; that without free speech
> and assembly discussion would be futile; that with them, discus-
> sion affords ordinarily adequate protection against the dissemi-
> nation of noxious doctrine; that the greatest menace to freedom
> is an inert people; that public discussion is a public duty; and that
> this should be a fundamental principle of the American govern-
> ment. They recognized the risks to which all human institutions
> are subject. But they knew that order cannot be secured merely
> through fear of punishment for its infraction; that it is hazardous
> to discourage thought, hope and imagination; that fear breeds
> repression; that repression breeds hate; that hate menaces stable
> government; that the path of safety lies in the opportunity to
> discuss freely supposed grievances and proposed remedies; and
> that the fitting remedy for evil counsels is good ones. Believing
> in the power of reason as applied through public discussion, they
> eschewed silence coerced by law—the argument of force in its
> worst form. Recognizing the occasional tyrannies of governing
> majorities, they amended the Constitution so that free speech and
> assembly should be guaranteed.
>
> Fear of serious injury alone cannot justify suppression of free
> speech and assembly. Men feared witches and burned women. It
> is the function of speech to free men from the bondage of irrational
> fears. To justify suppression of free speech there must be rea-
> sonable ground to fear that serious evil will result if free speech
> is practiced. There must be reasonable ground to believe that the
> evil to be prevented is a serious one. Every denunciation of ex-
> isting law tends in some measure to increase the probability that
> there will be violation of it. Condonation of a breach enhances
> the probability. Expressions of approval add to the probability.
> Propagation of the criminal state of mind by teaching syndicalism
> increases it. Advocacy of lawbreaking heightens it still further.

But even advocacy of violation, however reprehensible morally, is not a justification for denying free speech where the advocacy falls short of incitement and there is nothing to indicate that the advocacy would be immediately acted on. The wide difference between advocacy and incitement, between preparation and attempt, between assembling and conspiracy, must be borne in mind. . . .

Those who won our independence by revolution were not cowards. They did not fear political change. They did not exalt order at the cost of liberty. To courageous, self-reliant men, with confidence in the power of free and fearless reasoning applied through the processes of popular government, no danger flowing from speech can be deemed clear and present, unless the incidence of the evil apprehended is so imminent that it may befall before there is opportunity for full discussion. If there be time to expose through discussion the falsehood and fallacies, to avert the evil by the processes of education, the remedy to be applied is more speech, not enforced silence. Only an emergency can justify repression. Such must be the rule if authority is to be reconciled with freedom. Such, in my opinion, is the command of the Constitution.

Next consider Holmes's dissent in *United States v. Schwimmer*, which Lewis says is "close to poetry in its density." Like Brandeis, Holmes uses short, familiar words and connects his thoughts without wasteful transitions or windy phrases. He, too, speaks in a mild manner that strengthens the force of his argument. He is not being disagreeable; how can one disagree with him? Of course, in time, no one did: This dissenting opinion is now enshrined in our law.

The applicant seems to be a woman of superior character and intelligence, obviously more than ordinarily desirable as a citizen of the United States. It is agreed that she is qualified for citizenship except so far as the views set forth in a statement of facts "may show that the applicant is not attached to the principles of the Constitution of the United States and well disposed to the good order and happiness of the same, and except in so far as the same may show that she cannot take the oath of allegiance without a mental reservation." The views referred to are an extreme opinion in favor of pacifism and a statement that she would not bear arms to defend the Constitution. So far as the adequacy of her oath is concerned, I hardly can see how that is affected by the statement, inasmuch as she is a woman over fifty years of age, and would not be allowed to bear arms if she wanted to. And as to the opinion the whole examination of the applicant shows that she holds none of the now-dreaded creeds, but thoroughly believes in organized government and prefers that of the United States to any other in the world. Surely it cannot show lack of attachment to the principles of the Constitution that she thinks that it can be improved. I suppose that most intelligent people think that it might be. Her particular improvement looking to the abolition of war seems to me not materially different in its bearing on this case from a wish to establish cabinet government as in England, or a single house, or one term of seven years for the President. To touch a more burning question, only a judge mad with partisanship would exclude because the applicant thought that the 18th Amendment should be repealed.

Of course, the fear is that if a war came the applicant would exert activities such as were dealt with in Schenck v. United States. But that seems to me unfounded. Her position and motives are wholly different from those of Schenck. She is an optimist and states in strong and, I do not doubt, sincere words her belief that war will disappear and that the impending destiny of mankind is to unite in peaceful leagues. I do not share that optimism nor do I think that a philosophic view of the world would regard war as absurd. But most people who have known it regard it with horror, as a last resort, and, even if not yet ready for cosmopolitan efforts, would welcome any practicable combinations that would increase the power on the side of peace. The notion that the applicant's optimistic anticipations would make her a worse citizen is sufficiently answered by her examination, which seems to me a better argument for her admission than any that I can offer. Some of her answers might excite popular prejudice, but if there is any principle of the Constitution that more imperatively calls for attachment than any other it is the principle of free thought —not free thought for those who agree with us but for freedom for the thought that we hate. I think that we should adhere to that principle with regard to admission into, as well as to life within, this country. And, recurring to the opinion that bars this applicant's way, I would suggest that the Quakers have done their share to make the country what it is, that many citizens agree with the applicant's belief, and that I had not supposed hitherto that we regretted our inability to expel them because they believe more than some of us do in the teachings of the Sermon on the Mount.

Our survey responses on good writing were weighted against lawyers writing today. Judges such as Holmes and Brandeis are staples of literary excellence, known to everyone and studied by everyone. There is always a time lag before contemporary writing, of any age, is admitted to the canon. It's hard to be an icon when you are alive. Moreover, the number of lawyers writing today is vastly greater than in any age past, and it is therefore more difficult for a consensus to emerge.

Many strong, effective writers practice today. Jay Topkis of New York is confident enough of his abilities that he does not fear bucking a traditionalism that calls for "questions presented" to be stated only in the form of a question. Watch how Topkis builds up to his questions presented with a simple narrative statement:

QUESTIONS PRESENTED

For 64 years, ASCAP has offered the "blanket" license to commercial users of copyrighted music—the same blanket license which is the standard license in all nations of the world which recognize copyright. Since 1941, ASCAP has been required to offer such licenses by consent decrees with the Department of Justice in *United States v. ASCAP*, an antitrust case in the Southern District of New York.

The Court of Appeals for the Second Circuit has now held in this action that the blanket license constitutes price-fixing, that it is *per se* illegal under Section 1 of the Sherman Act, and that ASCAP's members misused their copyrights merely by offering an ASCAP blanket license to plaintiff CBS for its television network.

The Court of Appeals reached this extreme result only by expanding the *per se* doctrine far beyond the bounds sanctioned by this Court and in square conflict with decisions of the Ninth Circuit.

If the decision below is allowed to stand, the sure result will be years of turmoil in the music licensing business in the United States and around the world, confusion in the trial and appellate

courts charged with administering the antitrust laws, and a flood
of new litigation.

To avoid these consequences, we urge this Court to grant
certiorari to decide the following questions:

> 1. When individual sellers are willing and free to negotiate
> individual prices for their individual products in individual ne-
> gotiations, does their simultaneous offer of a package of all of
> their products through a common sales agent at a negotiated price
> constitute price-fixing which is *per se* violative of Section 1 of
> the Sherman Act?

This writing is so clear that even readers unlettered in the law can follow
the problem and understand the issue he wanted the Court to resolve.
From the start, the brief escorts the judges along a road that leads only
to Topkis's destination. By the end, it seems self-evident, as Topkis
argued later in his brief, that the lower court had "declared that the entire
artistic and economic community of music writers and publishers in this
country and the rest of the world—from Aaron Copland to Roberta Flack
to Sir Ralph Vaughan Williams to Edith Piaf—are price-fixers and guilty
of copyright misuse because of their membership in, or relation to,
ASCAP." And obviously that's preposterous. Who could suppose that
any of these were price-fixers? Not the justices of the Supreme Court,
which granted certiorari, reversed the court of appeals, and rendered a
decision in Topkis's favor.

> *Whene'er you speak, remember every cause*
> *Stands not on eloquence, but stands on laws:*
> *Pregnant in matter, in expression brief,*
> *Let every sentence stand with bold belief;*
> *On trifling points not time or talents waste,*
> *A sad offense to learning and to taste;*
> *Nor deal with pompous phrase, nor e'er suppose*
> *Poetic flights belong to reasoning prose.*
>   JOSEPH STORY, NINETEENTH CENTURY

We asked our respondents to send or cite examples of elegant, amusing, or bad legal writing. We received scores of examples, some of which

we have used in this book. Several judges called our attention to *United States of America v. Janet Leslie Cooper Byrnes*, a 1981 opinion of the Second Circuit. The author of the opinion is William Hughes Mulligan, a leading wit and toastmaster of the New York bar. *United States v. Byrnes* was his last opinion before leaving the bench for private practice. Mulligan, too, sent the opinion along, with this caveat: "Fairly amusing, though inelegant, and maybe overdone." This is how he begins:

> Who knows what evil lurks in the hearts of men? Although the public is generally aware of the sordid trafficking of drugs and aliens across our borders, this litigation alerts us to a nefarious practice hitherto unsuspected even by this rather calloused bench—rare bird smuggling. The appeal is therefore accurately designated as *rara avis*. While Canadian geese have been regularly crossing, exiting, reentering and departing our borders with impunity, and apparently without documentation, to enjoy more salubrious climes, those unwilling or unable to make the flight either because of inadequate wing spans, lack of fuel or fear of buck shot, have become prey to unscrupulous traffickers who put them in crates and ship them to American ports of entry with fraudulent documentation in violation of a host of federal statutes. The traffic has been egregious enough to warrant the empaneling of a special grand jury in 1979 in the Northern District of New York to conduct a broad investigation of these activities. Even the services of the Royal Canadian Mounted Police were mustered to aid the inquiry.

After a trial, a California woman was convicted of falsely testifying about her role in bringing into this country, with spurious entry papers, four trumpeter swans and two red-breasted geese. Judge Mulligan has a good time describing what happened at the grand jury and at trial. Like Will Rogers, he wryly comments on the facts as he leads the reader along. For example:

> No birds have been indicted and there is no indication in the record that they were even aware of, much less participated in, the criminal activity unearthed by the grand jury. They were at least as innocent as the horses whose jockeys were bribed to discourage their best efforts at Pocono Downs. . . .

The trumpeter swan makes a noise described by a trial witness, Cherie Perie, as "*weird.*" The appellant, on the other hand, in her grand jury testimony, stated that the male trumpeter during courtship "struts around with his neck and head held high and makes this marvelous little trumpeting sound." . . . *De gustibus.* The mute apparently courts in silence.

After a further learned discussion of birds and precedents, here is how Judge Mulligan ends:

The judgment of conviction is affirmed, justice has triumphed and this is my swan song.

And ours.

END NOTES

Chapter 1: Does Bad Writing Really Matter?

Page 4: Judge Alvin Klein: *Manhattan Lawyer*, Nov. 3–9, 1987, p. 9.

Page 7: George D. Gopen, "The State of Legal Writing: *Res Ipsa Loquitur*," 86 *Michigan L. Rev.* 333, 342–343 (Nov. 1987).

Chapter 2: Don't Make It Like It Was

Page 15: Fortescue: Cited in David Mellinkoff, *The Language of the Law* (Boston: Little, Brown, 1963), p. v.

Page 15: The hapless plaintiff with his head in the pleadings is recounted by Mellinkoff, ibid., p. 191.

Page 15: Chief Justice Hale quoted in Mellinkoff, ibid., p. 190; Bacon quoted p. 193.

Page 15: Jonathan Swift, *Gulliver's Travels*, in *The Writings of Jonathan Swift*, ed. by Robert A. Greenberg and William Bowman Piper (New York: W. W. Norton, 1973), p. 217.

Page 15: Jeremy Bentham, 3 Bentham *Works* 260 (Bowring ed. 1843); quoted in Mellinkoff, ibid., p. 262.

Page 15: Henry Fielding, *Tim Vinegar*, in 1 *The Champion* 127 (Dec. 25, 1739); quoted in Mellinkoff, ibid., p. 193.

Page 16: Jefferson, letter to Joseph C. Cabell, Sept. 9, 1817, in 17 *The Writings of Thomas Jefferson* 417–18 (Lipscomb ed. 1905), quoted in Mellinkoff, ibid., p. 253.

Page 16: Urban A. Lavery, "The Language of the Law," 7 *A.B.A.J.* 277, 283 (1921).

Page 16: Karl N. Llewellyn, "On What Is Wrong with So-Called Legal Education" 35 *Columbia L. Rev.* 651, 660 (1935).

Page 16: Fred Rodell, "Goodbye to Law Reviews," 23 *Virginia L. Rev.* 38 (1936).

Page 17: William L. Prosser, "English as She Is Wrote," 7 *J. Leg. Ed.* 155, 156 (1954); originally published in 28 *English J.* 38 (1939).

Page 17: Prosser, final exam excerpt: ibid. at 158.

Page 17: Arthur T. Vanderbilt, "A Report on Prelegal Education," 25 *N.Y.U. L. Rev.* 199, 209 (1950).

Page 18: Dean William Warren: "Fifty-Second Annual Meeting A.A.L.L.," 52 *L. Library J.* 341 (1959).

Page 18: Carl McGowan, "Law and the Use of Language," 47 *A.B.A.J.* 897, 900 (1961).

Page 20: Lawrence M. Friedman, "Law and Its Language," 33 *George Washington L. Rev.* 563, 567, 568 (1964).

Page 20: Robert W. Benson, on "strange style": "The End of Legalese: The Game Is Over," 13 *R. L. & Soc. Change* 519, 522 (1984–1985).

Page 21: Norbert Wiener, *The Human Use of Human Beings* (Garden City, N.Y.: Doubleday Anchor Books, 1954), p. 107.

Page 21: *Brown v. Board of Education* II, 349 U.S. 294 (1955).

Page 21: The complete recall notice: "A defect which involves the possible failure of a frame support plate may exist on your vehicle. This plate (front suspension pivot bar support plate) connects a portion of the front suspension to the vehicle frame, and its failure could affect vehicle directional control, particularly during heavy brake application. In addition, your vehicle may require adjustment service to the hood secondary catch system. The secondary catch may be misaligned so that the hood may not be adequately restrained to prevent hood fly-up in the event the primary latch is inadvertently left unengaged. Sudden hood fly-up beyond the secondary catch while driving could impair driver visibility. In certain circumstances, occurrence of either of the above conditions could result in vehicle crash without prior warning."

Page 22: "Herein" and "whereas" not precise: Mellinkoff, ibid., pp. 315, 321.

Page 23: Steven Stark, "Why Lawyers Can't Write," 97 *Harv. L. Rev.* 1389 (1984).

Page 23: Fred Rodell, *Woe Unto You, Lawyers* (New York: Reynal and Hitchcock, 1939; Pageant-Poseidon, 1957; Berkley, 1961), pp. 16, 17.

Page 23: Lawrence M. Friedman, ibid., p. 564.

Page 24: Mark Matthewson, "Verbatim," *Student Lawyer*, January 1988, p. 7.

Page 24: Holmes on Henry IV: "The Path of the Law," 10 *Harv. L. Rev.* 457, 469 (1897).

Page 24: Friedman, ibid., p. 571.

Page 25: Peter Lubin, "Happy Hereinafter," *The New Republic*, Apr. 11, 1988, p. 14.

Page 25: Mellinkoff, on the typewriter creating verbosity, ibid., p. 261.

Page 25: Mellinkoff on data retrieval, ibid., p. 403.

Page 26: Carl McGowan, "Lawyers and the Uses of Language," 47 *A.B.A.J.* 900 (Sept. 1961).

Page 27: Steven Stark, ibid., p. 1389.

Page 27: Richard Hyland, "In Defense of Legal Writing," 134 *Univ. of Pennsylvania L. Rev.* 599 (1986).

Page 27: Hyland, ibid., p. 608.

Page 28: "The Writing Gap," *Yale Alumni Magazine*, Jan. 1976, p. 16.

Pages 28–29: A. Bartlett Giamatti, on cultural longings: "Sentimentality," *Yale Alumni Magazine*, Jan. 1976, pp. 17–19.

Page 29: Jacques Barzun, "English As She's Not Taught," reprinted in *On Writing, Editing, and Publishing* (Chicago: University of Chicago Press, 1971), p. 19.

Page 29: Royal Society and Dryden: Jacob Bronowski and Bruce Mazlish, *The Western Intellectual Tradition* (New York: Harper Torchbooks, 1962), p. 192.

Page 29: Kathleen M. Carrick and Donald J. Dunn, "Legal Writing: An Evaluation of the Textbook Literature," 30 *New York Law School L. Rev.* 645, 653–654 (1985).

Page 30: Law faculty resentment: Carrick and Dunn, ibid.

Page 30: Robert A. Leflar, "Some Observations Concerning Judicial Opinions," 61 *Columbia L. Rev.* 810, 815–16 (1961).

Page 30: Pig latin: Rodell, *Woe Unto You, Lawyers*, ibid., p. 11.

Page 31: Arthur T. Vanderbilt, "A Report on Prelegal Education," 25 *N.Y.U.L. Rev.* 199, 209 (1950).

Page 31: McGowan, *ibid.*, p. 901.

Page 32: Orwell, "Politics and the English Language," reprinted in *In Front of Your Nose, The Collected Essays* (New York: Harcourt Brace Jovanovich, 1968), vol. 4.

Page 32: Exhorted to refrain from vouching personally for their clients' bona fides: See *Code of Professional Responsibility* DR 7-106(C) (4): A lawyer shall not "assert his personal opinion as to [*sic*] the justness of a cause, . . . as to the culpability of a civil litigant."

Page 32: Transport the masks that they wear in public: Compare John T. Noonan, Jr., *Persons and Masks of the Law* (New York: Farrar, Straus & Giroux, 1976), p. xi: "The responsibility [of lawyers] comes in the response to other persons; it is the greater the more one is conscious that he or she— not some imagined entity—is acting, and the more one is conscious that the action affects not a hypothetical *A* but a real Helen Palsgraf."

Page 32: Hyland, ibid., p. 620.

Page 33: Hyland, ibid., pp. 621, 623 (Latin and Greek).

Page 33: Ray J. Aiken, "Let's Not Oversimplify Legal Language," 32 *Rocky Mountain L. Rev.* 358, 363 (1960).

Page 33: Friedman, ibid., p. 572.

Page 34: Hyland, ibid., p. 625.

Page 34: "McLuhanacy": Marshall McLuhan's famous '60's aphorism "the medium is the message" encapsulated the notion, the *reductio ad absurdum* of modern communications theory, that content is meaningless—a notion absorbed by Hyland in his belief that prose is no longer (or soon will not be) the means by which we communicate thought. See J. Ben Lieberman, "McLuhanacy," in Gerald Emanuel Stearn, ed., *McLuhan: Hot & Cool* (New York: Signet, 1967), p. 217.

Chapter 3: *Ten Steps to Writing*

Page 40: *Sierra Club v. Morton*, 405 U.S. 727 (1972).

Page 41: On the nature of the writing process: Susan Horton, *Thinking through Writing* (Baltimore: Johns Hopkins University Press, 1982), pp. 156–57.

Page 44: Schiller: quoted in James L. Adams, *Conceptual Blockbusting* (New York: W. W. Norton, 2d ed., 1980), p. 119.

Page 46: Justice Holmes, on caving in of the knees, quoted in Catherine Drinker Bowen, *Yankee from Olympus* (Boston: Little, Brown, 1944), p. 324.

Page 49: Galbraith's ambassadorial appointment: *The New Industrial State* (Boston: Houghton Mifflin, 1st ed. 1967), pp. viii–ix.

Chapter 4: *Of Dawdlers and Doodlers*

Page 58: Susan R. Horton, ibid., pp. 6–7.

Page 58: V. A. Howard and J. H. Barton, *Thinking on Paper* (New York: William Morrow and Co., 1986), p. 22.

Page 59: Donald H. Murray, *Writing for Your Readers* (Chester, Conn.: The Globe Pequot Press, 1983), pp. 143–45.

Chapter 5: *The Mechanics of Getting It Down*

Page 61: Typing history is drawn from Bruce Bliven, Jr., *The Wonderful Writing Machine* (New York: Random House, 1954), p. 62 (Twain), p. 79 (George), pp. 103–104 (market), pp. 113–15 (McGurrin).

Page 61: David Mellinkoff on typing and verbosity: *The Language of the Law* (Boston: Little, Brown, 1963), p. 261.

Page 62: Mellinkoff, *Legal Writing: Sense and Nonsense* (St. Paul: West, 1982), p. 128.

Page 63: Judge Jasen's complaint about word processors: *Slater v. Gallman*, 377 N.Y.S. 2d 448, 38 N.Y.2d 1, 339 N.E.2d 863 (1975).

Page 63: The 1902 decision on prolixity: *Stevens v. O'Neill*, 169 N.Y. 375 (1902).

Page 63: Mary Edwards: Unpublished ms. in authors' files.

Page 63: Vivian Dempsey, "The Dangers of Junk Documents," *California Lawyer*, Oct. 1987, p. 4.

Page 63: David S. Levine, " 'My Client Has Discussed Your Proposal to Fill the Drainage Ditch with His Partners': Legal Language" in *The State of Language* (Berkeley: University of California Press, 1980), p. 406.

Page 64: Fran Shellenberger, "Who Should Type?" *Word Progress*, American Bar Association Section of Economics of Law Practice, winter 1988, p. 20.

Page 64: Simpson, quoted in the *New York Times Book Review*, Jan. 3, 1988, p. 12.

Pages 64–65: William K. Zinsser, *On Writing Well* (New York: Harper & Row, rev. 3d ed., 1988), pp. 205, 214.

Page 65: Bliven, quoted, from *The Wonderful Writing Machine*, pp. 133–34.

Page 67: Zinsser, "don't say anything in writing": ibid., p. 221.

Page 67: Edward H. Warren, on not dictating: *Spartan Education* (Boston: Houghton Mifflin, 1942), p. 31.

Chapter 8: Writing the Lead

Page 87: Charles Peters, *Tilting at Windmills* (Reading, Mass.: Addison-Wesley, 1988).

Page 88: *Larkin v. Grendel's Den, Inc.*, 459 U.S. 116 (1982), Brief of Appellee. The brief is reprinted in Veda R. Charrow and Myra K. Erhardt, *Clear and Effective Legal Writing* (Boston: Little, Brown, 1986), pp. 229–264.

Page 89: Brief for Appellee in *Larkin v. Grendel's Den*, footnote 6.

Page 92: Lahey lead quoted in James W. Carey, "The Dark Continent of American Journalism," in Robert Karl Manoff and Michael Schudson, eds., *Reading the News* (New York: Pantheon, 1987), p. 147.

Page 92: Marijuana lead, *Wall Street Journal*, Aug. 20, 1985.

Page 92: Dirt to eat, *New York Times*, Feb. 13, 1984.

Page 93: Roll call lead, *New York Times*, Apr. 26, 1986.

Page 93: Scarlet letter lead, *Miami Herald*, Jan. 29, 1984.

Page 93: Rene J. Cappon, *The Word* (New York: Associated Press, 1982), p. 31.

Page 93: Boccardi quoted in Cappon, ibid., p. 46.

Page 94: Judge Hand's lead paragraph is from *Sheldon v. Metro-Goldwyn Pictures Corp.*, 81 F.2d 49 (1936).

Chapter 9: "By the Way, I Forgot to Mention . . ." Form, Structure, and Organization

Page 96: On Prescott's memory: Allan Nevins, *The Gateway to History* (New York: Anchor Books, rev. ed., 1962), p. 376.

Page 101: Winston Churchill on sentences, from *A Roving Commission* (New York: Charles Scribner's Sons, 1941), pp. 211–12.

Page 101: David M. Balabanian, "Justice Was More Than His Title," 70 *California L. Rev.* 878 (1982).

Page 108: Noel Coward: Bowerstock, "The Art of the Footnote," 53 *American Scholar* 54 (1984), quoted in Arthur D. Austin, "Footnotes as Product Differentiation," 40 *Vanderbilt L. Rev.* 1131, 1152 (1987).

Page 108: Fred Rodell on footnotes: from "Goodbye to Law Reviews," 23 *Virginia L. Rev.* 38 (1936), p. 41.

Page 111: John E. Nowak, "Woe unto You, Law Reviews!" 27 *Arizona L. Rev.* 317, 323 (1985).

Page 111: On Jesse Choper's footnotes: Paul M. Barrett, "To Read This Story in Full, Don't Forget to See the Footnotes," *Wall Street Journal*, May 10, 1988, p. 1.

Chapter 10: Editing I: Wrong Words, Long Sentences, and Other Mister Meaners

Page 115: Dorothy Evslin, "In the Write Spirit," *New York Times*, Jan. 16, 1987, p. 27.

Page 118: Humpty Dumpty: Lewis Carroll, *Through the Looking Glass*, ch. 6, in Martin Gardner, ed., *The Annotated Alice* (New York: New American Library, 1960), p. 269.

Page 119: Wydick, *Plain English for Lawyers* (Durham: Carolina Academic Press, 2d ed., 1985), p. 53.

Page 119: Frank Gifford and Kathie Lee Johnson on "heretofore": Lisa Faye Kaplan, "Hot Stuff!" New Rochelle, N.Y.: *Standard-Star*, Oct. 22, 1986.

Page 119: Alfred E. Kahn, memorandum of June 16, 1977, on "The Style of Board Orders and Chairman's Letters."

Page 119: Kilpatrick, on Rehnquist, quoted in Ronald Goldfarb, "My Secretary, Hereinafter Referred to as Cuddles . . . ," *Barrister*, Summer 1978, p. 43.

Page 120: Kurland, book review of Rehnquist, *The Supreme Court: How It Was, How It Is*, New York Times Book Review, Sept. 20, 1987, p. 3.

Page 120: H. W. Fowler, *A Dictionary of Modern English Usage*, p. 342.

Pages 121–122: John L. Lewis quoted: Rudolf Flesch, *The Art of Readable Writing* (New York: Collier Books, 1949), p. 221; as quoted in Horton, ibid., p. 15.

Page 122: Edward Tenner, "Cognitive Input Device in the Form of a Randomly Accessible Instantaneous-Read-Out Batch-Processed Pigment-Saturated Laminous-Cellulose Hard-Copy Output Matrix," *Discover*, May 1986, pp. 58–59.

Page 122: Grocery baggers: "Could you, er, say that again?" *U.S. News & World Report*, Apr. 20, 1987, p. 71.

Page 122: Minimally adequate training: *Youngberg v. Romeo*, 457 U.S. 307 (1982).

Page 122: Wellness potential: "Could you, er, say that again?" *U.S. News & World Report*, Apr. 20, 1987, p. 71.

Page 122: Three Mile Island: Quoted in Joanne Lipman, "In Times of Trouble, Candor Is Often the First Casualty," *Wall Street Journal*, Dec. 15, 1986.

Page 125: On Chief Justice White's use of adverbs: Paul A. Freund, Arthur E. Sutherland, Mark DeWolfe Howe, and Ernest J. Brown, *Constitutional Law, Cases and Other Problems* (Boston: Little, Brown and Co., 2d ed., 1961), vol. 2, p. lxiii.

Page 126: Geraldine A. Ferraro, letter to the *New York Times*, July 17, 1988, p. E28.

Page 128: Thoreau, "spur of the moment": quoted in Sheridan Baker, *The Practical Stylist* (New York: Harper & Row, 6th ed., 1985), p.139.

Page 132: Orwell, ibid., p. 138, footnote 1.

Page 132: Haig quoted in the *New York Times*, Jan. 29, 1987, p. A10.

Page 138: Donald Freeman's example is drawn from materials he distributed at the Legal Writing Institute Conference, University of Puget Sound Law School, Tacoma, Washington, Aug. 6, 1988.

Page 141: Chief Judge Wald on the use of the passive: From her commencement address to the class of 1988, New York Law School, June 12, 1988, Lincoln Center, New York.

Page 146: Chief Judge Wald on the use of "I," ibid.

Page 150: Casey Miller and Kate Swift, *The Handbook of Nonsexist Writing* (New York: Harper & Row, 2d ed., 1988), p. 50.

Page 150: *Random House Dictionary of the English Language* (1987), p. 2470.

Pages 150–151: Richard H. Weisberg, *When Lawyers Write* (Boston: Little, Brown, 1987), p. xxi.

Page 151: Emily Brontë, *Wuthering Heights* (New York: Penguin Classics, 1965), p. 168.

Pages 155–156: Joseph Williams on emphasis within sentences: *Style: Ten Lessons in Clarity and Grace* (Glenview: Scott, Foresman, 2d ed. 1985), pp. 33–34.

Pages 156–157: Donald Freeman's example is drawn from materials he distributed at the Legal Writing Institute Conference, ibid.

Page 157: George Gopen's revision of the UCC: From materials distributed at his talk to the Legal Writing Institute, University of Puget Sound Law School, Tacoma, Washington, Aug. 5, 1988.

Page 159: Rudolf Flesch, *How to Write Plain English: A Book for Lawyers and Consumers* (New York: Harper & Row, 1979), pp. 22–23.

Page 160: Justice Cardozo on sentences: "Law and Literature," 52 *Harv. L. Rev.* 471, 474 (1939); reprinted from 14 *Yale Review* 699 (July 1925); and *Law and Literature* (New York: Harcourt Brace, 1931), pp. 7–8.

Page 160: "Headnote disease" is a term one of the authors introduced in 1983. See Jethro K. Lieberman, "To Reach and Teach the Public, Write Better," in Robert S. Peck and Charles J. White, eds., *Understanding the Law: A Handbook on Educating the Public* (Chicago: American Bar Association, 1983), p. 25.

Page 160: Urban A. Lavery, "The Language of the Law," 8 *A.B.A.J.* 269, 272 (1922).

Page 162: Utah Supreme Court: Our thanks to Prof. Stephen A. Newman of New York Law School for referring us to *In re Ann Goalen*, 30 Utah 2d 27, 542 P.2d 1028 (1973).

Chapter 11: Editing II: Revising Your Prose

Pages 164–165: Writers on rewriting: George Plimpton, ed., *Writers at Work: The Paris Review Interviews,* (New York: Viking, 7th series, 1986). Roth at p. 271.

Page 165: John Kenneth Galbraith, "Writing, Typing, and Economics," *Atlantic Monthly,* March 1978, p. 103.

Page 170: *Wall Street Journal* on Manion's spelling: editorial, June 2, 1986.

Page 170: Daniel Seligman, "Rotten Writing in High Places," *Fortune,* Aug. 18, 1986, p. 77.

Page 170: On the spelling of "accommodation," see Holly Stevens, *The Letters of Wallace Stevens* (New York: Alfred A. Knopf, 1981), p. 37 (journal entry of June 15, 1900).

Page 171: Theodore M. Bernstein on the comma that legalized slavery: *Dos, Don'ts & Maybes of English Usage* (New York: Times Books, 1977), p. 42.

Page 171: Supreme Court on punctuation: *Hammock v. Farmers Loan & Trust Co.*, 105 U.S. 77, 84 (1891). David Mellinkoff, *The Language of the Law*, (Boston: Little, Brown, 1963), p. 251.

Page 179: Our thanks to Erika S. Fine for the 1988 Harvard Law School fund-raising letter.

Page 181: *United States v. Nixon*, 418 U.S. 683 (1974).

Page 184: Kilpatrick, *The Writer's Art* (Kansas City: Andrews, McMeel & Parker, 1984), p. 138.

Page 184: Kilpatrick, Throttlebottom reference: ibid., p. 145.

Page 184: Bernstein, *Miss Thistlebottom's Hobgoblins* (New York: Farrar, Straus & Giroux, 1971), first page of preface.

Chapter 12: *Making Your Writing Memorable*

Pages 189–190: Our thanks to Christopher G. Wren for referring us to *State v. Rossmanith*, Wisconsin Supreme Court, 87–0353–CR (1988).

Pages 190–191: Judge Logan's opinion: *Edwards v. Sims*, 24 S.W.2d 619, 622–623 (Ct. App. Ky. 1930).

Pages 191–192: Judge Wright's opinion: *Goldin v. Artache*, New York Law Journal, Aug. 26, 1986.

Pages 192–193: Judge Curry's opinion: *Chicago National League Ball Club, Inc. v. Thompson*, No. 84Ch 11384 (Circuit Court, Cook County, Ill. 1985). Our thanks to George J. Siedel for calling our attention to this opinion.

Page 193: Justice Cardozo, "Law and Literature," 52, *Harv. L. Rev.*, (1939), p. 483.

Page 193: George Rose Smith, "Primer of Opinion Writing for Four New Judges," 21 *Arkansas L. Rev.* 197, 210 (1967).

Pages 193–194: Judge Becker's opinion in verse: *Mackensworth v. American Trading Transportation Co.*, 367 F.Supp. 373 (E.D. Pa. 1973).

Page 194: Judge Gillis's verse: *Fisher v. Lowe*, 122 Mich. App. 418, 333 N.W. 2 d 167 (1983).

Pages 194–195: *United States ex rel. Mayo v. Satan and His Staff*, 54 F.R.D. 282, 283 (W.D. Pa. 1971). Our thanks to Adam Kasanof for calling this opinion to our attention.

Page 195: Judge Easterbrook's opinion: *United States v. Sblendoriio*, 830 F.2d 1382, 1384 (7th Cir. 1987).

Pages 195–196: Justice Jackson's explanation for repudiating an opinion as attorney general: *McGrath v. Kristensen*, 340 U.S. 162, 177–178 (1950) (concurring) (citations omitted).

Page 196: Justice Rutledge: *Wolf v. Colorado*, 338 U.S. 25, 47 (1949).

Page 197: Judge Conner: *American Home Products Corp. v. Johnson & Johnson*, 654 F.Supp. 568 (S.D.N.Y. 1987).

Page 197: Legal writing specialists on Hemingway: Steven Stark, "Why Lawyers Can't Write," 97 *Harv. L. Rev.* 1389 (1984).

Page 197: Advice angers others: Richard Hyland, "In Defense of Legal Writing," 134 *Univ. of Pennsylvania L. Rev.* 612, 621 (1986).

Page 198: Judge Brown's "dark and stormy night": *Allied Chemical Corp. v. Hess Tankship Co. of Delaware*, 661 F.2d 1044, 1046–1047 (5th Cir. 1981).

Page 198: Patricia Presutti's sentence: Quoted in "The Best of the Worst," *Quarterly Review of Doublespeak*, July 1986.

Page 199: Judge Burnett's Rodriquez opinion: *State v. Baker*, 103 Idaho 43, 644 P.2d 365 (Idaho App. 1982).

Page 199: Judge Nolan's dissent: *Brophy v. New England Sinai Hospital, Inc.*, 398 Mass. 417, 497 N.E.2d 626, 640 (1986).

Pages 199–200: Leon S. Lipson, commencement address, from Yale Law *Report* No. 1, Fall 1979, pp. 3–4. 19 p. We thank Simon H. Rifkind for calling Prof. Lipson's address to our attention.

Page 201: Rochman on Attica: *New York Times*, Feb. 27, 1976, p. 1.

Page 201: Cardozo on the blundering constable: *People v. Defore*, 242 N. Y. 13, 21 (1926) (dissenting).

Page 201: Holmes on burning theaters: *Schenck v. United States*, 249 U.S. 47, 52 (1919) (dissenting).

Page 201: Thurgood Marshall on door signs: *Cleburne v. Cleburne Living Center*, 473 U.S. 432, 468–69 (1985) (concurring in part and dissenting in part).

Page 202: Loren Eiseley, *Darwin's Century* (Garden City, N.Y.: Doubleday Anchor Books, 1961), p. 2.

Page 203: Chief Justice Marshall, on the Constitution: *McCulloch v. Maryland*, 4 Wheat. 316, 407 (1819).

Page 203: Justice Harlan: *Plessy v. Ferguson*, 163 U.S. 537, 559 (1896) (dissenting).

Page 203: Justice Holmes, on free trade in ideas: *Abrams v. United States*, 250 U.S. 616, 630 (1919).

Page 203: Justice Holmes, on ideas as incitements: *Gitlow v. New York*, 268 U.S. 652, 673 (1925) (dissenting).

Page 204: Justice Cardozo: *Palko v. Connecticut*, 302 U.S. 319, 325 (1937).

Page 204: Judge Hand: *Sheldon v. Metro-Goldwyn Pictures Corp.*, 81 F.2d 49, 54 (2d Cir. 1936).

Page 204: Justice Jackson, on fixed stars: *Board of Education v. Barnette*, 319 U.S. 624, 642 (1943).

Page 204: Justice Jackson, on interstate commerce: *United States v. Women's Sportswear Manufacturers Assn.*, 336 U.S. 460, 464 (1949).

Page 204: Justice Jackson on infallibility: *Brown v. Allen*, 344 U.S. 443, 540 (1953).

Page 204: Chief Justice Warren: *Reynolds v. Sims*, 377 U.S. 533, 562 (1964).

Pages 204–205: Justice Douglas: *Griswold v. Connecticut*, 381 U.S. 479, 486 (1965).

Pages 206–207: Justice Brandeis, concurring in Whitney: *Whitney v. California*, 274 U.S. 357 (1927).

Pages 207–209: Justice Holmes, dissenting, in *United States v. Schwimmer*, 279 U.S. 644, 653–655 (1929).

Page 209: The Topkis brief is *A.S.C.A.P. V. CBS, Inc.*, 441 U.S. 1 (1979).

Page 211: *United States v. Byrnes*, 644 F.2d 107 (2d Cir. 1981).

Glossary

Page 238: Pamela Samuelson, "Good Legal Writing: Of Orwell and Window Panes," 46 *U. Pittsburgh L. Rev.* 149, 163 (1984).

Page 239: George D. Gopen, "The State of Legal Writing: *Res Ipsa Loquitur*," 86 *Michigan L. Rev.* 333, 362 (1987).

AN EDITING CHECKLIST

L IKE CHILDREN, flower gardens, and romantic relationships, your writing will benefit immeasurably from close attention. As a professional, you aim to tell, explain, advocate, persuade. You cannot succeed in those ambitions when your prose is unclear, and if you supply your audience with a first draft only, you will surely fail. No good writing goes unedited.

Here is a checklist that provides one reasonable way to ensure that your writing clearly expresses your thought and meaning. It is not the only way to proceed—after a little experimenting, you will surely find a procedure that suits you better. But the checklist should remind you that you will work more efficiently if you edit in steps, starting with the more comprehensive problem of organization and ending with the more minute and particular problems of proofreading.

Edit for Structure

Major Sections

☐ Will your reader understand why you have grouped each part of your document as you have? (p. 96) If your transitions between sections are confusing or don't work, parts of your discussion may be out of order.

☐ Have you consciously written a lead? (p. 85) Now that you have finished your paper, does your original lead still work? Does it tell why your reader should continue reading, what's to be found in the paper, and why? (p. 166)

☐ Have you written a conclusion that shows the reader you have accomplished what you set out to do? (p. 166)

Paragraphs

☐ Do your topic sentences express the sense of each paragraph? (p. 101) You must find a way to tell the reader what each paragraph is about.

☐ Is your topic flow consistent within each paragraph? (p. 103) The topics of each sentence must be closely related. If they are not, you may need to shift unrelated points to their appropriate places in your document. (p. 166) Look to see whether your sentence tells its story or disguises it in a faulty topic.

☐ Are the transitions between your paragraphs coherent? Will your reader understand why one paragraph follows another? (p. 158)

Edit for Length

☐ If you were in your reader's place, would you pore over every word in front of you? What subsidiary issues and minor points can you prune—or eliminate? (p. 167)

☐ Ruthlessly weed out redundancies. (p. 133)

☐ Ruthlessly eliminate verbosity. (p. 134)

☐ Are your sentences too long? Can you split some of them apart? (p. 159)

Edit for Clarity

☐ Excise Latinisms, legalese, bureaucratese, and pomposities. (p. 119)

☐ Ruthlessly eliminate fuzzy phrases. (p. 130)

☐ Scan for usage mistakes. (p. 122)

☐ Doublecheck troublesome words: do they mean what you think they do? (p. 118)

☐ Avoid throat-clearing phrases and clichés. (pp. 128–129)

☐ Look for negatives: can you rewrite in the affirmative? (p. 132)

☐ Rigorously search for nominalizations and replace whichever are unnecessary. (p. 137)

☐ Find passive verbs and justify them or remove them. (p. 141)
☐ Eliminate strings of prepositions. (p. 136)
☐ Minimize the "there is" construction. (p. 143)
☐ Are you using the word "which" too often and in confusing ways? (p. 147)
☐ Review your grammar and basic style: subject-verb agreement (p. 144), dangling and misplaced modifiers (pp. 151–152), problems of parallelism (p. 155), fused participles (p. 148), split infinitives (p. 145), antecedents (p. 146).

Edit for Continuity

Now start over with a clean version of your document, incorporating the changes you have made in your previous edits.

☐ Do first references to persons, cases, or other particular things fully identify them?
☐ Do your transitions still make sense?
☐ If you said something is "above" or "below" are their relative positions still accurate? (*Note:* Many word-processing programs now have automatic cross-referencing features that will "remember" and record references to page numbers even when blocks of material are moved around.)

Proofread

☐ Check your spelling. After you or your secretary has fed your document through a "spell-checker," go back and read it again. Spell-checkers aren't perfect, and they do not catch homonym errors ("there" for "their"). (p. 170)
☐ Correct typographical errors (missing words and the like). (p. 170)
☐ Make your style consistent (capitalization and the like). (p. 175)
☐ Punctuate properly. (p. 171)

GLOSSARY

This glossary lists the most common errors in grammar and syntax that we have observed among lawyers. Entries are drawn from a variety of sources: from usage books, from respondents to our survey, and from lawyers' memoranda on usage and style that we have collected. Since lawyers often misuse prepositions, this glossary includes the idiomatic prepositions for many nouns, verbs, and adjectives commonly used by lawyers.

abbreviations: Do not use abbreviations in text other than titles, such as Mr., Ms., Prof., and Dr., and commonly recognized initials, such as SEC.

absolute words: James J. Kilpatrick says certain words do not allow comparison or qualification. They are either-or words: Either their quality is present or it is not, so they can't be "partly" or "very" or "most" or "a little bit." His list: complete, dead, equal, essential, eternal, fatal, final, imperative, indispensable, perfect, pregnant, total, unanimous, unique, universal, and virgin.

absolve from or of

abstain from

accede to

accessory after, before, or to

accommodate, to or with: Frequently misspelled with either one "c" or one "m"; takes two of each.

accord in or to

accordance with

accountable for or to

accuse of

acquiesce in

adapt: See *adopt.*

adept at or in

adhere to

admit of, into, to: Normally connotes guilt; use sparingly. Gerald Stern: "It signifies a clear-cut statement of guilt. It should not be used in place of 'stated,' 'said,' or 'acknowledged.' "

adopt, adapt: *Adopt* means to take on as one's own, to espouse; *adapt* means to adjust, to make fit.

advantage of or over

adverbial excesses: See *emphatics.*

adversarial: Until 1969, the dictionaries recognized no such word, and most still do not. The proper phrase is "adversary system," not "adversarial system." Usually, "adversarial" is simply pompous.

advise of or about

affect, effect: *Effect* as a noun means "result" or "consequence." As a verb it means to bring about or accomplish. *Affect* as a verb means to influence; it is used as a noun only in psychological parlance, to mean something akin to mood.

affinity between or with

aforementioned: Avoid. See *lawyerisms.*

aggravate, irritate: *Aggravate* means to make worse, enhance, enlarge; *irritate* means to arouse, annoy, inflame. "He was irritated that she kept him waiting in the rain." "Her sarcasm aggravated his already hostile mood."

all ready, already: *All ready* means fully prepared; *already* means now, by this or that time, previously, before, so soon. You can't say, "They were already to go."

all right: Idiomatic and informal, inappropriate in writing. Note spelling; "alright" is incorrect.

all, not all: "All members of the band are not here yet." People write like that, but they don't mean it. The sentence means, literally, that no member of the band has arrived. The writer probably meant to say that some members of the band are still absent. The better way to construct the sentence is "Not all members of the band are here yet."

alleged: *Allege* is a serviceable verb meaning to state something is true without having proved it; plaintiffs allege that the defendant injured them in some manner. But as an adjective or adverb, *alleged* and *allegedly* are overworked and misused, signaling an overly cautious writer. "The Bible doesn't say 'Thou Shalt Not Commit Alleged Adultery,' " *Winners & Sinners*, a bulletin on usage published by the *New York Times*, advised its readers in 1981. "The weasel words *alleged* and *allegedly* turn up too often, giving our columns an unwelcome precinct-house odor. Why do they appear? Maybe because it's thought—mistakenly—that they shelter us from libel or editorializing. We're no less safe, and we're easier to read, if we say what we mean, in everyday English."

Examples of the unnecessary *alleged*: From the *Washington Post*: "The first grand jury to consider the case declined to indict Goetz for attempted murder, charging him only with alleged gun possession." Obviously, he was charged with *actual* gun possession; alleged possession of a gun is no crime, not even in New York or Texas. From the *Wall Street Journal*, quoting Oscar B. Goodman, a Las Vegas lawyer: "There is no question [that Ray Luca] was based on Mr. Spilotro's alleged life as perceived by law enforcement authorities." From a caption in *New York Newsday*: "Police pin down a pit bull that allegedly bit a woman in the East Village." The rights of the accused may be taken too far. See also p. 126.

allude, elude: To *allude* is to refer to something indirectly, to hint at; to *elude* is to avoid detection or capture or memory.

allusion, illusion: *Allusion* means a hinting at or indirect reference to; *illusion* is a deceptive appearance. One may "allude to" something but never "illude" to it. Something may be "illusory," but never "allusory."

already: See *all ready*.

also: *Also* must be near the word intended to be modified, or it can cause problems. Consider: "You are the bearer of this bad news." Insert "also" before "are," "bearer," or after "news" and watch the meaning change.

alternate, alternative: The meanings of these two distinct words are beginning to bleed at the edges. *Alternate* means to go back and forth between two positions, by turns; or, as a noun, a substitute: "alternate juror." *Alternately* means one after another, like boys and girls lined up at a dance. "Alternative" connotes choice—once limited to two, but now it is generally agreed that there may be "alternatives." In the early days of the dispute resolution movement in the late 1970s the movement was inaccurately called "Alternate Dispute Resolution"; it is properly "Alternative Dispute Resolution," because the choice is not between court one day and something else the second and then again court the third.

amenable to

amend, emend: *Amend* means to make formal changes in (amend the Constitution); *emend*, to correct a mistake.

among, between: Purists insist that *between* refers to two people or things; *among* to three or more. But many usage books agree that when contracts are negotiated among many parties, each considered as an individual, "between" is preferable: "The nine players struck a deal between themselves before approaching the owner."

and/or: Use sparingly or never. *And/or* rarely clarifies and it saves little space. See Mellinkoff, *The Language of the Law*, pp. 306–318.

antipathy against, to, between, or for

anxiety about or for

apostrophes: "The misuse of apostrophes is a particularly striking instance of recidivism [among students]," says Edward A. Dauer. See p. 175.

appreciation of or for

apprehensive of or for

arguendo: Pomposity. Avoid. *Arguendo* means "for the sake of argument"; say that. See also *Latin*.

as: *As* can be mishandled in many ways. Don't use it as a substitute for "because": "As he arrived late last night, I did not get a chance to see him until this morning." "Regarded as" does not require "being": "She is regarded as [not: as being] the best dancer in the world." Many writers tend to indulge in a surplus "as." For example, in "The class elected Sheila as president," omit "as." See also *like*.

as . . . as: The expression is *as much as* or *as large as* but not "as much than." The *New York Daily News* incorrectly allowed this sentence: "Black women had almost four times as high a risk of death than white women in the 35 and older group." The *New York Times*: "But the authorities make the visitors pay the rent to them—three times as much for foreigners than for Yugoslavs for the same accommodations."

The rule once was that in affirmative expressions, the appropriate phrase is *as . . . as*: "Mike is as quick as Lindy," but in negative expressions, the preferable phrase is *so . . . as*: "Mike is not so quick as Lindy." Few grammarians insist on the distinction any longer, and *as . . . as* may be used either affirmatively or negatively.

Do not say "as good or better than"; say, "as good as or better."

as of yet: Eliminate *as of* in a sentence such as this: "She hasn't posted bail as of yet."

as such: Ordinarily awkward and inappropriate.

as to: The worst modern offense by lawyers against the prepositional order is their use of *as to* to substitute for the idiomatic proper prepositions that go with nouns: clue to, debate over, issue of, rather than "clue as to," "debate as to," "issue as to," etc. This glossary lists the proper prepositions for many nouns, verbs, and adjectives common in legal writing. See also *prepositions*.

aspire to, after, or toward

assent to

assumption of

at least: Tom Rowe: "Often a dead giveaway for a weak citation: 'At least one court has held' probably means it is the only one you could find."

attest to

attorney: *Attorney*, technically, means something different from *lawyer*; see Mellinkoff, *Language of the Law*, p. 80. David S. Levine, in "My Client Has Discussed Your Proposal to Fill the Drainage Ditch with His Partners," says a lawyer may not have passed the bar while an attorney has.

averse to

awhile, a while: *Awhile* is an adverb; *while*, a noun. "She waited for a while," or "She waited awhile."

badly: Misused to mean "bad" in the expression "I feel badly." Verbs such as "feel," "appear," and "look" take the adjective, not the adverb.

based on: A film can be based on a book, and a hypothesis can be based on nothing much more than a guess, but a person can't be based on anything. "Based on the clue in the motel, we drove directly to the airport." "We" weren't based on it; the act of driving was. This is a dangling modifier. Consider this other example: "Axel and Hal allege in their complaint that First Park City Bank breached the January 15 agreement. *Based on* this so-called breach, *they* seek damages in excess of $10 million." The second sentence implies that Axel and Hal are themselves somehow based on a breach. The "based on" phrase is also somewhat redundant. Change it to: "Axel and Hal claim [or assert or allege] that First Park City Bank breached the January 15 agreement. Basing their suit on this so-called breach, they seek damages." Or: "Axel and Hal claim [or assert or allege] that First Park City Bank breached the January 15 agreement. They seek damages of more than $10 million." Or: "Axel and Hal seek damages of more than $10 million from First Park City Bank, which they claim breached the January 15 agreement."

being: Do not use as a substitute for "because": "He missed the speech being that the plane was late." Also, unnecessary after "regard as": "She is regarded as (being) the best dancer in the world."

between: See *among*.

between you and I: Ugh! Says Milton Gould: "Lawyers are untaught in elemental grammar; they seem to be engaged in an endless struggle with the accusative. 'Between you and I'—etc. They don't think grammar is important!" This is a prepositional phrase and requires pronouns in the objective case. It should *always* be "between you and me."

candid about

canvas, canvass: *Canvas* is a cloth, used for sails and paintings. *Canvass* means to examine systematically or to solicit, to question, as in a poll.

capable of

capital, capitol: *Capital* is the city in which the seat of government lies; *capitol* is the building. No excuses for mixing them up.

Cardozo: Often, mysteriously, misspelled with an "a" at the end and an "s" for the "z."

careless about, in, or of

case: Verbose; omit. Instead of "It is often the case that lawyers are long-winded," say: "Lawyers are often long-winded."

certainly: Certainly overused; to be avoided. If something's certain, show how or why it's certain, rather than merely asserting it.

character: Verbose, except when referring to a character in a play or a person's character. Omit in the sense of kind or nature: "Speech of a scintillating character" should be "scintillating speech."

choose among or between

claim: Restrict to sense in which plaintiff makes claim in complaint; distinguish from "assert," "insist," "declare," etc.

clue to

commence: Use "begin."

completely: To be avoided; a false emphatic.

comprise: *Comprise* means to embrace or include. "The law firm comprises sixty partners and twenty associates." It is generally considered wrong to invert the meaning: "Sixty partners comprise a law firm." Do not confuse with "compose" or "consist." The law firm "is composed of" or "consists of" sixty partners, but it cannot be "comprised of" them. "Comprised of" is nonstandard English, and although it is seen more and more, its use marks the writer as inelegant. Here are the rules: The whole comprises the parts. The parts are comprised in the whole. The whole is composed of its parts. The parts compose or constitute the whole.

concur in or with

confident of

contemptuous of

continuous, continual: *Continuous* refers to an uninterrupted occurrence over time, as in "continuous vigil"; *continual* means repeated at intervals, as in "continual banging of the shutters."

contractions: Never use in briefs or court memoranda. Say "do not," not "don't."

convince of (not to)

correlation between or of

correspond to or with

criterion, criteria: *Criterion* is singular, *criteria* plural. The Supreme Court incorrectly said, "No consideration of the second or third criteria is necessary if a statute does not have a clearly secular purpose." 472 U.S. at 56.

curriculum: *Curriculum* is singular, *curricula* plural. See also *plurals*.

data: A plural word. Correct: "The data are." See also *plurals*.

de minimis: If you must use this phrase, spell it correctly, not "de minim*u*s."

debate over or about

deem: Lawyers love it, for no apparent reason. As chairman of the Civil Aeronautics Board in 1977, Alfred E. Kahn wrote this memo to staff: "I once asked a young lawyer who wanted us to say 'we deem it inappropriate' to try that kind of language out on his children—and if they did not drive him out of the room with their derisive laughter, to disown them." Say, rather: "It is inappropriate."

delusion, illusion: *Delusion* is a false belief; *illusion* is a false perception.

dicta: Singular of *dicta* is *dictum*. Says Justice Stanley Mosk: "I have little tolerance for grammatical errors; e.g., when an attorney uses 'dicta' as singular." See also *plurals*.

differ with, on, or from

different: Often overworked. Omit in the following sentence: "We called on a dozen different people."

different from, than: Purists insist that only *different from* is correct: "Frogs are different from [not: than] toads."

differentiate among, between, or from

disappointed in or with

discreet, discrete: *Discreet* means judicious, circumspect, prudent, modest in approach or manner, unobtrusive; *discrete* means separate, disconnected, discontinuous.

disinterested, uninterested: *Disinterested* means not personally engaged in, impartial; *uninterested* means not interested, not caring, indifferent.

dissatisfied with

double negatives: See *negatives*.

due to: *Due to* should not be used adverbially as a substitute for "owing to" or "because of." It is a prepositional phrase that modifies nouns: "Our loss was due to our injuries." Its synonym is "attributable to." You can also use "because": "Steve opposed both sales because the price was inadequate."

educated about, for, or in

effect: See *affect*.

either-or words: See *absolute words*.

elude: See *allude*.

emend: See *amend*.

emphatics: Opposite of hedge words, equally undesirable. Judge Matthew Jasen lists as "pet peeves": "the use of trite and hackneyed phrases such as 'well settled,' or dogmatic statements such as 'clearly,' 'plainly,' and 'without doubt.' " Others include "completely," as in the phrase "completely untrue" (using "completely" there suggests that in some other part of the paper, referring to some other falsehood, it may be true), "surely," "certainly," "indeed," "obviously," "beyond question." Avoid these ambiguities by realizing that the unmodified "false" is stronger than the apparently stressed "completely untrue."

enormity: Not to be confused with "immensity." *Enormity* has a moral connotation and means a monstrous wrong; "immensity" and "immense" connote size.

equally as: Redundant. "I was entitled to the reward equally as much as him." Fix: "I was entitled to the reward equally with him" or "I was entitled to the reward as much as he." "Sam is equally as tall as George" should be "Sam is as tall as George."

equivalent in or to

essential in, of, to, or for

etc.: *Etc.* means "and so forth" or "and other things," so "and etc." is always incorrect. This Latin abbreviation (for *et cetera*) should be used sparingly and never at the end of a list introduced by "for example."

evoke, invoke: *Evoke* means to draw out or elicit; *invoke* means to call into use. "Only twice before had anyone attempted to evoke Florida Statute 104.38," a reporter erroneously wrote in the *New York Times*. "Invoke" is correct.

fact that: A barbarism; avoid. "Owing to the fact that it was raining, I took an umbrella" should be "Because it was raining, I took . . ." "In spite of the fact that it was dark out, I wore my sunglasses" should be "Although it was dark out . . ." "I was unaware of the fact that I was late": "I was unaware I was late." "The fact that he had not succeeded did not deter him": "His failure did not deter him" or "He was not deterred even though he failed."

factor: As a term of art in commerce, be our guest. But as a filler, it's verbose and avoidable: "Word processors are an important factor in getting out work" should be "Word processors are important to getting out work."

farther, further: *Farther* refers to physical distance; it does not mean more in the figurative sense. *Further* can refer to distance, but it has the additional sense of "in addition," "more," "to a greater extent." "They did not want to go to Lutece because of the cost; a further (not farther) consideration was the time it would take to get there."

fewer: See *less*.

first person: See *I*.

flagrant: Use sparingly; this is an overused emphatic.

flaunt, flout: *Flaunt* means to show off ostentatiously. *Flout* means to mock, to treat with contempt or disrespect, to disobey. "Flouting the laws of the city, some young people flaunted their nudity."

forbid to (never from)

foregoing: Avoid it.

forthwith: Avoid. Silly lawyerism.

fortuitous, fortunate: *Fortuitous* means coincidental or accidental; *fortunate* means lucky.

free from, of, or in

gamut, gantlet, gauntlet: See *running the gamut*.

garnishee: A noun; avoid using as a verb. It is incorrect to say: "The plaintiff seeks to garnishee the wages." The proper verb is "garnish."

gift: Not a verb, so don't ever use it that way. *Gift* means without consideration, so "free gift" is redundant.

graduate from: The verb *graduate* takes the preposition "from"; it is wrong to say that someone has "graduated law school." A person graduates from a law school. Older usage books insist, as a greater refinement, that a person "was graduated from" a school.

he/she: Pamela Samuelson admonishes the writer not to "get cute about personal pronouns" and then says that " 'he/she' is ok." No, it is not. See p. 149.

hedge words: Early on, lawyers learn to avoid speaking directly. They say: "It would seem that it is raining out" when what they mean is "look, it's pouring." See p. 126.

herein: Avoid. See *lawyerisms*.

hereinafter: Avoid. See *lawyerisms*.

heretofore: Avoid. See *lawyerisms*.

herewith: Unnecessary. One of our respondents, who complained about "overwriting" by lawyers, wrote in his cover letter: "I have completed and am returning to you *herewith* the questionnaire."

hint at

historic, historical: *Historic* means momentous; *historical* means pertaining to history.

honorifics, titles: Honorifics or titles should be used sparingly. Don't say, "Ms. Emily Jones." Reserve the honorific for the second use, if you are being formal. Be consistent: Don't refer to her sometimes as "Jones" and sometimes as "Ms. Jones." Exceptions to this rule: doctor (medical); professor; senator, judge (political).

hopefully: Commonly misused to mean "I hope." The word means "full of hope." This sentence is incorrect: "Hopefully, it will stop raining so we can go out for a walk." This sentence is correct: "Hopefully, he entered the examination room with his favorite pen."

however: A word with two meanings. In the sense of "in whatever manner" it is not set off by commas: "However you get to town, call me as soon as you arrive." In the sense of "nevertheless," it must always be set off by commas, or preceded by a semicolon: "She agreed to meet him at 10; however, she was not there when he arrived." "The cat, however, had climbed down the tree." It is now acceptable to begin a sentence with "however." Strunk and White mildly reprove its being positioned there; Williams finds it perfectly acceptable. See also p. 174.

I: Even the writers who write about writing succumb to the taboo against using "I." Here is George Gopen in his *Michigan Law Review* article on "The State of Legal Writing": "This methodology *has been used by the present author* since 1984." See Judge Wald's remarks, p. 146.

Tom Rowe: "Never use in court memoranda or briefs; in other writing, to the contrary, do not strain to avoid using "I." Rodell complained of this "taboo" on "I" in the law reviews as a "style quirk that inevitably detracts from the forcefulness and clarity" of the writing; "an 'I' or a 'me' is regarded as a rather shocking form of disrobing in print." Avoiding it, he suggests, through such phrases as "It is suggested," or "It would seem," often "lead to the kind of sentence that looks as though it had been translated from the German by someone with a rather meager knowledge of English" (*Goodbye to Law Reviews*).

I do not think: "I do not think this proposition is true." This puts the matter backwards. It is not that the writer has failed to think; it is that the writer believes otherwise. Hence, say: "I think this proposition is false." So say the purists, though the expression has been idiomatic English for centuries. Still, you shouldn't use expressions such as "I think" in the first place. Just state your premise: "The proposition is false."

identical with

if, whether: With words such as "say," "know," "ask," and "doubt," use *whether* rather than *if*: "I don't know whether this is the right size."

illusion: See *allusion*.

immensity: See *enormity*.

impact: *Impact* is not a verb. Don't say that the breach of contract "impacted" on their plans. It had an impact on their plans. Only teeth are impacted.

impervious to

imply, infer: *Imply* is what you do when you make a statement from which someone else will *infer* your meaning. "From all the footprints in the mud, she inferred that the fugitives were riding camels." "She was nervous about accusing the Senator directly, but she implied that he had cheated on his income taxes."

importantly: The usage books disagree, but more say that the introductory phrase should be "more important," not "more importantly." The phrase is an ellipsis of "what is more important." *Importantly* does have an independent meaning, however; it suggests self-importance, having a swelled head, as in "he walked about the room importantly."

impress into, upon, or with

improvement in, of, or upon

in terms of: Flabby, wooden, useless. A pet peeve of Justin A. Stanley: "How was your vacation in terms of the weather?" "It was a favorable case in terms of precedent" means "It was a favorable precedent." You wouldn't say "How are you in terms of health?" Why say it otherwise?

in the event that: Don't use; always prefer "if."

incentive to or for

inconsistent with

incredulous: Leonard H. Sandler: "I am glad to note that it has been some years since I have seen the expression in a brief, 'It's incredulous.' " Many a neophyte still confuses "incredulous" with "incredible." *Incredible* means unbelievable; *incredulous* means skeptical or unbelieving.

infer: See *imply.*

input: Not a verb. Wrong to say: "Please input your thoughts." If you must use this word, say: "I would like your input."

inquire into or of

inquiry into

insight into

instant case: "This case" is preferable.

intended for: "The secretary intended *for* those procedures to be the principal mechanism." Here, "for" is redundant. Omit.

inter alia: Use the English, "among other things," or better, don't say it at all. The phrase is overused and rarely necessary.

interest in

interface: This word should be restricted to technical electronic parlance. In any case it is not a verb.

interment, internment: *Interment* means burial; *internment* means imprisonment, usually in a prisoner-of-war camp.

invoke: See *evoke.*

involved: A weak verb that imparts little or no information. For instance: "The

Yarrow case involved a claim by an auctioneer for recovery of its expected commission on the sale of property which was never delivered to the auctioneer by the owner.'' The writer has wasted the opportunity to tell the story immediately. Rewrite: ''In the *Yarrow* case, an auctioneer tried to recover the commission it expected from selling a piece of property that the owner never delivered to the auctioneer.''

irony: *Irony* means an outcome contrary to what was generally expected or an expression contrary to the obvious meaning of the person making the utterance. What are we to make of these misuses of ''irony'': ''History will record as a profound irony that the most powerful word processing package ever created for the IBM Personal Computer wasn't created by IBM'' (from an advertisement for Leading Edge Products). Why? IBM leaves software development to many different companies. No irony there. Or Miss America, Vanessa Williams, who ''said that in the competition for her own crown she had correctly answered several questions about [Mayor Harold] Washington's campaign. 'I was crossing my fingers that he'd win,' she said. 'He did, and, ironically, so did I' '' (quoted in *Chicago Magazine* in 1983). You may find her statement ironic in retrospect, but there can be no irony in her winning her crown.

irritate: See *aggravate*.

it would seem that: ''A laborious circumlocution,'' says Stuart Taylor. ''It would seem that he is correct''—read: ''He is correct.'' Hedge words, such as ''it would appear that,'' are examples of lawyers' fear to say what they mean.

its: David Trager says: ''Law schools that have a large number of students who attended public school in the early '70s find themselves in the situation where even the good writers don't know the difference between 'its' and 'it's.' '' Without the apostrophe, the word is a possessive pronoun; with the apostrophe the word is a contraction for ''it is.'' Example: ''It's amazing that lawyers forget its roots.''

judgment: Not spelled ''judgement.''

kind: Verbose. ''Speech of a scintillating kind'' should be ''scintillating speech.''

late: Be wary of referring to someone deceased as ''the late.'' The effect is not always what you intend: ''The bill was signed by the late President Johnson.'' A neat trick. He wasn't dead when he signed it. The term is generally not useful.

Latin: *Res gestae, ratio decedendi, in pari delicto, inter alia.* Jay Wishingrad and Prof. Douglas E. Abrams: ''Why say in Latin what can be said in English? The reader who understands Latin is not impressed, while everyone else is unable to comprehend the writer's meaning without scurrying for a dictionary," Eugene R. Fidell says: "What I hate most is legalisms, such as 'assuming arguendo.' I once had a senior partner who said that he disapproved of the use of words in a foreign language—except on a menu."

lawyerisms: Avoid archaic words and phrases such as "whereas," "wherein," "aforementioned," "forthwith," "heretofore," "hereinafter," "thereunto appertaining," "goes to the question of." They serve no intelligible purpose. Any information they are thought to convey can be conveyed far more clearly in other ways. Robert Stuart Nathan, novelist and former legal editor, calls these "knee-jerk words, which make lawyers feel important but turn legal writing into gibberish."

In his last official act as general counsel of the U.S. Department of Commerce, Homer E. Moyer Jr. issued a memorandum on plain English and said this: "*Avoid legalisms.* Latin phrases, abbreviations, and other legalisms are the badges of legal writing. However, they are commonly redundant, usually pretentious, and invariably unnecessary. When legalisms punctuate a paragraph, readability suffers. Like lavish capitalization, frequent exclamation marks, and underscoring for emphasis, legalisms serve as crutches when plain English would nicely suffice. The addition of "*supra*," "*arguendo*," or "*inter alia*" rarely amplifies a thought. Even more dispensable are 'therein,' 'hereinafter,' 'provided, however,' and similar rhetorical baggage. In almost all instances, 'herewith' is redundant, as in 'a copy is enclosed herewith.' "

Justice George Rose Smith of the Arkansas Supreme Court says no lawyer should ever use these terms: "said" (in the sense of aforesaid: "I can do with another piece of that pie, dear; said pie is the best you've ever made"); "same" (similar sense: "I've mislaid my car keys; have you seen same?"); "such" (similar sense: "Sharon Kay stubbed her toe this afternoon, but such toe is all right now"); "hereinafter called" ("You'll get a kick out of what happened today to my secretary, hereinafter called Cuddles"); and "inter alia" ("it supplies information needed only by fools").

lay, lie: Perennial confusion exists between these two verbs and their tenses. *Lay* is a transitive verb (except as a nautical term: "laying about"). It means to put or make or set in motion. Present tense is "lay" ("watch as I now lay the book on the table"); past, "laid" ("he laid the book on the table"); present participle, "laying"; past participle, "laid" ("he has already laid his plans"). *Lie* is an intransitive verb. Present tense is "lie" ("the dogs lie about in the kitchen"); past, "lay" ("yesterday she lay on the bed in pain"); present participle, "lying" ("the dogs are lying on the floor"); past participle, "lain" ("the dogs had lain there for hours").

lead: Spelling problem here. As a noun, *lead* is a metal. As a verb, it is the present tense of the verb "to lead." The past tense is "led."

legalisms: See *lawyerisms.*

less, fewer: Although the distinction is breaking down in ordinary conversation, it is worth preserving. *Less* refers to amount or quantity, *fewer* to number. "She has less space in her house than you do." "She has fewer rooms in her house than you in yours."

lie: See *lay.*

like, as: *Like* connects nouns and pronouns; *as* connects phrases and clauses. "She is just like her mother," but "She visited her mother as she did long ago."

like, such as: A subtle, often misunderstood difference. In a series, *like* means similar to but not an example of. "Preachers like Jimmy Swaggart should be ashamed of themselves." That sentence does not say that Jimmy should be ashamed, but only that preachers like (who resemble) him should be. "Preachers such as Jim Bakker should be ashamed of themselves." Jim Bakker, take heed.

literally: Should not be used figuratively. "We worked so hard we literally died" is not literally true. As an overused term, "literally" has lost much of its force; use sparingly.

loan: *Loan* is a noun, the thing lent. The verb is "lend."

masterful, masterly: *Masterful* means domineering, imperious, vigorous, powerful. *Masterly* means possessing the skill or knowledge of a master.

mastery of or over

means of, to, or for

meddle in or with

media: *Media* is plural, *medium* singular. See also *plurals.*

minister to

minuscule: Often misspelled "miniscule."

mirandize: A vogue term used in police stations, meaning to read suspects their rights. Less than a quarter of the panel writing in the *Harper Book of Contemporary Usage* thought it a useful addition to the language. James Kilpatrick asks whether our public schools have been *Browned*? Calvin Trillin, on the other hand, says it may be useful for police officers: "If lawyers can say 'Shepardize,' why can't cops say 'Mirandize?' "

mistrustful of

mitigate, militate: *Mitigate* means to make less severe or soften; *militate* means to weigh heavily or have a substantial effect. "The budget deficit militated against increased spending." "The judge mitigated her sentence, reducing it to two years."

motive for

Ms.: The honorific "Ms." is widely acceptable. The *New York Times*, long a holdout, accepted it in 1986. When used lowercase, "ms." means manuscript.

nature: Verbose. "Speech of a scintillating nature" should be "scintillating speech."

negatives: See p. 132.

neither, nor: It's "neither . . . nor," not "neither . . . or." See also *not only, but also.*

noisome, noisy: *Noisome* means disgusting, foul smelling; *noisy* refers to sound.

nominalization: See p. 137.

not only, but also: English is full of small connecting phrases—"not only . . . but also," "neither . . . nor"—that hold disparate thoughts together. Their use is governed by specific rules. Lawyers often make an irritating mistake in failing to abide by these rules: "Not only" must be followed by "but [also]." For example: "Mr. Ciseros *not only fails* to cite a single Utah authority in support of his contention, *he utterly fails* to distinguish the authorities cited by defendants." Fix it: "Mr. Ciseros *fails not only* to cite a single Utah authority to support his contention *but also* to distinguish the authorities whom defendants cite."

null and void: Often redundant.

parameter: A mathematical term that does not mean perimeter or limit; it refers to a specifically defined type of variable and rarely is useful for lawyers.

pass muster: The expression means to measure up. It's not "past muster."

passive voice: See p. 141.

per se: Not necessary per se; useful mainly to antitrust lawyers.

peradventure: Overused, as in "beyond peradventure."

plagiarism: Variously misspelled "plagearism" and "plagerism."

plainly: See *emphatics.*

pleased at, by, with

plurals: Some nouns cause lawyers unnecessary grief. Although a few usage experts disagree, and many people abuse the words, "data," "media," "curricula," and "dicta," are plural nouns requiring the plural verb: "The data *are* missing." Another type of noun, the collective noun, can cause similar confusion—words like staff, couple, class, management, team, company, number, all, what, and none. Whether they are plural or singular depends on context. Thus, "all," which seems plural, is obviously singular in the sentence: "All was lost." Likewise, "number," which is usually singular, takes a plural verb in a sentence such as this: "A number of judges agree" because the sense intended is "many." (Theodore Bernstein suggests an easy rule: When the subject is "the number," it is singular; when "a number," plural.) One thing is certain about these uncertain words: They cannot be both singular and plural at once: "When the judge excuses them, the jury stands up to leave." If "jury" is a "them," then they must "stand" up to leave. (For avoiding sexism, see p. 150; for noun-verb agreement, see p. 144.

pomposities: Lawyers are masters of the pompous word or phrase. They use them often without even knowing it. Here's a lawyer writing an appreciation of a deceased colleague: "I remember many occasions in which I appeared in his courtroom prefatory to our lunching together." Why not "before lunch"? Rene J. Cappon lists words all can avoid: ameliorate (use improve), approximately (about), commence (begin), endeavor (try), finalize (end), implement (carry out), initiate (begin), proliferation (spread), purchase (buy), remuneration (pay), underprivileged (poor). See also p. 119.

portentous, pretentious: "The new line of thought," reads a sentence in the *New York Times*, "puts a stress on logic and the methods of science, dismissing earlier philosophy as portentious verbiage." Ain't no such word. The writer probably meant "pretentious," meaning full of pretense, ostentatious. "Portentous," the word with which the writer conflated it, means momentous.

pre-: Many people think that the prefix "pre-" adds weight to their actions. Thus we are told that the picnic has been "preplanned," that a chance meeting was in fact "prearranged," that they must excuse themselves from the party because of a "preexisting" commitment. What are they pretending? In all those circumstances, the "pre-" may safely be dropped. The *Wall Street Journal* in 1988 said: "While television networks typically allow advertisers to pre-screen series in order to avoid awkward segues, most publishers and TV news departments don't permit such preview because it might compromise editorial integrity." "Preview" is permissible, because it means to look at something beforehand, but "pre-screen"? That's what "screen" means. Any pretext for pretense, we suppose. We couldn't pretermit the comment.

precipitate, precipitous: As an adjective, *precipitate* means speeding headlong, moving rapidly and heedlessly, lacking deliberation; *precipitous* means extremely steep physically, not relating to action.

prefer . . . than: Mangled syntax. "The President prefers delegating the duty of firing his subordinates than doing it himself." Should be: "The President prefers delegating the duty of firing his subordinates to doing it himself."

prejudice against, by, for, or in favor of

preoccupied with

prepositions: Short words, such as "in," "on," "through," "around," "by," "of," "from," and "under," that connect parts of sentences, prepositions seem to cause lawyers sleepless nights, or ought to. Prepositions are highly idiomatic, not logical. The wrong preposition linked to a verb or noun can change meaning drastically, or make the writer appear stupid. Consider the various prepositions that attach to the verb "look": look after, look around, look at, look back, look down, look down on, look for, look forward to, look in, look in on, look into, look on, look out, look out for, look over, look to, look up, look up to, and look upon.

Lots of people have problems with prepositions. In her book *The Elements of Grammar*, Margaret D. Shertzer, in a section on prepositions, tells the reader to consult a dictionary "in case of doubt as to correct usage." That usage is incorrect.

A milder sin, but irritating nonetheless, is the omission of a preposition when called for. For example, "she graduated law school" and "he shopped a store." It should be "graduate from" and "shopped in."

A long time ago, students were told prepositions were something you could never end a sentence with. This old saw recalls the story of the city slicker who went out to Wyoming on vacation and bumped into a fellow who asked the vacationer whether he could tell him "where the theater's at?" The city slicker drew himself up and said, "My good man, don't you know you're not supposed to end your sentences with prepositions." The local thought about that for a moment and then responded: "Okay, well then, can you tell me where the theater's at, jackass?" See also *as to*.

prerequisite to

presently: Alfred E. Kahn: "For at least from the 17th through most of the 20th century, 'presently' meant 'soon' or 'immediately' and not 'now.' The use of 'presently' in the latter context is another pomposity: why not 'now?' "

principal, principle: *Principal* is the main thing, head of a school, or the money borrowed; *principle* is the rule or course of action we should follow.

prior to: Pompous. Use "before." See also *subsequent to*.

prioritize: Not a word.

pro tanto: Learned Hand could get away with this. Why should you try? It means "for as much as may be," "for so much," "as far as it goes."

process: Redundant in phrases such as "editing process," "educational process," "litigation process," "preboarding process." Editing, education, litigation, and boarding are all processes. Compare the flabby political catchphrase of the 1980s, "the peace process." What's wrong with peace negotiations?

pursuant to: An ugly lawyerism that can almost always be avoided. Why say "pursuant to your phone call" when you can as easily say, "As we discussed"? And why say "pursuant to Rule 61," when you can say "under Rule 61" or "by Rule 61" or "Rule 61 requires"?

pursuit of

quid pro quo: One of the rare Latinisms with no ready English substitute. It means "giving one valuable thing for another."

quotation marks: Do not use quotation marks around a lengthy passage indented in the text. When using quotation marks, put them outside punctuation, except for colons and semicolons.

quote: *Quote* is a verb. You quote the Supreme Court, but you put a Supreme Court quotation in your brief.

ravage, ravish: *Ravage* means to destroy; *ravish* means to enrapture, enchant, or rape. "The marauding Union army ravaged Atlanta." "The Beethoven sonata ravished the audience." "The soldiers ravished the woman in the barn."

reason about, on, with, or for

reason is because: A redundancy: "The reason he shivered is because it's freezing outside." Say either "The reason he shivered is that it's freezing outside" or "He shivered because it's freezing outside." Similarly, most usage books consider "reason why" a redundancy. Say "reason that" instead.

redundancy: See p. 133, for general discussion. Here are some lawyer redundancies to avoid: subject to future mutual agreement, written instrument, over and above and in addition to, inhabitant actually resident, become progressively more difficult as you go along, not identically the same, connected together. In *Usage and Abusage*, Eric Partridge lists dozens of redundancies; here are some: adequate enough, appear on the scene, collaborate together, continue on, equally as, file away, joint cooperation, meet together, mix together, new innovation, pair of twins, past history, penetrate into, really realize, renew or repeat again, revert back, seldom ever, sink down, still continue, unite together, Sahara Desert, skirt around, Sierra mountains, advance planning, as never before in the past, strangled to death, true fate.

And who can top Alexander Hamilton, who wrote in *Federalist* 33 that America must develop a "capacity to provide for future contingencies as they may happen."

reference to: A grotesque nominalization. Instead of "the letter makes reference to," say "the letter refers to."

regard for or to

regret to, over, or about

reluctant: See *reticent*.

remand back: Redundant. *Remand* means to send back.

render: Use "give."

requirement for or of

res gestae: Means "things done," but why say it? Use English.

resemblance among, between, of, or to

resentment against, at, or for

respect to

responsibility for

reticent, reluctant: *Reticent* means shy, unwilling to talk; reluctant means unwilling to act.

revert back: Redundant. *Revert* always means to go back.

rhetorical questions: "Are often a weak device, aren't they?" asks Tom Rowe.

role, of

run-on sentence: See p. 173.

running the gamut, gantlet, gauntlet: *Running the gamut* means going across the whole range of something. *Running the gauntlet* (or gantlet) means taking whatever criticism or punishment is handed out. A *gauntlet* is also a glove you wear or throw down to challenge someone to a duel.

said: Use only as a verb. Never use this archaic legalism as an adjective.

satisfaction of, in, or with

save harmless: Archaic. Use "hold harmless." See also *indemnify*.

secure in

serious: Use sparingly; this is an overused emphatic.

sexism: "He/she" and "him/her" are bad form. Use "he" or "she" or "they." See also p. 149.

she: Using the feminine form without warning can be jarring; that may be a sexist conclusion, but writers must reflect on the nuances of their society and, unless they intend to be jarring, should avoid unsettling the reader. Use "he" or "he or she" says Pamela Samuelson, who declares that the bare feminine form is overdone: " 'she' is too cute."

singular and plural: Examples: "Court" is singular, and the pronoun reference should be "it," not "they." In a series connected with "or," the verb agrees with the last item in the series. See also *plural.*

so . . . as: See *as . . . as.*

split infinitives: See p. 145.

strident, stringent: *Strident* means harsh, grating, shrill, or irritating. *Stringent,* means exacting, strict, or severe. Thus the court that spoke of meeting "strident criteria" did not edit stringently enough.

subject matter: Redundant, though often heard. Outside the discourse of jurisdiction, in which the rule writers have forced us to think about "subject matter jurisdiction," it is never necessary. Even worse is the sometimes heard variant: "Subject matter area."

subsequent to: A stuffy phrase that leads to trouble and means "after." Asked whether he had taken the Fifth Amendment before, John Dean, in one of the Watergate trials, said "subsequent to my appearance here." A neat trick!

such as: See *like.*

suitable for or to

supersede: Frequently misspelled supercede.

supportive of: Avoid. "The court was supportive of plaintiff's position" can easily enough be recast: "The court supported the plaintiff's position."

surely: Avoid; it's surely a false emphatic.

surprised at or by

sympathetic with, to, or toward

sympathize in or with

taboo words: Many vogue words in English serve only to make the writer sound self-important. We all have favorites: utilize, infrastructure, parameter. Here is a partial list of taboo words compiled in 1984 by Murray J. Rossant of the Twentieth Century Fund: additionally, address (as a verb), articulate (as a verb), at this point in time, bottom line, cohort, component, contact (as a verb), criterion, crucial, determinant, dichotomy, dimension, disadvantaged, disfunction, elements, explicate, factor (in a nonmathematical context), finalize, first priority, hopefully, illuminate, impacts on, incipient, in-depth, input, insoluble (meaning unsolvable), interaction, interface, key (meaning critical or major), leanings, lifestyles, meaningful, menu (other than in restaurant), mode, module, normative, ongoing, outcome, output, quantum, replicate, resonance, rubric, segmented (meaning divided), seminal, solidarity, stance, subsystem, supportive, symbiosis, time frame, upgrade, verbalize, viable.

taste for, in, or of

tendency to or toward

tortuous, torturous: *Tortuous* means winding, twisting, devious; *torturous* means inducing pain.

total and absolute: Redundant; avoid.

totaled: "Mileti totaled his Saab in the accident." That's slang or low colloquial speech, and should be avoided in writing. "Mileti demolished [or destroyed] his Saab."

trust in, to, or with

try and, try to: Correct usage is "try to."

turbid, turgid: *Turbid* means muddy, opaque, unclear. *Turgid* means pompous, swollen.

un-: "If you use awful expressions like 'not unlikely,' it is not unlikely that you will find my red ink on them," says Tom Rowe. See p. 132.

undeniably: Do not use. Few things are undeniable with two lawyers in town. It is lazy to suppose you can carry the day simply by asserting that your position is undeniably true or plainly so.

unfavorable for, to, or toward

uninterested: See *disinterested.*

unique: An either-or word, capable of no shadings. So don't try to be precise by saying "almost unique." See also *absolute words.*

unmindful of

unpopular with

up: Overused as a verbal modifier: climb up, end up, finish up, head up, loom up, polish up, rest up, rise up, saddle up, settle up, study up. These verbs can stand on their own.

utilize: Pompous and unnecessary. Use "use" instead.

vary from or with

venal, venial: *Venal* means corruptible, purchasable; a politician who takes a bribe is venal. *Venial* means forgiveable, hence minor; jaywalking is a venial sin.

very: Use sparingly; this is an overused emphatic.

vexed at or with

virtually: *Virtually* is a weasel word; it's a signal that the writer isn't sure that he can assert some universality, so he hedges. "In virtually every year from 1896 through 1981—with the exception of 1977 and 1978, when we incurred a tremendous oil bill because of the second OPEC crisis—we sold more goods and services abroad than we bought in return," wrote Robert Heilbroner in the *New Yorker.* Why "virtually?" Here, Heilbroner knows exactly; he even tells us. Or again, "Numerous courts have examined pollution exclusions virtually identical to those contained in the policies." The author is lazy. The exclusions are either identical or they are not. If they vary by only a word or two, the writer should say so, and tell us how. Omit "virtually" or rephrase your point.

vulnerable to

wary of

was, were: The subjunctive use of "were" sometimes trips up the unwary. When you are talking about something contrary to fact, use "were" rather than "was" or "am" or "are." "If I were (not *am*) back in law school again, I would (not *will*) study harder." "If this were (not *was*) 1964, we would have a clear choice for President."

well settled: Avoid unless your precise point is that the matter is well settled. This phrase is overused.

were: See *was.*

where and when: Lawyers tend to say "where" for "when." For instance: "The risk of unintended hardship where a defendant dies during direct appeal is even more pronounced." The defendant did not die in the unintended hardship. *Where* refers to space, location, geography, *when* to time or condition. The "where" in the quoted sentence should have been "when."

whereas: Avoid. See *lawyerisms.*

wherein: Avoid. See *lawyerisms.*

whether: See *if.*

whether or not: Whether to use "or not" depends on your meaning. When the point you wish to make is that on either condition something will happen, then you must include the "or not." For example: "The game will go on whether or not it rains." Otherwise, the "or not" may be dispensed with: "Whether the terrorist spoke the truth is unknown."

which: See p. 147.

who, whom: *Who* is the subject of a sentence or a clause, *whom* the object. "Who poisoned whom?" "The defendant became angry and often violent with whoever opposed her." "Sally Smith, who the state says killed six husbands, is on trial here."

with respect to: Art Rovine: "The single phrase most overworked [by lawyers] is 'with respect to.' " Reword.

without doubt: Few things are without doubt. This is an emphatic to be avoided.

would appear: See p. 126.

THE LEGAL WRITER'S
REFERENCE WORKS

During the 1980s there has been a torrent of writing about lawyers' writing. For a comprehensive bibliography, see George D. Gopen, "The State of Legal Writing: *Res Ipsa Loquitur*," 86 *Mich. L. Rev.* 333 (1987). The books listed below are generally available in bookstores (although we list some school texts and some especially noteworthy older books available in libraries). Books are listed alphabetically by author within each topic. (Entries preceded by an asterisk indicate availability in paperback.)

The Essential Reference Shelf

Some books are for fun, some for study, and some for instant reference. Here are ten books that should be within easy reach at your desk:

1. A comprehensive dictionary, something more advanced than the one you had in college. The most recent comprehensive American dictionary is the 1987 *Random House Dictionary of the English Language.*

2. A competent thesaurus, with words arranged in alphabetical order. Perhaps the Merriam-Webster.

3. An up-to-date usage book. Probably Roy H. Copperud, *American Usage and Style, The Consensus* (Van Nostrand Reinhold, 1980).

4. A basic work on grammar. Either George O. Curme, *English Grammar* (Barnes & Noble, 1947), the standard work, or Karen Elizabeth Gordon, *The Transitive Vampire: A Handbook of Grammar for the Innocent, the Eager, and the Doomed* (Times Books, 1984), sugarcoated for delightful reading.

5. H. W. Fowler, *A Dictionary of Modern English Usage* (Oxford, 2d ed. revised by Sir Ernest Gowers, 1965). Somewhat dated but still authoritative and encyclopedic in range.

6. Joseph M. Williams, *Style: Ten Lessons in Clarity and Grace* (Scott Foresman & Co., 3d ed., 1988). The best short work on how to achieve clarity in prose.

7. William Strunk, Jr., and E. B. White, *The Elements of Style* (Macmillan, 3d rev. ed., 1981). Thin but essential.

8. David Mellinkoff, *The Language of the Law* (Little, Brown, 1963). Magisterial, a work no lawyer should ignore.

9. A competent book on editing. One of the best is Claire Kehrwald Cook, *Line by Line* (Houghton Mifflin, 1985).

10. A standard composition handbook. One of these will do: Edward D. Johnson, *The Handbook of Good English* (Facts on File Press, 1982); Thomas S. Kane, *The Oxford Guide to Writing* (Oxford University Press, 1983); or Richard M. Weaver, *A Rhetoric and Composition Handbook* (Morrow, 1974).

Books on writing and language are plentiful. Listed below are works that we have found interesting, helpful, fun, or quirky.

Books on American Usage

Theodore M. Bernstein, *The Careful Writer* (Atheneum, 1968).

*———, *Miss Thistlebottom's Hobgoblins* (Atheneum, 1971).

*———, *Dos, Don'ts & Maybes of English Usage* (Times Books, 1977).

*Robert Claiborne, *Saying What You Mean* (W. W. Norton, 1986).

*Roy H. Copperud, *American Usage and Style, The Consensus* (Van Nostrand Reinhold, 1980).

*Wilson Follett, *Modern American Usage* (Hill & Wang, 1966).

*J. N. Hook, *The Grand Panjandrum* (Macmillan, 1980).

*James J. Kilpatrick, *The Writer's Art* (Andrews, McMeel & Parker, 1984).

*William and Mary Morris, *Harper Dictionary of Contemporary Usage* (Harper & Row, 1985).

*William Safire, *On Language* (Avon, 1981).

*Laurence Urdang, ed., *The New York Times Everyday Reader's Dictionary of Misunderstood, Misused, Mispronounced Words* (Quadrangle, 1972).

General Books on Style and Writing

*Theodore Bernstein, *Watch Your Language* (Atheneum, 1983).

*Sheridan Baker, *The Practical Stylist* (Harper & Row, 6th ed., 1985).

*Howard S. Becker, *Writing for Social Scientists: How to Start and Finish Your Thesis, Book, or Article* (University of Chicago Press, 1986).

*Rene J. Cappon, *The Word: An Associated Press Guide to Good News Writing* (The Associated Press, 1982).

*Claire Kehrwald Cook, *Line by Line* (Houghton Mifflin, 1985).

*Peter Elbow, *Writing with Power* (Oxford University Press, 1981).

*David W. Ewing, *Writing for Results in Business, Government, the Sciences, and the Professions* (John Wiley & Sons, 2d ed., 1979).

*Natalie Goldberg, *Writing Down the Bones* (Shambhala, 1986).

*Susan R. Horton, *Thinking through Writing* (Johns Hopkins, 1982).

*Edward D. Johnson, *The Handbook of Good English* (Facts on File Press, 1982).

Thomas S. Kane, *The Oxford Guide to Writing* (Oxford University Press, 1983).

*David Lambuth et al., *The Golden Book on Writing* (Penguin, 1963).

Richard A. Lanham, *Style: An Anti-Textbook* (Yale, 1974).

*Donald Murray, *Writing for Your Readers* (Globe Pequot Press, 1983).

*Lucile Vaughan Payne, *The Lively Art of Writing* (Mentor Books, 1969).

*Herbert Read, *English Prose Style* (Pantheon, 1952).

*William Strunk, Jr., and E. B. White, *Elements of Style* (Macmillan, 3d rev. ed., 1981).

*Jan Venolia, *Rewrite Right!* (Ten Speed Press, 1987).

*Marie L. Waddell et al., *The Art of Styling Sentences* (Barron's, 1972).

*Richard M. Weaver, *A Rhetoric and Composition Handbook* (Morrow, 1974).

*William Zinsser, *On Writing Well* (Harper & Row, 4th ed., 1988).

Books on Grammar and Punctuation

*George O. Curme, *English Grammar* (Barnes & Noble, 1947).

Karen Elizabeth Gordon, *The Transitive Vampire: A Handbook of Grammar for the Innocent, the Eager, and the Doomed* (Times Books, 1984).

————, *The Well-Tempered Sentence, A Punctuation Handbook for the Innocent, the Eager, and the Doomed* (Ticknor & Fields, 1983).

*John B. Opdycke, *Harper's English Grammar* (Fawcett Popular Library, 1965).

*Margaret Shertzer, *The Elements of Grammar* (Collier Macmillan, 1986).

Other Usage Books

H. W. Fowler, *A Dictionary of Modern English Usage* (Oxford, 2d ed. revised by Sir Ernest Gowers, 1965).

*Eric Partridge, *Usage & Abusage* (Penguin Books, rev. ed., 1973).

*Mario Pei and Salvatore Ramondino, *A Dictionary of Foreign Terms* (Dell, 1974).

Books on Legal Style

Veda Charrow, *Clear and Effective Legal Writing* (Little, Brown, 1987).

Rudolf Flesch, *How to Write Plain English: A Book for Lawyers & Consumers* (Harper & Row, 1979).

*Ronald L. Goldfarb and James C. Raymond, *Clear Understandings: A Guide to Legal Writing* (Random House, 1982).

George D. Gopen, *Writing from a Legal Perspective* (West, 1981).

Lucy V. Katz, *Winning Words: A Guide to Persuasive Writing for Lawyers* (Harcourt Brace Jovanovich, 1986).

*David Mellinkoff, *Legal Writing: Sense and Nonsense* (West, 1983).

Richard H. Weisberg, *When Lawyers Write* (Little, Brown, 1987).

*Richard C. Wydick, *Plain English for Lawyers* (Carolina Academic Press, 2d ed. 1985).

Books on Legal Language

David Mellinkoff, *The Language of the Law* (Little, Brown, 1963).

*Fred Rodell, *Woe unto You, Lawyers* (1939, Berkley ed., 1961).

*James Boyd White, *The Legal Imagination* (University of Chicago Press, 1985).

————, *Heracles' Bow: Essays on the Rhetoric and Poetics of the Law* (University of Wisconsin Press, 1985).

Books on the State of the Language

Jacques Barzun, *A Word or Two Before You Go* (Wesleyan University Press, 1986).

Stuart Chase, *The Tyranny of Words* (Harcourt, Brace & Co., 1938).

*Robert Claiborne, *Our Marvelous Native Tongue* (Times Books, 1983).

Donna Woolfolk Cross, *Word Abuse* (Coward McCann & Geoghegan, 1979).

Leonard Michaels and Christopher Ricks, *The State of the Language* (University of California Press, 1990).

*Richard Mitchell, *Less Than Words Can Say* (Little, Brown, 1979).

*————, *The Gift of Fire* (Simon & Schuster, 1987).

*Edwin Newman, *Strictly Speaking: Will America Be the Death of English?* (Warner Books, 1980).

———, *A Civil Tongue* (Warner Books, 1980).

*Joseph T. Shipley, *In Praise of English* (Times Books, 1977).

Books on Creativity and Writing

*James L. Adams, *The Care and Feeding of Ideas* (Addison Wesley, 1986).

*———, *Conceptual Blockbusting* (W. W. Norton, 2d ed., 1979).

*M. Neil Browne and Stuart M. Keeley, *Asking the Right Questions: A Guide to Critical Thinking* (Prentice-Hall, 2d ed., 1986).

*Brewster Ghiselin, ed., *The Creative Process* (Mentor, 1955).

*V. A. Howard and J. H. Barton, *Thinking on Paper* (William Morrow, 1986).

*Arthur Koestler, *The Act of Creation* (Dell, 1967).

*David Lewis and James Greene, *Thinking Better* (Rawson, Wade, 1982).

Books on Metaphor

*Anne E. Berthoff, *The Making of Meaning* (Boynton/Cook Publishers, 1981).

*Mark Johnson, ed., *Philosophical Perspectives on Metaphor* (University of Minnesota Press, 1981).

*George Lakoff and Mark Johnson, *Metaphors We Live By* (University of Chicago Press, 1980).

*Andrew Ortony, ed., *Metaphor and Thought* (Cambridge University Press, 1979).

*Sheldon Sacks, ed., *On Metaphor* (University of Chicago Press, 1979).

ACKNOWLEDGMENTS

We wish to thank Joe Spieler, Bobbi Mark, and Lisa Frost for their exceptional guidance; Jennifer Crewe for her encouragement; Martha Cooper, Sandor Frankel, Lawrence Grauman Jr., Nancy Ramsey, and Amy Stevens for editing suggestions that greatly improved the manuscript; Elizabeth K. Lieberman for proofreading the galleys; for their research help, Paul Mastrangelo and Mary lin Raisch and the staffs of the libraries at New York Law School, Park City, Utah, and the University of California, Berkeley; Beth Pickett for her administrative help; and Terry Pristin, Mike Keiser, and Phil Friedmann for providing us shelter while we worked on the manuscript. We have also benefited greatly over the years from the published work of and discussions with Joseph Williams and George D. Gopen.

We gathered this material from many people, including lawyers in several firms and students at New York and Fordham law schools and the Graduate School of Journalism, University of California, Berkeley.

We are grateful to the following people who took the time to answer our questionnaire. Others answered whom we are unable to acknowledge. Some preferred anonymity. And because of a temporary glitch at the post office, some responses which friends told us had been sent never arrived (and, we suspect, others did not arrive as well). We list respondents with their affiliations as of publication of our hardcover book in 1988.

Beryl A. Abrams, Associate General Counsel, Columbia University, New York City

Prof. Douglas E. Abrams, Fordham University School of Law, New York City

Floyd Abrams, Cahill Gordon & Reindel, New York City

Thomas F. Ahrensfeld, Senior Vice President & General Counsel, Philip Morris, Inc., New York City

Susan Alexander, lawyer and writer, Wilmette, Illinois

C. David Anderson, Tuttle & Taylor, Los Angeles

William L. Anderson, Minnesota Law Review, Minneapolis

Lori B. Andrews, American Bar Foundation, Chicago

Hon. Richard T. Andrias, State Supreme Court, New York City

Louis S. Auchincloss, lawyer and author, New York City

Stuart Auerbach, The Washington Post, Washington, D.C.

Richard Babcock, New York Magazine, New York City

David M. Balabanian, McCutchen, Doyle, Brown & Enersen, San Francisco

Robert S. Banks, Vice President & General Counsel, Xerox Corp., Stamford, Connecticut

Fred Barbash, The Washington Post, Washington, D.C.

David A. Barrett, Duker & Barrett, New York City

Prof. Jacques Barzun, Columbia University, New York City

Prof. Paul A. Bateman, Southwestern University School of Law, Los Angeles

James Bays, Vice President & Assistant General Counsel, TRW, Inc., Cleveland

David E. Beckwith, Foley & Lardner, Milwaukee

Hon. Joseph W. Bellacosa, New York Court of Appeals, Albany

Prof. Rebecca White Berch, Arizona State University College of Law, Tempe

Prof. Curtis J. Berger, Columbia University School of Law, New York City

Curtis G. Berkey, Indian Law Resource Center, Washington, D.C.

Albert L. Beswick, Senior Counsel, International Telephone & Telegraph Co., New York City

Lawrence Bodine, Editor, American Bar Association Journal, Chicago

Michael Boudin, Covington & Burling, Washington, D.C.

Michael A. Boyd, General Counsel, Donaldson Lufkin & Jenrette, Inc., New York City

Hon. Stephen Breyer, United States Court of Appeals, First Circuit, Boston

David M. Brodsky, Schulte Roth & Zabel, New York City

Prof. Susan L. Brody, Director, Legal Writing, The John Marshall Law School, Chicago

Helman R. Brook, Office of Special State Prosecutor, New York City

Howard D. Burnett, Holly, Troxell, Ennis & Holly, Pocatello, Idaho

W. Peter Burns, Steel Hector & Davis, Miami

Margaret B. Carlson, Time Magazine, Washington, D.C.

Bradley Carr, New York State Bar Association, Albany

James H. Carter, Sullivan & Cromwell, New York City

Prof. David Chang, New York Law School, New York City

Richard Cheney, Chairman, Hill & Knowlton, New York City

Dean Jesse Choper, Boalt Hall, University of California, Berkeley

Arthur H. Christy, Christy & Viener, New York City

Roy Peter Clark, The Poynter Institute for Media Studies, St. Petersburg, Florida

Hon. Avern Cohn, United States District Court, Detroit

Henry S. Cohn, State Attorney General's Office, Hartford, Connecticut

John T. Connor, Jr., Vice President & General Counsel, PHH Group, Inc., Hunt Valley, Maryland

Randal R. Craft, Jr., Haight, Gardner, Poor & Havens, New York City

L. Gordon Crovitz, The Wall Street Journal, New York City

Dean Edward A. Dauer, University of Denver College of Law, Denver

Evan A. Davis, Counsel to the Governor of New York, Albany

James F. Davis, Howrey & Simon, Washington, D.C.

Prof. Joel C. Dobris, University of California School of Law at Davis, Davis

Jean Dubofsky, University of Colorado School of Law, Boulder

Victor Earle III, Cahill Gordon & Reindel, New York City

Charles D. Edelman, Vice President and General Counsel, Fortress Re, Inc., Burlington, North Carolina

Renee Edelman, Edelman Group, New York City

Mary Frances Edwards, Federal Publications, Inc., Washington, D.C.

Richard D. Emery, Lankenau Kovner & Bickford, New York City

Thomas Engel, Engel & Mulholland, New York City

Eli N. Evans, President, The Revson Foundation, New York City

Thomas W. Evans, Mudge Rose Guthrie Alexander & Ferdon, New York City

Lisa Evren, New York University Law Review, New York City

Herald Price Fahringer, Lipsitz, Green, Fahringer, Roll, Schuller & James, New York City

Kenneth R. Feinberg, Kaye, Scholer, Fierman, Hays & Handler, Washington, D.C.

Jeffrey Feinstein, Inspector General's Office, Department of Health, New York City

Franklin Feldman, Stroock & Stroock & Lavan, New York City

Charles K. Fewell, Jr., Senior Counsel & First Vice President, Deutsche Bank AG, New York City

Eugene R. Fidell, Klores, Feldesman & Tucker, Washington, D.C.

Erika S. Fine, WestLaw, New York City

Frank Fioromonti, New York State Attorney General's Office, New York City

Josh Fitzhugh, lawyer, Burlington, Vermont

Stuart Berg Flexner, Random House Dictionary of the English Language, New York City

Hon. Marvin E. Frankel, Kramer, Levin, Nessen, Kamin & Frankel, New York City

Sandor Frankel, Bender & Frankel, New York City

Prof. Eric M. Freedman, Hofstra University Law School, Hempstead, N.Y.

Prof. Monroe H. Freedman, Hofstra University Law School, Hempstead, N.Y.

David Freeman, writer, Los Angeles

James C. Freund, Skadden, Arps, Slate, Meagher & Flom, New York City

Prof. Leon Friedman, Hofstra University Law School, Hempstead, New York

Stanley Friedman, Shereff, Friedman, Hoffman & Goodman, New York City

Donald Fry, The Poynter Institute for Media Studies, St. Petersburg, Florida

Martin Garbus, Frankfurt, Garbus, Klein & Selz, New York City

Michael G. Gartner, President, NBC News, New York City

Gibson Gayle, Jr., Fulbright & Jaworski, Houston

Warren B. Gelman, McGee & Gelman, Buffalo

Ted Gest, U.S. News & World Report, Washington, D.C.

Robin Gibson, Gibson & Lilly, Lake Wales, Florida,

Prof. Stephen Gillers, New York University Law School, New York City

Prof. Donald Gillmor, Silha Center for the Study of Media Ethics and Law, University of Minnesota, Minneapolis

Prof. I Cathy Glaser, New York Law School, New York City

Marshall Goldberg, writer, Brentwood, California

Robert M. Goldberg, Offices of Robert M. Goldberg & Associates, Anchorage

Sondra Gamow Goldenfarb, Tanney, Forde, Donahey, Eno & Tanney, Clearwater, Florida

Ronald Goldfarb, Goldfarb & Singer, Washington, D.C.

Marshall L. Goldstein, Goldstein and Van Nes, White Plains, New York

James C. Goodale, Debevoise & Plimpton, New York City

Prof. George D. Gopen, Department of English, Duke University, Durham, North Carolina

Robert H. Gorske, Vice President & General Counsel, Wisconsin Electric Power Co., Milwaukee

Milton S. Gould, Shea & Gould, New York City

Joseph Goulden, writer, Washington, D.C.

Chester Graham, Cross Lake, Minn.

Fred Graham, WKRN-TV, Nashville

Lawrence Grauman, Jr., editor, Mill Valley, California

Prof. Eric D. Green, Boston University School of Law, Boston

Matthew Greenberg, Office of Special State Prosecutor, New York City

Jeff Greenfield, ABC-TV, New York City

Linda Greenhouse, The New York Times, Washington, D.C.

Robert Gruendel, Burlingham, Underwood & Lord, New York City

Philip Hager, The Los Angeles Times, San Francisco

David Halston, Hale & Dorr, Boston

William Hannay, Schiff Hardin & Waite, Chicago

Jane Frank Harman, Surrey & Morse, Washington, D.C.

Hon. Bertram Harnett, Dreyer and Traub, Boca Raton, Florida

Prof. Geoffrey C. Hazard, Jr., Yale University Law School, New Haven

William E. Hegarty, Cahill Gordon & Reindel, New York City

Prof. William E. Hellerstein, Brooklyn Law School, Brooklyn, New York

Lawrence F. Henneberger, Arent, Fox, Kintner, Plotkin & Kahn, Washington, D.C.

Joel F. Henning, writer and lawyer, Chicago

Coleman S. Hicks, Covington & Burling, Washington, D.C.

George V. Higgins, author and lawyer, Milton, Massachusetts

Joseph D. Hinkle, Hill & Barlow, Boston

Alan J. Hruska, Cravath, Swaine & Moore, New York City

Hon. Shirley Hufstedler, Hufstedler, Miller, Carlson & Beardsley, Los Angeles

Prof. Patrick Hugg, Loyola Law School, New Orleans

Prof. Dennis Hynes, Co-Director of Legal Writing, Univ. of Colorado School of Law, Boulder

Linda Ishkanian, Siegal & Gale, New York City

Hon. Jack B. Jacobs, Court of Chancery, Wilmington, Delaware

Herb Jaffe, Newark Star-Ledger, Newark, New Jersey

Hon. Matthew Jasen, Moot & Sprague, Buffalo

Alan Jenkins, Harvard Civil Rights-Civil Liberties Law Review, Cambridge

Robert D. Joffe, Cravath, Swaine & Moore, New York City

William J. Jones, General Solicitor, AT&T, Berkeley Heights, N.J.

Kenneth Jost, writer, Washington, D.C.

Roberta S. Karmel, Brooklyn Law School and Kelley, Drye & Warren, New York City

Adam Kasanof, Department of Police, New York City

Robert Kasanof, Kasanof & Shannon, New York City

Frank Katz, lawyer, Santa Fe

George Kaufmann, Dickstein, Shapiro & Morin, Washington, D.C.

Hon. John F. Keenan, United States District Court, Southern District of New York, New York City

James M. Kindler, New York County District Attorney's Office, New York City

Dean James M. Klebba, Loyola University School of Law, New Orleans

Hon. J. Anthony Kline, California Court of Appeal, San Francisco

Steven H. Kruis, Higgs, Fletcher & Mack, San Diego

James Simon Kunen, People Magazine, New York City

Jack L. Lahr, Foley & Lardner, Washington, D.C.

Newton Lamson, Donley Communications, New York City

A. Van C. Lanckton, Craig & Macauley, Boston

Jay F. Lapin, Wilmer Cutler & Pickering, Washington, D.C.

Mark D. Lebow, Coudert Brothers, New York City

Hon. James J. Leff, State Supreme Court, New York City

Prof. Robert Leflar, University of Arkansas, Fayetteville

Donald G. Leka, General Counsel, Teradyne, Inc., Boston

Thomas B. Lemann, Monroe & Lemann, New Orleans

Prof. Arthur Leonard, New York Law School, New York City

William H. Levit, Jr., Godfrey & Kahn, Milwaukee

Anthony Lewis, The New York Times, Boston

Hal R. Lieberman, Disciplinary Committee, Appellate Division, First Department, New York City

Prof. Carol B. Liebman, Boston College Law School, Boston

Carl D. Liggio, General Counsel, Arthur Young Co., New York City

Prof. James Lindgren, University of Connecticut School of Law, Hartford

Martin Lipton, Wachtell, Lipton, Rosen & Katz, New York City

Prof. Daniel H. Lowenstein, University of California at Los Angeles School of Law, Los Angeles

Weyman I. Lundquist, Heller Ehrman White & McAuliffe, San Francisco

Judy Lynch, City Attorney's Office, San Francisco

James E. Lyons, Skadden, Arps, Slate, Meagher & Flom, Los Angeles

Patrick J. Mahoney, Cooley, Godward, Castro, Huddleson & Tatum, San Francisco

Jonathan R. Maslow, editor, San Francisco

Prof. Robert McKay, New York University School of Law, New York City

John F. Meigs, Saul Ewing Remick & Saul, Philadelphia

Prof. David Mellinkoff, University of California at Los Angeles School of Law, Los Angeles

Prof. Michael Meltsner, Northeastern University School of Law, Boston

Elizabeth Mertz, Northwestern Law Review, Chicago

Harry Meyer, Hodgson, Russ, Andrew, Woods & Goodyear, Buffalo

Stephen B. Middlebrook, Vice President & General Counsel, Aetna Insurance Co., Hartford

Prof. Arthur R. Miller, Harvard Law School, Cambridge

Prof. Richard H. Miller, Brooklyn College, Brooklyn, New York

Herbert Mitgang, The New York Times, New York City

Prof. Norval Morris, University of Chicago School of Law, Chicago

Alan B. Morrison, Public Citizen, Inc., Washington, D.C.

Justice Stanley Mosk, California Supreme Court, San Francisco

Daniel B. Moskowitz, McGraw-Hill, Inc., Washington, D.C.

Homer E. Moyer, Miller & Chevalier, Washington, D.C.

Hon. William Hughes Mulligan, Skadden, Arps, Slate, Meagher & Flom, New York City

Betty Southard Murphy, Baker & Hostetler, Washington, D.C.

Hon. S. Michael Nadel, Criminal Court, New York City

Stan Naparst, Albany, California

Stephen Natelson, Natelson & Ross, Taos, New Mexico

Robert Stuart Nathan, writer, New York City

Hon. Richard Neely, Supreme Court of West Virginia, Charleston

Maurice N. Nessen, Kramer, Levin, Nessen, Kamin & Frankel, New York City

Prof. Charles R. Nesson, Harvard Law School, Cambridge

Prof. Richard K. Neumann, Jr., Director, Legal Writing, Hofstra University School of Law, Hempstead, New York'

Prof. Stephen A. Newman, New York Law School, New York City

Prof. Jacqueline Nolan-Haley, Fordham University School of Law, New York City

J. Michael Parish, LeBoeuf, Lamb, Leiby & Macrae, New York City

Hon. Robert Patterson, Jr., United States District Court, Southern District of New York, New York City

Robert S. Peck, American Bar Association, Washington, D.C.

Prof. Michael Perlin, New York Law School, New York City

Kenneth A. Plevan, Skadden, Arps, Slate, Meagher & Flom, New York City

Milt Policzer, San Francisco Recorder, San Francisco

Hon. Richard A. Posner, United States Court of Appeals, Seventh Circuit, Chicago

Prof. Michael Powell, Department of Sociology, University of North Carolina, Chapel Hill

Llewelyn Pritchard, Karr, Tuttle, Koch, Campbell, Jawer, Morrow & Sax, Seattle

Anthony E. Pucillo, West Palm Beach, Florida

Henry Putzel, Jr., Retired Reporter of Decisions, United States Supreme Court, Munsonville, New Hampshire

Henry Putzel III, lawyer, New York City

Prof. Jill J. Ramsfield, Georgetown University Law Center, Washington, D.C.

Charles A. Reich, writer, San Francisco

Prof. Chris Rideout, University of Puget Sound School of Law, Tacoma, Washington

Simon H. Rifkind, Paul, Weiss, Rifkind, Wharton & Garrison, New York City

Marjorie Rawls Roberts, Bureau of Internal Revenue, St. Thomas, V.I.

Charles Robinowitz, lawyer, Portland, Oregon

T. Sumner Robinson, Editor, The National Law Journal, New York City

Timothy Roble, Ducker, Gurko & Roble, Denver

Salvatore A. Romano, Arent, Fox, Kintner, Plotkin & Kahn, Washington, D.C.

Prof. Marjorie D. Rombauer, University of Washington School of Law, Seattle

Andrew A. Rooney, CBS-TV, New York City

Prof. Maurice Rosenberg, Columbia University School of Law, New York City

Hon. Albert M. Rosenblatt, Appellate Division of State Supreme Court, New York City

David Rosenbloom, Orrick, Herrington & Sutcliffe, San Francisco

C. Thomas Ross, Craige, Brawley, Lipfert & Ross, Winston-Salem, North Carolina

Prof. Donald Rothschild, George Washington Law School, Washington, D.C.

Arthur W. Rovine, Baker & McKenzie, New York City

Prof. Thomas D. Rowe, Jr., Duke University School of Law, Durham, North Carolina

Prof. Zick Rubin, Brandeis University, Waltham, Massachusetts

Prof. David Rudenstine, Benjamin N. Cardozo School of Law, New York City

Jerry W. Ryan, Crowell & Moring, Washington, D.C.

Elizabeth Sacksteder, Articles Editor, Yale Law Journal, New Haven

Joseph R. Sahid, Cravath, Swaine & Moore, New York City

Hon. Leonard B. Sand, United States District Court, Southern District of New York, New York City

Prof. Frank E. A. Sander, Harvard Law School, Cambridge

Justice Leonard H. Sandler (deceased), Appellate Division of State Supreme Court, New York City

David L. Sandor, Simon, McKinsey, Miller, Zommick, Sandor & Dundas, Irvine, California

John P. Scanlon, Edelman Group, New York City

Milton R. Schlesinger, Arter & Hadden, Cleveland

Prof. David Schoenbrod, New York Law School, New York City

Prof. Peter H. Schuck, Yale Law School, New Haven

Allen G. Schwartz, Proskauer Rose Goetz & Mendelson, New York City

Victor E. Schwartz, Crowell & Moring, Washington, D.C.

Melvin L. Schweitzer, Rogers & Wells, New York City

Eric A. Seiff, Scoppetta & Seiff, New York City

Prof. David. L. Shapiro, Harvard Law School, Cambridge

Prof. E. Donald Shapiro, New York Law School, New York City

Ronald M. Shapiro, Shapiro & Olander, Baltimore

Prof. Marjorie Silver, New York Law School, New York City

Leon Silverman, Fried, Frank, Harris, Shriver & Jacobson, New York City

Robert Siverd, Penn Central lawyer, Stamford, Connecticut

Neil Skene, Executive Editor, Congressional Quarterly, Washington, D.C.

Jonathan A. Small, Debevoise & Plimpton, New York City

Chesterfield Smith, Holland & Knight, Miami

Prof. Eva M. Soeka, Marquette University Law School, Milwaukee

Justin A. Stanley, Mayer Brown & Platt, Chicago

John H. Stassen, Kirkland & Ellis, Chicago

Jacob A. Stein, Stein, Mitchell & Mezines, Washington, D.C.

Carl Stern, NBC-TV, Washington, D.C.

Gerald Stern, Administrator, New York State Commission on Judicial Conduct, New York City

Prof. Christopher D. Stone, University of Southern California Law Center, Los Angeles

Fred M. Stone, Executive Vice President & General Counsel, Jamie Securities, New York City

Hon. Eugene B. Strassburger III, Court of Common Pleas, Allegheny County, Pittsburgh

Prof. James F. Stratman, Graduate School of Industrial Administration, Carnegie-Mellon University, Pittsburgh

Prof. Peter L. Strauss, Columbia University Law School, New York City

Fern Sussman, Executive Secretary, Association of the Bar of the City of New York, New York City

Phil Talbert, UCLA Law Review, Los Angeles

Peter Tannewald, Arent, Fox, Kintner, Plotkin & Kahn, Washington, D.C.

Stuart Taylor, Jr., The American Lawyer, Washington, D.C.

M. Margaret Terry, Lubell & Lubell, New York City

Texas Law Review staff, 1987–1988, Austin

Evan Thomas, Newsweek, Washington, D.C.

Robert Tierney, AT&T, New York City

Sean Tierney, Mudge Rose Guthrie Alexander & Ferdon, New York City

Richard J. Tofel, Gibson, Dunn & Crutcher, New York City

Jay Topkis, Paul, Weiss, Rifkind, Wharton & Garrison, New York City

R. Edward Townsend, Townsend Rabinowitz Pantaleoni & Valente, New York City

Dean David G. Trager, Brooklyn Law School, Brooklyn, New York

Prof. Nicholas Triffin, Pace University School of Law, White Plains, New York

Thomas R. Trowbridge III, Donovan Leisure Newton & Irvine, New York City

Scott F. Turow, Sonnenschein Carlin North & Rosenthal, Chicago

Gerald Uram, Davis & Gilbert, New York City

Andrew Vachss, lawyer and author, New York City

Prof. Jon M. Van Dyke, University of Hawaii, William S. Richardson School of Law, Honolulu

Cyrus Vance, Simpson Thacher & Bartlett, New York City

Prof. Robert Volk, Director, First-Year Writing Program, Boston University School of Law, Boston

George Vradenburg III, General Counsel, CBS, New York City

Hon. Sol Wachtler, New York Court of Appeals, Albany

Hank Wallace, consultant, Washington, D.C.

Irene C. Warshauer, Anderson Russell Kill & Olick, New York City

Kelly R. Welsh, Corporation Counsel, Chicago

Stephen Wermiel, The Wall Street Journal, Washington, D.C.

Edwin J. Wesely, Winthrop, Stimson, Putnam & Roberts, New York City

Roger Wilkins, Institute for Policy Studies, Washington, D.C.

Christopher Wren, Wisconsin Department of Justice, Madison

Melvin Wulf, Beldock Levine & Hoffman, New York City

Hon. William G. Young, United States District Court, Boston

Prof. Irving Younger (deceased), University of Minnesota Law School, Minneapolis

Lois Young-Tulin, Wyncote, Pennsylvania

Prof. Donald H. Zeigler, New York Law School, New York City

Sidney Zion, writer, New York City

INDEX

In addition to the topics discussed throughout the text, this index lists (1) all people referred to in the book (except for those named solely in the End Notes as authors of works); (2) set in small caps, specific words or phrases discussed in the text (but not those separately alphabetized in the Glossary beginning on p. 229). This index does not name those who answered the survey, all of whom are listed alphabetically in the Acknowledgments beginning on p. 259.